How to open more doors

as a

Software Engineer ?

By

Arulkumaran Kumaraswamipillai
Sivayini Arulkumaran

Opening more doors as a software engineer

Copy Right 2013

Please e-mail feedback & corrections to
java-interview@hotmail.com.

blog: http://www.java-success.blogspot.com

First Edition : Oct 2013

Table of Contents

Section-1:

What can you do as a software engineer to open more doors?

It is a competitive world out there and being in the know how can open more doors and make a huge difference to your career success. You need to make a lasting impression on those who communicate, interview, and interact with you. This impression will be partly influenced by how knowledgeable you are about **your industry** and **the challenges it faces** and partly by your passion and imagination. It will also be influenced by your soft skills, attitude, marketing skills, job hunting skills and networking skills. This book outlines things you must know and can do to open more doors as a software engineer.

All the breaks you need in life wait within your imagination, Imagination is the
workshop of your mind, capable of turning
mind energy into accomplishment and wealth.

-- Napoleon Hill

What can you do as a software engineer to open more doors?

Why this book?

I learned a lot from the mistakes I made in my career as a software engineer. Here are my **top 5 mistakes**

- **Mistake #1**: Naively believing that I could easily find a job with my M. Eng. degree led to being unemployed for about 16 months. I under estimated the power of **hands-on experience** and much needed **job hunting skills**. I wish I had taken on unpaid internships or volunteer work. More on this in Section 4: <u>Write effective resumes to open doors</u> - **how to get some experience on your CV.**

- **Mistake #2**: When I was interviewed for my first IT job, I was asked how I would go about working with a person who is difficult to work with. Only after taking up the job, I realized that I had to work with a such person, and my lack of soft skills and immaturity resulted in leaving the job just after 5 months. I learned the lesson that just being a techie is not enough to open more doors.

  - I think of it as this -- If I am paid $50k as a software developer, then $25k is for my technical skills add value, and the remaining $25K is to get things done by working with people. In other words for being a team player, having good interpersonal and communication skills, and right attitude to get things done.

- **Mistake #3**: Squandered great job opportunities due to lack of good resume writing and interviewing skills. I also let others around me decide what is best for me in terms of my career path. For example, letting the recruitment agents decide what is best for me and how much I should get paid.

  - An interview is a two way street. As a prospective employer is assessing your suitability, you must assess the suitability of the position to see if it is inline with your career goals. Failing to ask the right questions can land you in a dilemma as to accept the offer or not.

  - Treat each interview as a **free training session** to control your nervousness and to be in a win/win situation.

- **Mistake #4**: Fear of change, false understanding of job security, and fear of job interviews made me get into a comfort zone. Didn't realize that the real job security stems from having the right and up to date skills until the software house I was working for closed down.

- Nowadays, I make it a point to learn at least 1 new thing a week. With so many quality resources around you, why have excuses to learn. After I learn, I blog about it on my own style to expand my understanding and for my future reference.

- **Mistake #5**: As everyone does, from time to time stagnated at my job without enough work or challenging tasks. Didn't realize that what other avenues I could have explored as a software engineer to open more doors in and outside work. Most good software engineers are self-taught and there are plenty of things to learn and myriad of free and paid resources to learn from. There are a number of paths to take, and some paths are less traveled than the others. The big picture diagram in this section will inspire you as to what you can do as a software engineer.

  - You are the captain of your ship, and best placed to decide when to jump the ship versus when to steady the ship. I became a freelancer working exclusively for a client due to my mistake #2, but that is the best thing happened to my career.

I learned a lot from my mistakes, and these mistakes made me grow stronger. Here are my **Top 4 things that I got right**.

Getting it right #1: Realized early enough that IT salary starts well, but then plateaus in years 8 to 10. To get beyond this, you need to be someone with highly sought after skills that can not be found anywhere else, or be in a senior management position. Alternatively, I explored the other avenues like starting my blog, learning Search Engine Optimization techniques, and then publishing a number of Print-On-Demand books that sold over 25,000 copies.

Getting it right #2: Pro-actively learned the 16 technical key areas discussed in this book, and used them as my weapon to impress my superiors and peers at work to earn a reputation as a go to person.

Getting it right #3: As a freelance developer, recognized the importance of preparing prior to job interviews, which led to collecting over 400 Java job interview questions and answers. This was the motivation for my books and blogs. Also, immensely helped me in my job interviews to get multiple job offers and negotiate better rates. Job interview preparation along with building relationships are my risk mitigation strategies to continuously find work as a freelancer.

Getting it right #4: Always believed in taking the road less traveled. In other words, doing something out of the norm. So, never bothered acquiring certifications, but invested on getting a good handle on the 16 technical key areas and sought-after technologies/frameworks that add real value to the business. Translated my learnings to questions and answers based approach with lots of diagrams, practical examples, and code snippets. This empowered me to share my experience via my blog and books.

This book is not for super star engineers who are already going places. This is a career companion book with technical and non-technical information that can inspire you to fast track your career as a software engineer by exploring different avenues. The focus of this book is not to progress just as a techie, but as a well-rounded professional with good technical and non-technical skills. Good things take time, but if you **relentlessly** put these recommendations to practice, you will definitely achieve your career goals.

People more often buy the best advertised product than the best product

The same is true in marketing your personal services. If you want to market a product successfully, you must know the product. Many of you do not think in a marketing oriented way when it comes to selling your personal services. For example,

---

Product = Your personal services.

Targeted market = Your current or prospective employer(s).

Product features = Your achievements, experience, and capabilities to solve business problems.

Product benefits = Add value to the business.

Marketing plan

– Get a good handle on the **16 key technical areas** of software development.

- Become a **facilitator** or a **change agent** of those key areas to design and build quality software to solve business problems.
- Produce a highly effective resume that can attract more interviews.
- Perform well in job interviews that lead to multiple job offers.
- Share and enhance your experience and success with others through blogs and books.
- Create an **online brand** for your-self that can open more doors for you.

The key focus of this book is to motivate and guide you to present yourself in a better light with your technical and non-technical skills.

- Getting a good handle on the 16 key technical areas.
- Complimenting your technical skills with good soft skills, marketing skills, job hunting skills, and networking skills.
- Writing effective resumes.
- Being in the know how about the industry and the challenges it faces.
- Understanding what the current or prospective employers are looking for.
- Building an online persona that can not only open more doors, but also can keep you motivated in your quest for learning and helping others.

Building new income streams

As a software engineer, there are many avenues to look at depending on your interests, strengths, and career goals as shown in the ensuing diagram. With these avenues, you can not only open more doors to fast track your career by **acquiring much needed experience** in technical and non-technical areas, but also can open doors to new active and passive income streams.

- **Finding a side job**

    - as a freelancer via freelancer.com, elance.com, odesk.com, and guru.com.
    - part-time job as a teacher, an instructor, or a lecturer at your local training institute, technical college or university.
    - offering part-time consulting services in your field of expertise through networking.

Check your employment contract to see if it allows any side job. The contract jobs are different from freelancing work. Freelancing tends to be on a per-assignment

What can you do as a software engineer to open more doors?

basis, while the contract options could be on a monthly/daily/weekly rate for providing certain services for a pre-determined period like 6 months or 1 year to one client. The key focus of the side job is to enhance your experience.

- **Starting an ad-supported blog** – via wordpress.com, blogger.com, etc with Google adsense advertisements. There are other avenues to monetize your blog that you can research on the net. Firstly, build an interesting and informative blog before start advertising. Build up a reasonable size readers and followers before including advertisements. As a rule of thumb have at least 500 page views per day. Sign up for "Google analytics" to see what key words are bringing in the traffic, and where the traffic is coming from. Learn the SEO (i.e. Search Engine Optimization) techniques.

You could have blogs for your other passions like photography, music, movies, sports, or investments. The main focus should be on writing quality content that will help you and others, and not spraying your blog with advertisements everywhere. The #1 blogging tip that I can give you from my experience is that write blogs for people and not for Google adsense or SEO robots. So, focus on unique content, content, more content. Good content will drive traffic to your blog. Blogging is all about building relationships. If you want some sample blog examples, have a look at:

- javapapers.com (I think it is a wordpress based blog)
- jenkov.com

I am sure that you will find many more good examples. Research for "blogging tips" before you start.

As a general rule of thumb, 3,000 page views can bring in around $5-$30 in revenue via advertisements. This is only a pocket money, and the real benefits are realized from promoting and monetizing your books, services and products, enhancing your learning, capturing your experience, networking, and letting the world know of your capabilities to go places. It takes time and lots of patience to build a decent number of followers and subscribers, so start early. You also need to be patient.

Think of it as a small long-term savings account that gradually grows. All you have to do is regularly invest in publishing quality content to make it grow.

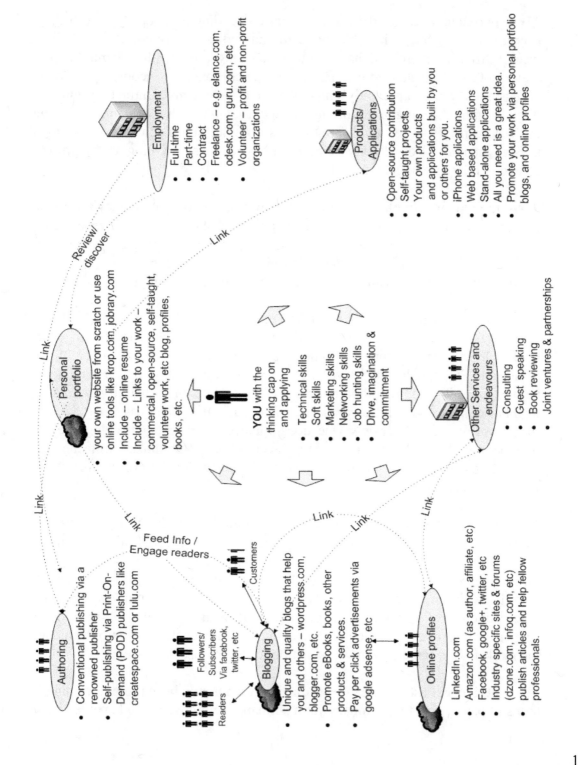

What can you do as a software engineer to open more doors?

My experience: In early 2012, actively started building my blog http://www.java-success.blogspot.com using blogger.com and dedicated around 12 – 15 hours a week. After 15 months, I have around 165 blog posts with 1.5 million page views, 600+ dedicated followers, a very small passive income via Google adsense, and most importantly empowered me to find my contract assignments directly without having to go through an agency and the blog contents are paving the way to my POD self publishing that is bringing in a much higher additional passive income. Also, while working on a project, I use my blog as my primary source of reference to get things done.

- **Writing your own book**. Publishing has never been easier and is very affordable through the print on demand (aka POD) publishing like createspace.com, lulu.com, iUniverse.com, and Lightningsource. The quality blog entries you had created over a period can become the inspiration and the content for your book. Unique content and titles are more sought-after than reinventing the wheel.

My experience: In 2005, self published my first book entitled "Java/J2EE Job Interview Companion" via lulu.com, which costed me less than $150.00 to get my book sold via amazon.com and other major channels. It has sold over 25,000 copies and POD publishers let you keep around 40% to 75% of the earnings as royalty. Does it sound too good to be true? The catch is that I had to promote my own books. I used google adwords (i.e. placing advertisements via Google search for keywords "Java Interview Questions") and more recently my blog itself to promote my books. Over time, the SEO (Search Engine Optimization) techniques has placed my blog in first page, when searched for keywords like "Java Interview Questions".

- **Becoming an independent contractor:** Contract jobs with the right skills are paid very well. If you have the well rounded skills, you could take up contract roles with the confidence that you could find a suitable employment even in a difficult job market. Building up a good network will help you find your contracts directly with an employer as opposed to going via recruitment agencies. Alternatively, you can build a good rapport with a handful of recruitment agencies who are happy to do door knocking on your behalf to tap into the hidden job market. This can be a win/win situation for both. I use both avenues.

My experience: Last 10 years of contracting has not only been more rewarding in terms of pay as cost to a company for a permanent employee with benefits can be

1.5 to 2.5 times the amount they see in their pay check and some contractors do bring in specialized and wide range of skills to get mission critical projects over the line. Another major plus for contracting is that you can afford to take some time off in between your contracts to pursue other avenues listed in the diagram. This gives you the much needed "professional freedom" to explore and grow.

Working as a consultant/contractor for more than 5 companies in the last 10 years has expanded my skills and ability to continuously find work. In most occasions, I was in a position to choose from 3-5 job offers and negotiated better rates. Contracting has also empowered me to blog on wider range of topics with good practical examples to standout from other blogs on similar topics. The major challenge to freelance is to find work continuously, and this risk can be mitigated by building relationships via online presence, writing quality resumes, good job hunting skills, and great interviewing skills.

- **Other avenues your creative mind can think of** in terms of new products and applications. A colleague of mine was working full-time as a software engineer and created an online application for "tennis court booking system" on a part-time basis. He basically combined his passion for playing tennis and writing software. Another example would be to build iPhone applications by getting a mac, SDK for iPhone development, learning objective C, and start writing an application. Alternatively, if you have a great idea, hire an iPhone developer (e.g. a freelancer via odesk.com) to implement your idea. The idea is more important. So, if you are not ready to sell a product or an application, sell your services or ideas by establishing the right contacts via your network.

Additional streams may not -- at least initially -- make enough money to replace a full-time job, but they can help you acquire new skills while expanding your professional network. Have you heard the phrase – it is not what you know, but who you know? In a *Harvard Business Review* article entitled "How to build your network", Brian Uzzi and Shannon Dunlap contend that "networks determine which ideas become breakthroughs, which new drugs are prescribed, which farmers cultivate pest-resistant crops and which R&D engineers make the most high-impact discoveries." Publishing articles via industry specific sites like dzone.com can also build a professional profile online. The web has become a very valuable tool for communicating your value as a professional, expressing your capabilities, and networking. You don't have to be a jack of all trades or a brilliant professional to build your own brand online. All what takes is to be creative and express your unique value with passion and perseverance. If things are looking more promising, you can promote your online products, books and services through your blogs and web sites. Each avenue brings in tangible and intangible benefits by complementing each other. So, put your thinking cap on, and expand your horizon as described in the diagram and see where it takes you.

Do IT salaries plateau?

From my personal experience and observation, a real growth in salary for a software engineer is between his/her second year to tenth year. Somewhere around the tenth year mark the salary tends to plateau. To get beyond this you need to be someone with highly sought after skills that can not be found anywhere else, or be in a management position. Alternatively, you need to set the foundation early enough so that you can explore the other avenues illustrated in the above diagram. You are only limited by your imagination, action and momentum to try different things to open more doors.

Don't let additional income let you lose focus

While it is encouraging to have additional income streams, it is imperative to put things into perspective. For many, full-time employment will be the main source of income. So, the main focus of this book is to achieve that and your key focus must be on

- Growing as a well-rounded professional with technical skills, soft skills, networking skills, job hunting skills, and marketing skills.

- If you are a beginner, acquiring the much needed hands-on experience via voluntary work, internships, self-taught projects, open-source experience, and creating an online portfolio to promote your work and passion will be a better choice than going down the path of enhancing your academic qualifications through post-graduate degree or certifications. The prospective employers are more interested in **hands-on experience**. The knowledge is only a potential power, and the real power to open more doors lies in the **action** of that knowledge.

- Ideas are products of your imagination. Without action, your imagination faculty can become dormant. You need to rekindle your imagination through action in one or more avenues described in the diagram. You don't always have to have an

16

original idea or plan. You can come up with a unique combination.

"Logic gets you from A to B. **IMAGINATION** will take you everywhere"

-- Albert Einstein

Recently, came across some creative article/blog titles like "How I taught my dog polymorphism", "If you are serious about your, quit your job now", etc.

My experience: Most of my ideas for my blog, book or to solve a pressing problem at work pops up in my head when I am relaxed. For example, after a 40 minute walk or an hour tennis session, or while commuting to work. Understanding and trying to solve others' problems via industry forums and soliciting others' views and perspectives on a problem can also spark new thoughts.

- If you are a blogger, then pay more attention to writing quality and unique blogs that will be useful to you and others. Quality blogs can impress your potential employers, help you network with like minded professionals, help you capture your thought bubbles and experience, and conducive to turning into a book. I have worked with many talented professionals who wished they had written a book too to share their experiences, but their main excuse was "didn't have time".

- Building an online persona and networking will help you discover like minded professionals to form an alliance to carry out your ideas and plans. For example, jointly writing a book or creating an application/product, guest posting on blogs and having mutual links, etc. When you collaborate, clearly define what benefits you offer individual members of your alliance. It does not have to be always in the form of money. It could be in the form of recognition, free copies of your book, mutual growth, etc.

- Don't just expect your first idea or plan to always work. If it did not work, come up with more ideas and plans until it works. For example, your first online article, blog, or book might receive bad reviews. Don't let those criticisms stop you from writing. Learn from your mistakes and grow stronger.

- A great idea, plan, or product must be backed with good marketing to reach the target audience. Harness the power of digital media to promote your idea, product, service, blog, and yourself. There are paid avenues like Google adwords, placing advertisements on industry specific websites, paid SEO, etc and unpaid avenues like mutual links or leaving comments on others' blogs, providing your signature with a link in technical forums while helping others, publishing articles in industry specific sites with your link in the signature, and creating profiles with your URL in LinkedIn.com, Facebook, Twitter, Amazon, and Google+. So, if you are contemplating further study, please include digital marketing to your list.

Do you have real 3-5 year experience as opposed to repeating the same year 3-5 times?

Most of us will stagnate in our careers from time to time. When you have many avenues to explore as a software engineer, there is no excuse to stagnate. Getting a good handle on the 16 key areas discussed in the next section will make your career more enjoyable and rewarding. It will help you open more doors by empowering you to present yourself in a better light at code review sessions, team meetings, brain storming sessions, project retrospective sessions, design review sessions, and job interviews. If you just rely on your experience alone, it can take a number of years to master these key areas. The best way to fast tack your career is to pro-actively learn and apply these key areas in paid, unpaid, and self-taught projects. There are plethora of online articles, quality blogs, and books for you to expand your knowledge and skills in these key areas. So, have "*real 3-5 year experience as opposed to repeating the same year 3-5 times*".

Earn a reputation as a "go to person"

Become a facilitator or a change agent of the 16 key technical areas discussed in the next section to solve business problems and build quality software. Take the initiative to solve some of the common problems faced by your organization. This will earn you the reputation as a "**go to person**". If you want to progress or survive lay offs, you need to stay visible by being pro-active and contributing. Contribute not only in terms of producing a quality software, but also in terms of contributing at daily stand-ups, code review sessions, team meetings, design review sessions, brain storming sessions, and project retrospective sessions. Volunteer and take on new work and challenges that are conducive to not only enhancing your capabilities in these key areas, but also improving your domain knowledge and soft skills. Technical skills alone can be replaced more easily than technical skills complemented with good domain knowledge and soft skills. Help others where possible as it will help you improve your skills and knowledge as well.

A well written resume can secure you more interviews

Your resume on average has to standout from 20-100 other competitors unless you are a high profile candidate like Rod Johnson (Founder of Spring framework). Today many prospective employers embrace **networking** as the key source for finding a new position. Even when candidates are brought through a networked source, the first thing one would say is "Ask them to send their resume and I will see what I can do". When a prospective employer is scanning through piles of resumes, it is an art to capture his or her attention to read your resume from beginning to end by making them concise and interesting to read. After reading the first few paragraphs, the prospective employer/recruiter needs to think, "Wow, this is exactly the type of professional I'm looking for and would like to learn more about him/her!'. *More often simple tips and being in the know how can make a huge difference*.

Ineffective resumes result in prolonged job searches, and very often, lower salary offers. It can also negatively impact your self confidence. When people get a poor response to a job application, they think that they are the problem, but fail to think that their resume could be the problem. If you really stop to think what benefits an effective resume can bring, you will be motivated to put the extra effort. Even, if you are already in an employment, multiple-job offers can increase your power to negotiate better salaries. The section 4 of this book focusses on writing effective resumes to open more doors.

Job interview questions are generally based on your resume

Writing an effective resume is also an excellent interview preparation. It will help you learn about yourself and empower you to walk into interviews knowing that you are highly capable. The first step in preparing for an interview is to do a thorough self-assessment. It is very important to develop a complete inventory of your technical skills, soft skills, experience, and personal attributes that you can use to market yourself to your prospective employers at any time during the interview process. Also, take a mental picture of the technical and soft skills you would like to acquire from your next job along with your goals and objectives. This will help you ask intelligent questions at the interview to evaluate if this is the right job for you without having to let the recruitment agencies and prospective employers decide what is best for you. The sections 5 and 6 focusses on interview preparation.

What can you do as a software engineer to open more doors?

What skills are IT employers looking for?

"Do you consider yourself to be a Java or .Net guru? Technical skills alone are no guarantee of success. Acquiring certifications is not going to bring your next promotion or save you from being laid off".

Who are the people I would like to work with? Here is a list of top 5 things I would look for:

1. Good handle on the **16 key technical areas** to get things done through collaboration and taking initiatives.
2. Very good **interpersonal skills** to work as a team and **help others** achieve common team goals.
3. **Passion** for the chosen profession.
4. Ability to **communicate** well, look at things from both **business** and **technical** perspective, and ability look at both the **big picture** and pay attention to **details**.
5. Right **attitude**. Big no for attitudes like "I know it all", "I always want to do it my way", "being negative", and "bad mouthing others".

The software engineers with good technical skills complimented with great soft skills are a minority and that is why you have mangers and team leaders to bridge the gap. Otherwise, all you need is a highly motivated self organizing teams.

Candidates who can demonstrate a personal interest in programming are regarded as hot property on account of the fact that they demonstrate initiative, passion, and illustrate a can-do attitude to their work. Old languages die out to be replaced with new dynamic technologies, so employers are on the hunt for people who can move with the times. The 16 key areas discussed in the next section are easily transferable from one technology to another by learning to ask the right questions.

Piling up of your certifications and learning new frameworks alone don't lead to recognition, promotion, and most importantly opportunity. Employers look for well-rounded professionals, who are good thinkers, problem solvers, communicators, and most importantly **get the job done** in a complex real life environment without whingeing. If you are deciding, which professional skill to improve next, then dig deep beyond just academic qualifications and identify the next set of skills that will open more doors as a software engineer. For example,

- you could pick a soft-skill to improve on. For example, communication skills.
- blogging can improve your writing, communication, and technical skills.
- pro-actively applying the technical key areas to self-taught projects or contributing to open-source projects can improve your technical know-how and most importantly the hands-on experience.
- Non profit organizations are generally eager to find volunteer help. Why not build a simple website for them while acquiring some hands-on experience at the same time. Don't over commit yourself.
- search engine optimization (aka SEO) and other digital marketing techniques like RSS feeds, tweeting, pod-casting, video streaming, etc can help you build your online brand and expand your network to open more doors.

Your marketing needs to be targeted

Your value proposition must be relevant to your target market. So, it is imperative to define your target audience first. Your resume, interview preparation, blogging, books, products, applications, services, etc need to be properly targeted. For example,

Q. If you put yourself in a prospective employer's shoes, will you interview candidate A or Candidate B?

Resume for candidate A:

Summary: A certified, results-driven, customer-focused, articulate and analytical Senior Software Engineer who can think "out of the box". Strong in design, application integration and problem solving skills. Expert in Java, C#, .NET, and T-SQL with database analysis and design. Skilled in developing technical specifications, user documentation, and architectural artifacts. Strong in written and verbal communications. Interested in a challenging technical track career in an application development environment.

Experienced in:

- Engineering web development, all layers, from database to services to user interfaces.
- Integrating modern systems with legacy systems.
- Analysis and design of databases and user interfaces.

What can you do as a software engineer to open more doors?

- Managing requirements.
- Implementing software development life cycle policies and procedures.
- Managing and supporting multiple projects.
- Highly adaptable in quickly changing technical environments with very strong organizational and analytical skills.

Resume for candidate B

Summary: Looking for a challenging position as a senior Java/JEE professional where my experiences are blogged at http://www.myblog.com and experience in summary include

- Over 6 years in building and solving business problems for organizations like BigInsurance1 and BigRetail2 of which recent 4+ years in Java/JEE and 2+ years in C# and .NET.

- 3+ years in finance sector, and 2.5 years in retail sector. Spent last 1.5 years as a lead developer for a complex finance system that has over 2 million registered users.

- Instrumental in successfully managing and implementing a mission critical .NET and C# based "Pay pass" system that increased the retail sales by 35%.

- One of the 7 key representatives selected among 45 professionals, as a core project team contributor to provide effective technical, business, and process ideas, solutions, improvements, and recommendations to a project budgeted at $25 million for XYZ Consulting.

I would be more temped to interview the candidate B. I will also be tempted to check out his/her blog as online persona can tell a lot about a candidate. The resume for candidate A is full of fluff and no stuff. Just being certified alone does not make him/her a better candidate. It even makes you think when candidate-A prides more on certification(s) than commercial experience, if he/she is an experienced professional or not. Anyone can say she/he is an "expert in **Java, C#, .NET, and T-SQL** ". Just certification or 5 year experience does not quantify you as an expert. It is your contributions and quantifiable accomplishments make you a better professional. The resume for candidate A is also not targeted. It is a very generic resume. The resume for candidate B is more focused and interesting with quantified statements. Favor multiple targeted resumes over a single generic resume.

Why is it important to build an online persona?

Employers are realizing that what you do online can actually prove your value as a potential hire. A positive "virtual you" featuring a blend of your life and work achievements through online portfolios, blogs, and LinkedIn.com profiles can strengthen your job hunt. If people Google you and find your work to be interesting, it can open more doors for you in terms of potential job interviews, requests for book reviews, and opportunities to meet like minded or influential people. You can turn your readers and followers into customers or employers with some clever ideas. My current employer had read my books before he actually hired me.

How to become an architect?

In industry specific forums I see questions like "what certification do I need to become an architect?". The simple answer is that you don't need a certification to become an architect. **You can't just only study to become an architect**. The best way to become an architect is to start thinking and acting like one. In other words, emulate the best in the business. If you start thinking like one, you will start to observe the architects at current work, and learn from them. You will start to follow good blogs and articles by other architects and invest in highly rated books. This is true for other roles like becoming a manager, lead developer, etc.

Any self-help book will tell you -- **what you think and do is what you become**. This is why many interviewers ask open-ended questions like who are your role models? what books did you read recently? how do you keep your knowledge up to date? tell me about yourself? what are your short term and long term goals?, etc. These questions can reveal a lot about your passion, enthusiasm, attitude, communication skills, and technical strengths.

Here is my take on the road map to become a software architect.

- **Get a good handle on the 16 key areas** discussed in the next section and proactively apply these key areas to experience them. Learn to ask the right questions -- what if ...? how about ...?, etc. Think in terms of scalability, transactional boundaries, best practices, exception handling, development process improvement, etc. Learn to analyze design alternatives, pros vs cons, tactical versus strategical, strategical vs political, weight the risks against the benefits, build vs buy, etc.

- **Look at things from both business and technical perspective**: architects form a bridge between many cross functional teams like business analysts, stake holders, project managers, developers, testers, infrastructure team, operational and support staff. Know your target audience and learn to convey technology to the business non-technically and the business requirements to the techies technically. Learn to draw high-level conceptual and UML diagrams. Know the various architectural styles, layered multi-tier architectures, and various integration styles. You must be confident to draw these diagrams on a white board with regards to the actual application you had worked on or how you would go about designing a new application.

- **Learn to look at the big pictures and also pay attention to details** where required. Get a well rounded hands-on experience. For example, client side, server side, application integration, full SDLC, etc. Nothing beats experience, and you can proactively fast-track your career by learning from others' experience via good books, blogs, industry specific web sites, and helping others on the forums.

- Lastly, but most importantly have a good grip on the domain knowledge and the much needed soft skills. You don't have to be the "jack of all trades", but as a technical leader and a bridge between various stake holders and the development teams, you need to have good soft skills to make things happen by engaging the right teams and expertise. The key soft skills to have are communication, interpersonal, leadership, analytical, negotiation, and problem solving to get things done.

What if your current job is not conducive to acquiring the relevant skills?

This is possible if you are either working for the wrong team or the organization. This is also possible if you are not putting your hand up to take on more challenges or your contributions are not visible enough in the relevant areas. You must always give before you take, but there are times in your career that you might strongly feel that you are working for the wrong organization. You will even feel that why you had waited so long.

One of the dilemmas many professionals face is **when to jump the ship?** versus **when to steady the ship?** There is no right or wrong answer to this question, and the answer depends on the individual circumstances. But here are some of my thoughts that might aid in your decision making. People jump the ship for a number of reasons like life style changes, feeling bored, burnt or stressed out, feeling stagnated, and wanting to earn more money. People steady the ship for a number of reasons like already jumped the ship too often, not ready to take on new challenges due to personal reasons, bad economy, etc. When my parents were in their working years, the prevailing notion was that an employer would "take care of you" for a long time with a secure job and a decent pension. But that's not true any more. Today, it's not uncommon to change jobs voluntarily every few years. Changing jobs has the following benefits.

- Gives you the opportunity to enhance your skills in the sought-after technologies, frameworks, and tools. The longer you stay at one company, the less motivated you become to learn new technologies, frameworks, and tools.

- You don't have to put up with things like "this is how we have always did it" syndrome. Getting different perspectives on development processes, agile practices, architectures, etc will give you an opportunity to understand not only what works and what doesn't, but also when it does work without getting into the hype. Some businesses are not set up to embrace the latest and greatest technologies. They are more business focused than technology focused. So, it really pays to work in different sectors like telecommunication, finance, insurance, software house, etc to see how the similar problems are solved differently in different sectors or organizations. This will enable you to become a better problem solver.

- Helps you build up a wider network. Networking is key to open more doors to your career. Knowing the right people is equally important as knowing the right technologies/frameworks.

- Helps you progress in you career a lot quicker. It also gives you the confidence that you can find a job whenever you need to. Now a days, there is no real job security in being with a company for 10+ years unless you feel that you are going places within the organization and foresee a good future there by acquiring the relevant domain knowledge and soft-soft skills. The real job security comes from keeping your skills and knowledge up to date without feeling stagnated.

What can you do as a software engineer to open more doors?

- Increases your earning potential. If you are lucky enough to get a promotion with your current company, they will only give you a small increase in salary, just enough to justify the promotion and keep you. If you however require a decent promotion and increased package, changing jobs and the employer might be the way to go.

Having said this, a few do progress well within the same organization. Quitting your job is not always the right solution. A better solution would be to ask for what you want. Your boss may not realize you feel undervalued. You also want to make sure your boss understands your value and what you have recently accomplished.

Here are a few tell tale signs to jump the ship when the time is right.

- Your skills are not respected. If you feel that your employer doesn't recognize your value to the company, then it may be time for a change. When you hand in your resignation, you might be asked questions like -- what can I do to keep you here? You might even think – why did I wait so long?

- You're stuck in the same position, doing the same things, for nearly the same pay, for a long time, it's time to shake things up. Be realistic of the situation, rather than deluding yourselves into believing that things will miraculously improve or what your boss tell you to convince you to stay back.

- Constantly looking at your watch and being unhappy at work.

- Sinking feeling about going back to work after your leave period.

- Talking to other people about the jobs they do in a greater depth.

Even if you are in the process of steadying the ship, there is no excuse to stagnate at work as you can take up a lot of things outside work as described in the big picture as to what you can do as a software engineer.

"Love your job but don't love your company, because you may not know when your company stops loving you. " – by A. P. J. Abdul Kalam

Balance is the key

You need a balance between "changing ships too often" and "not changing ships at all". Some employers in selected industry segments will wonder "what's wrong" with an individual who has not changed jobs in X years, and on the other hand, there are still many employers who will look on frequent changes unfavorably. The obvious implications for them are, that you won't stay long enough to make any significant contributions, and that if you were hired, perhaps your tendency to leave quickly will inspire many otherwise loyal employees to leave as well. Steadying the ship is important to convince your future employers that stability and permanence are at the top of your list of priorities, and that the targeted company appears to be one. It is also imperative that your current and past employers will vouch positively for your capabilities by providing positive references. This is why it is vital to always move on in good terms. Never burn bridges. You need to include your current employer and the other colleagues as part of your network via linkedIn.com.

A common sentiment from:

- an employee leaving a company is "I feel bad about leaving."
- an employer losing an employee is "**Absolutely NONE**".

A company's responsibility is to make profits. This means that for some reason you no longer help the employer reach this aim, the company can and will terminate your services. This dynamic should work both ways. When an employer no longer provides you what you need in the form of compensation and professional development then you have every right to terminate the relationship without any guilt. So, don't be afraid of change.

My experience: Changing from being a mechanical engineer to software engineering was the best thing I ever did to my career. The second best thing was to become an independent consultant/contractor to build a rewarding career. My increase in salaries and responsibilities were mostly brought on by changing jobs. My resignation letters often prompted salary discussions from my employers, and often made me think why I waited so long. This taught me a valuable lesson that I will have to make things happen and no one else is going to do that for me.

You are the captain of your ship, and best placed to solve your dilemma based on your current circumstance and career aspirations. It is not an easy decision to make. What ever your decision is, **don't base it on monetary value alone.** Use the multi-attribute decision approach discussed next.

How to choose from multiple job offers?

In career forums many interview candidates ask how to choose between company A, B and C. While it is a nice feeling to be in with multiple job-offers, it is not an easy decision to make and often this dilemma is made worse due to **not asking the right questions about the position or role at the interview**. An interview is a **two way process** where the interviewer(s) assess the suitability of the candidate to the position or role whilst the candidate assesses the suitability of the position or role to his/her interests and career aspirations. Asking the right questions can not only help you make an informed decision to choose the job of your dreams, but also can help you negotiate your remuneration and market your skills & strengths more effectively based on the answers.

Some of the questions you can ask are:

- If I am successful, what type of projects will I be involved in and what type of technologies/frameworks will I be exposed to? Will this role involve liaising with the business users and/or mentoring opportunities?

- What types of candidates succeed in your organization?

- Is this a mission critical project? How big is the team? What is the budget for this project?

- What are the key tasks and responsibilities involved with my role? Does this involve new development, enhancement or support work?

How would you go about choosing from multiple job offers?

It is not an easy decision to make, but here is my analytical approach with a list of things to consider. For each consideration, give a weight based on its importance to you.

- Remuneration and other benefits: This is an important criteria, but not the only one. You need to look long term. [e.g. weight = 30%]

- Opportunity to learn and/or work with popular, emerging and sought after technologies, frameworks, commercial tools, and architectural styles. By acquiring experience and skills in emerging and sought after technologies, frameworks, and products, you can stand out from your competition and get more interview calls next time you start hunting for a job. Specialized skills are more sought-after and paid well. For example, there are hordes of Java developers, and many with Spring experience, and a few with Spring and SOA or Spring and BPM or Spring and FIX protocol experience. Be mindful that some skills can be acquired through self-study whilst other skills require commercial experience. Java and Spring can be self-taught, but SOA, BPM, and FIX protocol experiences require commercial exposure. [e.g. weight = 20%].

- Type of project (new project, enhancement to existing project, support): You tend to learn more on new projects. Is it a mission critical project? how many other developers are working on it or you are the only developer? The more rigorous the interviewing process the greater the opportunity to work with talented fellow professionals to learn from each other. This is an important criteria for me. [e.g. weight = 20%]

- Brand name, company culture, business acumen, etc. Brand name does matter as it helps you get more interview calls next time you start hunting for a job, but what skills and experience you will be acquiring matters more. You may get more interview calls but may find it difficult to get through your interview stages if your skills are not enhanced through good hands-on experience. [e.g. weight = 10%]

- Type of role like mentoring, team leading, etc and other opportunities like liaising with the business, travel, customer facing, etc. Would this role have active involvement with the business users or will you be sitting in some obscure location and just coding away without being visible? [e.g. weight = 10%]

- Type of organization (Insurance, Finance, Software house, multinational, etc). In some types of organizations like finance, insurance, etc you tend get better remuneration. In some software houses and consultancy roles you tend to acquire wider range of skills. Some organizations favor professionals with prior experience in similar industry. [e.g. weight = 5%]

- Location and lifestyle choices. Other preferences like contract versus permanent

What can you do as a software engineer to open more doors?

role. [e.g. weight = 5%] .

Total weight should be 100%. The weights are for illustration purpose only and may vary from individual to individual.

You can analytically work it out as follows: You can give some weight to each of the criteria as shown above. The weights need to add up to 100%. Now say you have offers from company A, B and C. You give some points out of say 10 to each of the above criteria and then multiply each point by the weight (i.e. importance to you) and then add them all up. If the difference is negligible or not conclusive enough then go with your heart. Otherwise you know which one(s) to choose or pursue with further negotiations.

How do you find out how popular you are in online space?

Have you ever Googled you or your blog keywords to see how popular you are? Would you be interested in how many other people are searching for your name or blog? You can use the "**Google keyword tool**" to analyze the search volumes for yourself or your blog. This tool is very handy when you are deciding – what to blog on? You would not want to blog on keywords that are very competitive unless you are prepared to use paid advertisements to market your blog. If you would like your prospective employers and others to find you by Googling, you can set up a full profile at http://www.linkedIn.com and share your blog and upload your resume. Your profile will be indexed after sometime by the search engine. You can also use a number of free **search engine ranking tools** like

- http://www.searchenginegenie.com/google-rank-checker.html
- http://www.seocentro.com/tools/search-engines/keyword-position.html

to see how well your blog or website is doing for keyword searches on Google.

Regardless of many good tips you find online for SEO techniques for better search engine ranking of your blog or website, the most important tip is to write quality contents that are search engine friendly and engage readers to read, subscribe, leave comments on your blog, and create back links to your blog. The "**Google analytics**" is a very handy tool to gather relevant statistics. Review – where the traffic is coming from? which blog entries are more popular? how many are repeated visits?, what is the frequency of visits?, etc. Try to keep the bounce rate under 75%.

How to become a freelancer?

Anyone can become a freelancer, but the **hardest part of becoming a freelancer is finding work**. You just can't go to a freelance site like elance.com or odesk.com and expect to pull jobs that will give you a steady income. Those are low-dollar markets as you will be competing against people around the world. You can work for multiple clients, but this approach is favored when your objective is to acquire additional hands-on experience and income. If you want a more steady and decent income like 1.5 to 2.0 times the permanent staff salary, then favor working for a single client locally on a longer term contract basis like 3 months to 24 months. This assignment is also known to be freelancing as a contractor, consultant, or a contingent worker. No matter which approach you take, the key is to **find work continuously.** So, you should not only have relevant technical skills, but also good non-technical skills.

> You need to **"talk the talk"** in your job interviews to get hired as a freelancer,
> and **"walk the walk"** at your freelance work
> to impress your client and consequently get repeated extensions.

Step 1: Develop the experience and skills required to become a freelancer. Build at least 3 year hands on experience.

- Get a good handle on the 16 technical key areas discussed in the next section to solve real business problems and to better market your skills at the job interviews and on the job. These are transferrable skills that you can take from one programming language to another.
- Get a good handle on the sought-after frameworks and tools relating to your mainstream language. Check your local job advertisements to see what the prospective employers are looking for.
- You can be a front-end developer (i.e. focusing mainly on GUI development), back end developer (i.e. integrating various systems via web services, messaging, ETL, etc), or do both, but you tend to have more strength either on front-end or back-end development. I do both, but stronger on the back end development. In my experience, the backend tends to pay more.
- Develop good marketing skills -- **1.** Good resume writing **2.** Good interview preparation by knowing your resume well enough and brushing up on the fundamentals.
- Build your network via LinkedIn.com and regular catch ups with your former

What can you do as a software engineer to open more doors?

bosses and colleagues. You will be under less scrutiny when you find your next contract via your previous contacts.

- Build an online presence so that others can discover you. You can also show off your skills to your prospective employers or clients.

Step 2: Register yourself with the recruitment and consulting agencies.

Send your CV or resume to consulting or recruitment agencies so that they have your details in their databases. Big clients prefer to deal with consulting or recruitment agencies as they do not directly want to keep in touch with hundreds of freelancers and negotiate rates. Also, if you prematurely leave a client for unforeseen reasons, then the consultancy or recruitment agency can quickly find a replacement.

Join the relevant professional bodies like software forums like javaranch.com, professional networking sites like LinkedIn.com and its relevant groups like software groups (e.g. Java enthusiasts, Java jobs, etc), and job boards like indeed.com to advertise your availability.

As only 5% to 15% of the real vacancies are advertised, build your network to find your future contracts via your contacts. Make it a point to regularly catch-up with your former colleagues and bosses. Build a good rapport with a handful of consultancy or recruitment agencies so that they can proactively look for work on your behalf to create a "win/win" outcome for both. I have done this very successfully.

Step 3: Talk to an accountant about setting up your own company versus joining an umbrella contracting company to take care of the administration work in your jurisdiction. There are pros and cons for each approach.

Step 4: Be selective about the jobs you choose to work on. Freelancers are hired for 3 main reasons.

- To get freelancers to do the boring tasks or work that other permanent staff don't want to take on.
- To get the project over the line. In other words meet the deadline.
- To bring in expertise that are lacked within the current team.

So, it is imperative to learn more about the position at the job interviews to ensure what you are getting into. You would ideally want points 2 and 3 to be the reason where you can acquire more skills and experience. So, ask the right questions at your interviews.

Endeavor to build specialized skills to increase your rates and reduce your competition. So, build niche skills by having [main stream language] + [something niche]. When you choose your next assignment, pick the one that is more conducive to acquiring that [something niche]. That something niche could be a commercial application on SOA, BPM, BigData, etc that is in demand.

You will gain more confidence as you go through the above steps. Freelancing is not everyone's cup of tea, but can give professional freedom and better income streams for some. Some may prefer doing it for a short while and then settle down with a company to grow within that organization. Some love to go freelancing, but fearful of or too comfortable in the current role to take the first step. First step is always the hardest. Freelancing or not, more and more organizations are becoming leaner and meaner to make profit for their stake holders, and **staying relevant with the technologies and frameworks** without being too complacent about your current role is **your only job security** as a software developer.

"Any intelligent fool can make things bigger, more complex, and more violent. It takes a touch of genius -- and a lot of courage -- to **move in the opposite direction**."

- Albert Einstein

What can you do as a software engineer to open more doors?

Section 2:

Get a good handle on the 16 key areas of software

engineering to open more doors

- Motivate yourself to learn, and apply these key areas to impress your peers and superiors by pro-actively and re-actively solving the problems and challenges faced by your organization in software engineering.

- Make a real difference by building a quality software that satisfies the business needs.

- Highlight your experience and accomplishments in these key areas through your resumes and job interviews to differentiate yourself from the other software engineers.

If your efforts and contributions in these 16 technical key areas are not recognized, you might be either working for the wrong team/organization or your non-technical skills need to be reviewed. It could also mean that someone else is reaping the benefits of your contributions.

What are the 16 technical key areas?

Writing a quality software is a very complex process. It must not only meet all the functional requirements, but also should address non-functional requirements like robustness, responsiveness, maintainability, testability, scalability, security, supportability, monitor-ability, and disaster recoverability to meet the immediate business needs. It must also be flexible enough to adapt to growing and changing business needs. Anyone who has been in the software industry for a while will vouch for how quickly the business priorities can change. They also strongly understand that the following aspects need to be properly thought through from the beginning of a software project.

- Capture and document the functional and non-functional requirements. Conduct workshops and brain storming sessions to fully understand and close any gaps in the requirements and design. It is also important to look at the big picture to ascertain if existing services or processes can be either leveraged or enhanced. In larger organizations, expertise are scattered, and proper engagement and facilitation of relevant teams like infrastructure management, quality assurance, security, release management, production support, and other internal project teams that could be impacted is necessary.

- Hardware (CPU, memory, storage, etc), networking (latency, routing, clustering, DNS look-ups, load balancing, SNMP traps, etc), and access control requirements to various UNIX/WIN32 boxes, database servers, application servers, and message oriented middle-ware servers need to be sorted out. Proper capacity planning needs to be carried out to ensure that the relevant SLAs (i.e. Service Level Agreements) are met.

- Choice of development, dependency management, build, unit testing, continuous integration, deployment, and release management tools, frameworks, libraries, standards, and processes needed to be in place to get the team into the rhythm of code, build, release, test and deliver cycle. The continuous build, integration, and delivery are hot topics in SDLC (Software Delivery Life Cycle).

- Building the first end to end vertical slice for a typical use case can validate the design and choice of technologies, frameworks, and tools along with the realization of how some of the key areas discussed below like design consideration, design patterns, transaction management, memory/resource management, concurrency management, security, exception handling, scalability, best practices, and coding fit together like a puzzle to build a quality application. This initial vertical slice is generally built by a lead developer, architect, or technical lead with strong technical skills. The rest of the team will be required to provide feedback before taking the lessons learned and the approach into subsequent use cases.

- Adequate logging, auditing, and monitoring requirements need to be considered to provide better problem diagnostics and customer support. Contextual logging can be Splunked to gather key metrics and diagnose issues.

- Service assurance requirements like being up 24x7, gathering performance metrics, adherence to SLAs (Service Level Agreements) like peak and off-peak response times, service timeouts, system fail over, data retention, data archival, data backup, and disaster recovery strategies need to be incorporated to improve customer trust and experience in the system.

- The project needs to be taken through the full software development life cycle (SDLC) process by adopting waterfall, agile, or hybrid development practices with proper release and hand over procedures and documentation.

So, it really pays to have the right people in the team. People with the technical know how to manage complexities and get things done. It is also imperative to have a well balanced team with varying strengths to complement each other in these key areas.

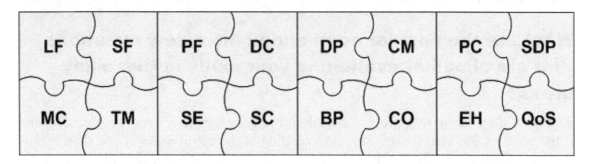

1. Language Fundamentals (LF)
2. Specification Fundamentals (SF)
3. Platform Fundamentals (PF)
4. Design Considerations (DC)
5. Design Patterns (DP)

Get a good handle on the 16 key areas of software engineering to open more doors

6. Concurrency Management (CM)
7. Performance Considerations (PC)
8. Memory/Resource Considerations (MC)
9. Transaction Management (TM)
10. Security (SE)
11. Scalability (SC)
12. Best Practices (BP)
13. Coding (CO)
14. Exception Handling (EH)
15. Software Development Processes (SDP)
16. Quality of Service (QoS)

In most of my contracts, I was in a position to impress my team leads, architects, peers, and superiors by pro-actively pinpointing some of the critical performance, memory, transactional, and threading issues, and subsequently fixing them. If you happen to be in an interview with an organization facing issues with regards to their applications relating to these key areas, then you are likely to be quizzed on them. If the team leads/architects of the organization you are being interviewed for feel that the current team is lacking skills in these key areas then you are likely to be asked questions on these key areas. Even if you don't get quizzed on these key areas, you can bring it up yourself as an answer to many of the open-ended questions to differentiate yourself from your competitors who fail to sell themselves on these key areas. **If you don't invest in acquiring the relevant skills in these technical key areas to market yourself, someone else will and clinch the deal.**

What are the popular open-ended interview questions that are aimed at evaluating your skills in these key areas?

As part of the interviewing process, besides other things, interviewers like to understand if the person being interviewed has understanding of the applications he/she develops as a whole. He/she must understand the entire architecture of the application and, most importantly, why a specific architecture is in place for that application and its specific needs.

Q. Could you please describe, from your perspective, what should be a typical .NET architecture for, let's say, a medium-size web-based application?
Q. Can you give a bird's eye view of the last application you had worked on?

Q. What frameworks and tools would you use to build your next application?
Q. How would you go about designing an online shopping cart application?

The interviewer is not expecting you to design a shopping cart application in 10-15 minutes. He or she is more interested in how well you understand the key areas, how you think, how you approach a problem, and how well you communicate your thoughts. The interviewer is not only expecting you to describe how you would go about designing an application, but also expecting you to draw some diagrams, and speak out your thinking. You will not only have to describe the conceptual architecture, but also you will be probed on the design decisions. For example, why a RESTful web service was used as opposed to a SOAP based web service?, why do you need separate tiers and layers?, etc. Layered applications are easier to maintain, extend, and test. If you are asked to design an online 2 player "tick tack toe" system, the interviewer might probe that how you will know that your opponent has moved. This is where the good understanding of the HTTP paradigm comes in handy. The browser pages can be refreshed by either "server push" or "client pull". In this case, you could use "client pull" to refresh the page every 5 seconds.

```
<META HTTP-EQUIV="REFRESH" CONTENT="5">
```

You will also be judged on relevant questions you ask. Good software engineers gather requirements by asking relevant questions prior to designing a system. For example -- what types of products or services will you be selling? what volumes are you expecting to sell during peak and off peak period? how will you accept online payments? should it integrate with any other internal or external systems like loyalty programs for discounts, data warehousing for aggregate reporting, and content management systems for publishing promotional and system outage messages?, what are the sensitive data that needs to be protected? how many concurrent users can we expect during peak hours? what information needs to be archived and audited? how will you maintain and provide support for the system? what system metrics need to be gathered?, etc. They might not know the answers to all the questions, but asking the right questions will lead to finding the solutions through good soft skills like researching, analyzing, collaborating and taking initiatives.

Q. What is the current trend in developing a web application?

The current trend in web development is to build single-page rich internet applications (RIA) using HTML5, CSS3, and JavaScript based MVW (Model-View-Whatever) frameworks like Angular JS, Backbone, etc. The data for the GUI is served up via

Get a good handle on the 16 key areas of software engineering to open more doors

RESTful web service calls made via ajax requests. The CORS (Cross Origin Resource Sharing) is used for cross domain calls. The web resources can be served via the Content Delivery Networks (CDN) for faster access and the data can be served via RESTful services hosted on the cloud.

Even though the "devil is in the details", your career success depends on your "**abstract thinking**" and how well you **communicate that thinking**.

Good developers are opinionated about a piece of technology or framework from their personal experience. They like/dislike some features and aware of the common pitfalls. They would also like some new features to be added in the future releases. The following questions are aimed at evaluating your experience.

Q. What features of language X do you like, dislike, and would like to be added in the future versions?
Q. In your observations, what are the common pitfalls or common mistakes junior developers make?

There are other open-ended questions to evaluate not only your technical skills, but most importantly to evaluate your experience, attitude towards software quality, enthusiasm for the chosen profession, and how well you fit in with the team without the "I know it all" attitude.

Q. If you are reviewing some one else's code, what would you look for?
Q. Why do you like software engineering?
Q. What do you like the most about your current job?
Q. What are some of the technical challenges you faced in your current job? How did you go about solving them?

Q. How do you ensure code quality?
Q. What tools do you need to manage complexities, fix issues and get your job done?
Q. How would you go about ..... improving performance, fixing memory leaks, identifying concurrency issues, fixing security holes, etc?

Q. Did you have to use any design patterns in your project?
Q. Tell me about yourself, and some of the projects you have worked on?
Q. Can you describe a situation where you applied your problem solving skills?
Q. Can you describe a situation where you fixed a concurrency issue?

Q. Give me an example of a time when you set a goal and were able to achieve it?

Q. Give me an example of a time you showed initiative and took the lead?

Q. Tell me about a difficult decision you made in the last year?

Q. Tell me about a most complex project you were involved in?

Q. What is a deadlock and how would you detect, and get rid of deadlocks?

The open-ended questions give you a great opportunity to promote your strengths and accomplishments on these key areas. Relate these key areas to your past experience using the **SAR** (Situation-Action-Result) technique described below.

Example -1:

At the job interview:

Situation: Performance problem where the application server had to be restarted every day.

Action:
- Used JMeter to simulate the load conditions and reproduce the issue.
- Identified the cause of the problem to be leaking database connections due to not properly closing the connections under an exceptional scenario.
- Fixed the issue by closing the database connections in the finally block.
- Tuned the JVM settings and configured proper service timeouts.
- Load and endurance tested the fixed code with the load testing tool JMeter to confirm that the issue has been fixed.

Result: The application became a true mission critical 24x7 type with a much improved performance.

You can now mention this in your CV as

- Re-factored and performance tuned a JEE based online insurance application, which *previously came down almost daily, became a true 24x7 application*.

Example -2:

At the job interview:

Situation: C# code that is hard to maintain and reuse. Changes to one module may break another module.

Get a good handle on the 16 key areas of software engineering to open more doors

Action:
- Wrote unit tests with proper mock objects for the existing unmaintainable code.
- Re-factored the code with OO concepts and design patterns in a test driven manner to improve maintainability.
- Reran the unit tests to ensure that the functionality is not broken due to refactoring.

Result: The application became easier to maintain, extend, and reuse.

You can now mention this in your CV as

- Re-factored inefficient code by applying OO concepts and design patterns (GoF & .NET) in a test driven manner to make it more maintainable and reusable.

Let's briefly look at these key areas as a good understanding of these key areas will greatly help you market your skills and open more doors for your career progression.

Even though the examples are aimed more towards Java, the similar approaches are available and useful for other programming languages as well. The knowledge and skills acquired in these key areas are easily transferable to other languages by asking the right questions. The following section provides a high level road map as to what you need to know, and in depth discussion is out of scope. A little online research with the key words used here will reveal more on these key areas. For example, "what is Aspect Oriented Programming?", "what is a post-back?", "AOP in Java", "HTTP forwards vs redirects", SQL injection attack, Aspect Oriented Programming (AOP) for deadlock retries, and functional programming for lots of concurrency/parallelism and mathematical computation.

Language Fundamentals (LF)

If you want to become a professional programmer, then you should be able to easily write code in multiple programming languages and ask the right questions pertaining to other key areas like – how do we prevent cross site scripting and SQL injection attacks?, will my code be thread-safe?, will the connections get closed if an exception is thrown?, will the transactions get rolled back?, are these operations atomic?, does this regular expression backtrack?, what data structure and sorting algorithm should I apply here?, what best practices can I apply here?, etc. Skills acquired in most of these key areas are transferable from one language to another. If you know what can go wrong and what question to ask, you will find the answer by Googling. So, if you are new to programming, don't be overwhelmed by all the technologies, frameworks, libraries, and acronyms. Learn the key concepts and the key areas, the rest will slowly fall into place with a little bit of research.

If you are new to programming or learning a new language, first thing you will need to learn is its fundamentals. You will also have to understand its gotchas, pitfalls, and the common mistakes the beginners make. For example, data over flows, using float variables for exact comparisons, using improper data types to represent monetary values, using the wrong data structures, not understanding deep versus shallow copy/comparisons, not understanding pass-by-reference versus pass-by-value, and writing substandard functions instead of reusing functions from proven APIs and libraries to name a few. It is also imperative to understand the programming paradigms like Object Oriented Programming (OOP), Aspect Oriented Programming (AOP), procedural programming, functional programming, and declarative programming (e.g. SQL, XSLT, Regular Expression, etc) .

I find some books to be unnecessarily verbose and the 3 corner stones to explain or learn the fundamentals are

- A good conceptual diagram that explains the big picture.
- A simple working code with relevant real life examples.
- Asking the right questions like when to use it and when not to, and any best practices, potential pitfalls and common mistakes to be aware of relating to other key areas like performance, scalability, security, etc.

The enterprise programmers should at least learn a main stream language like Java, C, C++, Objective-C, C#, or PHP. The SQL for database access, regex for pattern matching and JSON/XML for data exchange are must know languages for all enterprise developers.

The scripting languages like Ruby, Perl, Python, etc are handy when speed of development is more important. The scripting languages compliment the enterprise languages. The scripting languages are handy for prototyping, data mining, parsing text and log files, and writing test scripts. Dynamic languages like Ruby can be used for specialized areas such as gluing other systems together. For example, JRuby can pull data from one system, transform it and insert it into another. This is also known as the ETL (Extract, Transform and Load) operations. When the requirements change, modifying a JRuby script is as easy as changing a configuration file, thereby avoiding the complex compile-and-deploy cycle of a mainstream language like Java. Often you can combine the robustness of a mainstream language with the clarity and conciseness of dynamic languages like Python or Groovy by using its existing libraries in an application.

If you are a web programmer, you must know JavaScript. Like me, many seem to have a love/hate relationship with JavaScript. Google, Apple, Amazon, Microsoft, Facebook, and many other companies are using JavaScript to build rich web applications. Most websites nowadays have some element of JavaScript or Ajax present. It is probably the main element in developing the web 2.0 (i.e. Rich Internet Application - RIA) movement. The latest creative trend in web design is "**single page website design**" where the relevant content is refreshed via ajax calls. This design provides better user experience as navigating through content is quicker and more responsive than having to go to a new web page. It can be easier to maintain as you will have to maintain only a fewer pages with proper includes.

There are many popular JavaScript frameworks like jQuery, EXT JS, Dojo Toolkit, etc. No matter what your main language of choice is like Java, C#, or PHP, applications developed by any one of these languages will need JavaScript to manipulate the DOM (Document Object Model). In addition to browser based rich clients, desktop and mobile applications are using web-oriented technologies like HTML, CSS, and JavaScript. You will be a smarter, better, and more in-demand web developer by learning JavaScript. JavaScript can be used for building server side applications as well. Look at nodejs.org for more info.

So, you can increase your productivity and manage complexity a bit better by using the right language based on its strengths to solve the task at hand. So, it really pays to be able to sell yourself as someone who is skilled in some of the dynamic scripting languages in addition to having a good grasp on enterprise language(s) of your choice and other must know languages like SQL, regex, and XML based technologies. The XML based technologies/protocols like XSD, WSDL, XPath, XQuery, SOAP, BizTalk, Burlap, etc are language/platform neutral and widely used in system integration. Two different systems written in different mainstream languages/platforms can be integrated using XML. Having said this, there are scenarios where XML may not be the right choice as it is verbose and can put awkward constraints on syntax, especially when used to represent logical statements like a programming language or used to represent simple, non hierarchical data. JSON (i.e JavaScript Object Notation) is more popular in exchanging data.

Choose your languages astutely as some languages never become mainstream. Do your research before learning a programming or scripting language. For example

- Online advertisements in your area.
- Google trends – www.google.com/trends
- Good blogs & industry specific forums/sites to see what the experts are tipping for.
- Google research on keywords like "TIOBE Programming Index" or "RedMonk Programming Ranking" can reveal more.
- You can also determine the rank by number of projects on GitHub (https://github.com/) using that language and/or number of questions tagged with that language on Stack Overflow (http://stackoverflow.com/tags)

Specification Fundamentals (SF)

Once you learn an enterprise language, you will be using it in a framework like JEE (Java Enterprise Edition) or JME (Java Micro Edition) for Java developers and .Net framework for the C# developers. These frameworks provide a large library of APIs and enterprise level services to common programming problems. When you write enterprise level code to these frameworks, they need to adhere to the specifications of that particular framework. For example, in Java EE, you have JDBC for database connectivity, JMS for messaging, JNDI for LDAP naming & directory server access, etc.

Nowadays, most applications are web based, and it is really worth understanding the fundamentals of the HTTP paradigm like how the state is maintained between the client and the server as HTTP is a stateless protocol, differences among post-backs, forwards and redirects, and basic understanding of common HTTP headers and the use of cookies. You will be surprised to know that even some intermediate to senior level developers don't get this right. It is also worth learning the specification fundamentals for access to the database servers, messaging servers, directory servers, mail servers, and other applications and services using various standard protocols like TCP, LDAP, POP3, SMTP, IMAP, HTTP(S), and SOAP. There are other industry specific protocols like FIX for exchanging financial information. Each protocol and integration technology has its applicability in terms of its intended use, reliability, speed, delivery guarantee, synchronous versus asynchronous (i.e. blocking or non-blocking) invocations, and data formats. If you take messaging, the intended use will dictate whether a queue (i.e. single consumer) or topic (i.e. multiple consumer) to be used as the destination.

It also really pays to learn the sought-after third-party frameworks and libraries relevant to your primary choice of enterprise language and specification. While it is true that a software professional with the know how in the language and specification fundamentals can easily learn a new framework or library, many recruiters value immediate usefulness more than the true potential. This approach has the potential danger of screening out quality candidates with strong technical and problem solving skills for someone who happens to just know the required framework or library. But as a potential employee or interviewee, you have no choice but to cover all grounds by at least being familiar with the sought-after frameworks and libraries to open more doors for yourself. When there are many quality online tutorials, books, and open-source projects, there is no excuse to not invest in your marketability and job security by **staying relevant**. The local job advertisements, industry specific web sites like www.infoq.com, www.dzone.com, etc and monitoring www.google.com/trends should help you ascertain what to learn next to stay relevant. Some emerging technologies/frameworks will never make it to be mainstream. So, it really pays to research prior to learning without getting caught in the hype.

Platform Fundamentals (PF)

The platforms provide an environment for developing, compiling, interpreting, and executing your applications. The applications you develop can be run directly on operating system platforms like WIN32 and Unix or indirectly via virtual machine platforms like Java Virtual Machine, VMware, web servers, application servers, and message oriented middle-ware servers. The platform fundamentals can vary from learning the operating system basics to virtual machine basics, and from learning the compile-time, build-time, and runtime essentials to understanding the command-line and graphical user interface (GUI) tools provided to develop, debug, build, deploy, and monitor the applications.

Many production systems run in a Unix environment. The Unix environment is very robust, and offers powerful tools to automate and simplify tasks. You can replace a given text or phrase from 5000+ web templates in minutes if not in seconds. Being skilled with Unix commands will help you quickly search for files and contents in log files to see if a particular user is logged on, or to list all the log files that have a particular search text. You can also monitor processes, memory usage, connections, and sockets. You can diagnose connectivity problems by testing if a host or URL is reachable across the network. It is also very handy if you want to recursively delete folders. For example, when creating a new subversion project (or folder) based on an existing subversion project, it is imperative that the .svn folders containing the metadata are deleted before checking in the copied and subsequently modified project. Otherwise you run the risk of corrupting the original subversion project with the newly copied and modified project.

Sometimes you need to be lazy because only this laziness will avoid redundancy by motivating you to identify the tools and processes that will speed up productivity and improve code quality without having to write monotonous and repetitive code. So, having a good exposure to a list of handy development, build, deployment, communication, and change management tools will not only help you better manage software complexities, but also will help you open more doors to your career by getting things done more efficiently. Prospective employers could judge your experience with software development with questions like

Q. What are some of the tools you would need to manage complexities and improve efficiency?
Q. What tools would you normally require to get your job done in software development?

The experienced professionals have a variety of commercial and open-source tools at their disposal to get things done. The above open-ended questions will help employers determine your experience at the job interviews.

Thread analyzers help you identify thread-safety issues, and debuggers and decompilers help you identify general programming errors. Coding standards tools help programmers write code that adheres to coding standards. The code coverage tools measure the extent to which your code has been tested.

There are so many free and commercial third-party tools to make your life easier and get things done efficiently to impress your peers and superiors. For example,

- *RegexBuddy* and regexpal.com to test and debug regular expressions
- Automated regression testing tools like *BadBoy*, *Selenium*, and *OpenSTA* to record/playback tests without learning a test scripting language. The *OpenSTA* can perform scripted HTTP and HTTPS for heavy load tests with performance measurements. *BadBoy* can convert captured scripts to load testing tools like

JMeter. The Karma test runner, which used to be called Testacular from Google is a popular and light weight web testing tool.

- *SoapUI* is a popular functional testing tool for various protocols such as SOAP, REST, and HTTP. The Firefox "poster" plug-in is handy for posting messages via Restful services.
- Administration and deployment tools in a Message-Oriented Middleware (aka MOM) like *HermesJMS* for Java to help you interact with messaging providers like web Methods, making it simpler to publish, edit, browse, search, and delete messages.
- *Wireshark* is handy for monitoring network traffic. It is quite often handy to sniff what is being sent between a client and a server for debugging purpose.
- *FileZilla* is an efficient FTP and SFTP client.
- *BeyondCompare* makes comparing ASCII and binary files and folders a breeze.
- *FireFox* plug-ins like *FireBug, YSlow, LinkChecker, Tamper data*, etc to analyze web pages and tamper HTTP data. *Fiddler 2* is an HTTP(S) debugging proxy server to capture and fiddle with the HTTP(S) traffic as it is being sent. By default, traffic from Microsoft's WinINET HTTP(S) stack is automatically directed through Fiddler 2 at runtime, but any browser or application can be configured to route traffic through *Fiddler*.
- The *skipfish* is an application security tool from Google, and it is really easy to run your website through a fairly comprehensive set of security penetration tests.

Sonar is an open web based platform to manage code quality. It has built-in support for Java, and open-source and commercial plugins for C, C#, PHP, COBOL, Visual Basic 6, PL/SQL, and Flex. It covers the 7 axes of code quality as shown below.

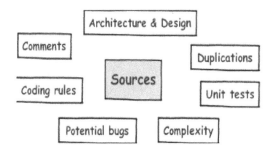

The continuous build and integration tools like Bamboo, Hudson, CruiseControl, Jenkins, Apache Continuum, Draco NET, etc keep track of the messy software development process with great ease. Application servers and monitoring tools like Nagios, Introscope, etc provide runtime support for your applications by monitoring their performance, memory, and socket usages.

Changes need to be tracked and properly versioned through software change management (SCM) tools like Borland StarTeam or BMC Remedy Change Management. Bugs, issues, and change requests can be tracked with tools like JIRA or HP Quality Center. Source control tools like Subversion or CVS are a must to manage concurrent code changes and multiple streams of work. The github.com provides public and private repositories for collaborative software development. The document management systems (DMS) like OpenDocMan or Microsoft SharePoint provide a centralized document storage, access control, change tracking, version control, and search tools. Communication within your team can be improved with tools like wiki or confluence. So, you will find tools for just about every task to be more productive.

Design Considerations (DC)

If you ask me to pick a key area that is most popular with the interviewers, this is it. Especially, the OO concepts, SOLID design principles, DRY (i.e. Don't Repeat Yourself), KISS (i.e. Keep It Stupid and Simple), and YAGNI (You Are not Going to Need It – i.e. don't over plan and build things that you might need it in the future) and the high level architecture of the system you have been involved in. This is the key area that takes lots of experience, practice, asking the right questions, and information gathering. This is also the area that can not only relatively take longer time to get good handle on compared to the other key areas, but also the area that makes the real difference to the quality of the software you build and to your career success.

Each functional and non-functional requirement needs to be mapped to the technical solution. Gaps in requirements need to be identified. If you just take technical design alone, there will be many possible design alternatives, and each alternative has its own pros and cons along with likely trade-offs to be made in your design decisions. You will have to list the relevant assumptions, potential risks, likelihood and impacts of those risks to the business. At times, tactical solutions need to be favored over strategical solution due to business demands, budgetary constraints, and time to market. List all design choices and pros and cons for each choice. It is also imperative to not cut corners as a particular choice might look attractive now, but in a longer term require more rework and budget. So, design is often all about making the **informed choices** and **trade offs**. You make the design choices based on the functional and non-functional requirements, budgetary and non-budgetary constraints, environmental and political factors, and collective experience. Your architectural decisions need to adhere to the frameworks, policies and standards in place and need to be approved by the relevant stake holders, architecture review board, superiors, and peers. So, this requires good communication skills both written and oral to convince the relevant stake holders. You need to look at things from both business and technology perspective, and present it based on the target audience without too much technical jargon.

The design considerations also entail physical architectures like 2-tier, 3-tier, and n-tier systems, and logical architectures like Model View Controller (MVC), Service Oriented Architecture (SOA), and Event Driven Architecture (EDA) with a clear separation of concerns into layers like presentation layer, service layer, data access layer, integration layer, etc. Put differently, a good software system consists of small, reusable building blocks, each carrying its own responsibility. In a good system, no cyclic dependencies between components are present and the whole system is a stack of layers of functionality. Conceptual diagrams and layering are probably the simplest way to discuss software architecture. The main goals of design are simplicity, flexibility, extensibility, re-usability, portability, deployability, maintainability, and testability. Appropriate **conceptual, ER** and **UML** diagrams need to be used to communicate the ideas more effectively to the relevant target audience. Also, be prepared to draw conceptual diagrams of a system you had worked on.

2 tier Vs 3 to n tier systems

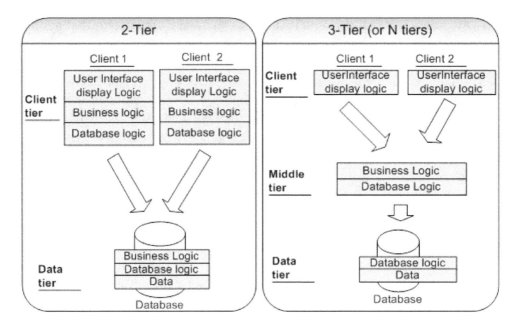

In a 2 tier system, if the developers are not disciplined, the display logic, business logic, and data access logic can get muddled up and duplicated. The 3 to n-tier systems force separation of display logic, business logic and data access logic. The data access logic includes retrieving data via databases, service calls via SOAP or RESTful web service and other remoting protocols, and file systems.

Separation of concerns into layers

The terms tier and layer are frequently used interchangeably, but actually there is a difference between them as tiers indicate a physical separation of components and layers refers to a logical separation of components.

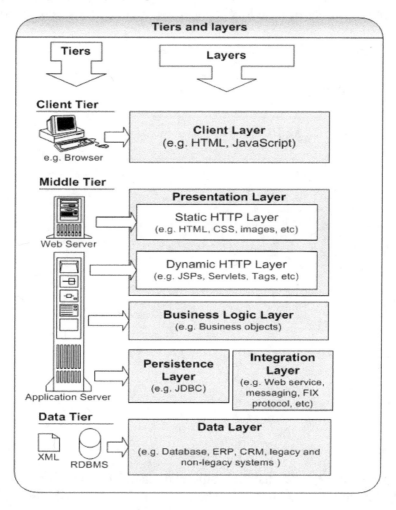

Get a good handle on the 16 key areas of software engineering to open more doors

The layered architecture has the benefits like

- Layers can be distributed over multiple physical tiers and reused by other applications. Have a deployment plan to distribute the layers over multiple physical tiers.
- Easier maintenance of your applications due to low coupling between the layers.
- Layering improves testability, scalability, and fault tolerance.

How many tiers you have is driven by the non-functional requirements such as scalability, availability, performance, and decisions such as build versus reuse existing service. There are a number of high level conceptual architectures as discussed below.

Model-View-Controller Architecture

Most web and stand-alone GUI applications follow this pattern.

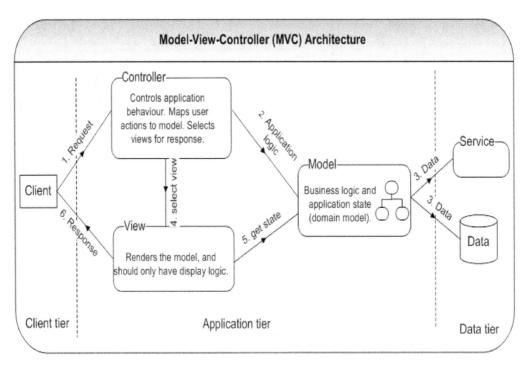

The model represents the core business logic and state. The view renders the content of the model state by adding display logic. The controller translates the interaction with the view into action to be performed by the model. The actions performed by a model include executing the business logic and changing the state of the model. Based on the user interactions, the controller selects an appropriate view to render. The controller decouples the model from the view.

Service Oriented Architecture (SOA)

The business logic and application state are exposed as reusable services. An Enterprise Service Bus (ESB) is used as an orchestration and mediation layer to decouple the applications from the services.

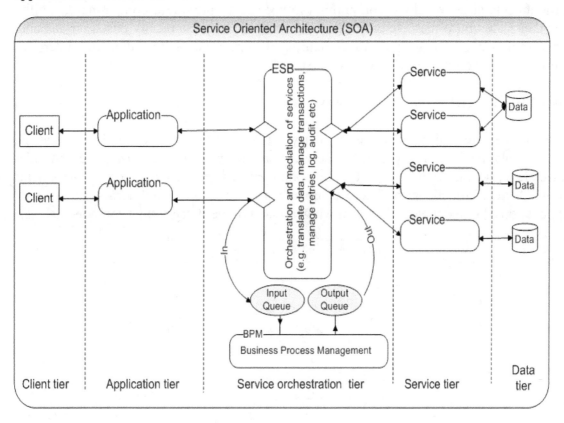

The above architecture has 5 tiers. The application tier could be using a typical MVC architecture. The service orchestration tier could be using ESB products like Oracle Service Bus, TIBCO, etc and BPM products like Lombardi BPM, Pega BPM, etc. In the above diagram, the ESB integrates with the BPM via messaging queues. The service tier consists of individual services that can be accessed through SOAP or RESTful web services. The SOA implementation requires change agents to drive adoption of new approaches. The real-time business process management via BPM tools and service integration via ESB are dynamically changing how business users do their jobs. So, it needs full support from the business, requiring restructuring and it can take some time to realize the benefits of SOA and BPM. The SOA provides **orchestrated** and **mediated** services. The service orchestration involves coordination of multiple implementation services exposed as a single, aggregate service. The mediated services involve adapting other services via protocol conversion, data transformation, and service mapping.

Cloud computing is at the leading edge of its hype and as a concept compliments SOA as an architectural style. Cloud computing is expected to provide a computing capability that can scale up (to massive proportions) or scale down dynamically based on demand. This implies a very large pool of computing resources either be within the enterprise intranet or on the Internet (i.e on the cloud).

User Interface (UI) Component Architecture

This architecture is driven by a user interface that is made up of a number of discrete components. Each component calls a service that encapsulates business logic and hides lower level details. Components can be combined to form new composite components allowing richer functionality. These components can also be shared across a number of applications. For example, JavaScript widgets, Java Server Faces (JSF) components, etc.

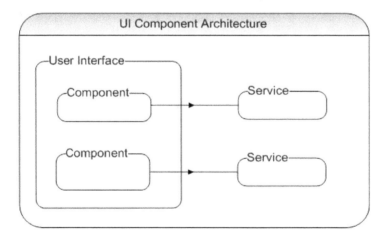

A number of individual web applications could use a single shared menu component that retrieves the data from a database via a RESTful Web service. This shared menu component will be used for navigating between separate web applications to provide a holistic experience of a single application. This shared menu data needs to be cached for performance. There are other components that can be shared like generic search functionality, header and footer information like contact us, site map, and other static links. For example, a generic ajax based drop down list search button can be built using jQuery and reused in a number of search screens like account search, report search, user search, etc.

The amazon affiliate program that enables you to add amazon products to your website or blog via their widgets make use of this style. These types of widgets are very common when you are building your online persona via blogs. In your blog, you will be adding RSS feeds, Facebook like button, twitter follow button, share link, and so on, which are JavaScript based widgets invoking external services.

RESTful data composition Architecture

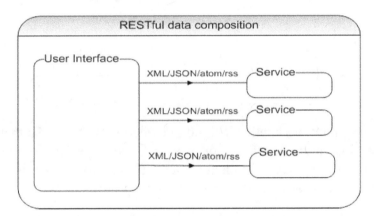

Google has raised the bar by designing single page web applications with JavaScript and ajax calls to RESTful services. The user interface can be built by calling a number of underlying services that are each responsible for building part of a page. The user interface translates and combine the data in different formats like XML(translate to HTML using XSLT), JSON (Java Script Object Notation), ATOM (feed for mail messages and calendar applications), RSS (for generating RSS feeds), etc. For example, a client information search page could retrieve client details from a database as JSON or XML data via ajax calls. The JSON format is less verbose and could perform better than XML format. The retrieved data can be paginated on client side using a JavaScript widget for faster navigation between records on client side. The retrieved data needs to be limited by prompting the user to refine the search criteria when it exceeds a certain limit. For example, 2000 records.

The client side JavaScript based MV* frameworks like Angular, Backbone and Ember use MVVM (**M**odel **V**iew **V**iew**M**odel) pattern. For example, the Angular framework uses the $scope object as the **ViewModel** that gets decorated by controller functions. The controller is responsible for making RESTful web service calls to get data in JSON format. The MVW (i.e. Model View Whatever) or MV* is a pattern that can be considered either MVC or MVVM.

HTML composition Architecture

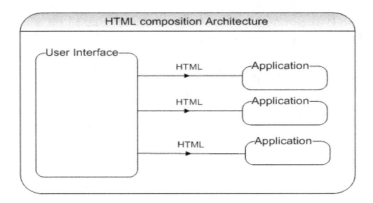

In this architecture, multiple applications output fragments of HTML that are combined to generate the final user interface. For example, Java portlets used inside a portal application server to aggregate individual content. This generally requires a portal server to aggregate a number of contents from various applications.

Plug-in Architecture

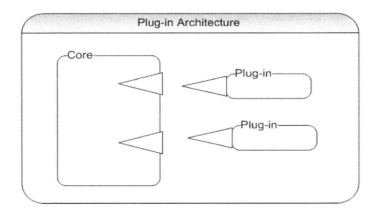

In this architecture, a core application defines an interface, and the functionality will be implemented as a set of plug-ins that conform to that interface. The plugins depend on the core application, and the reverse is not true. For example, Firefox and its plugins like Firebug, YSlow, Live HTTP headers, etc, Eclipse RCP framework and its plugins, Maven build tool and its plugins like Surefire, Enforcer, etc and plugins for .NET or .COM. The best way to write plugins in your application is using Interfaces.

Event Driven Architecture (EDA)

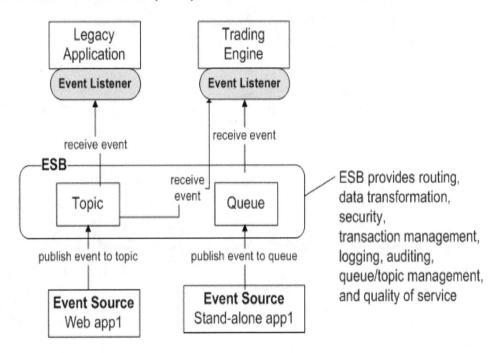

The EDA pattern decouples the interactions between the event publishers and the event consumers. Many to many communications are achieved via a topic, where one specific event can be consumed by many subscribers. The EDA also supports asynchronous operations and acknowledgments through event messaging. This architecture requires effective monitoring in place to track queue depth, exceptions, and other possible problems. The traceability, isolation, and debugging of an event can be difficult in some cases. This architecture is useful in scenarios where the business process is inherently asynchronous, multiple consumers are interested in an event(e.g. order status has changed to partially-filled), no immediate acknowledgment is required (e.g. an email is sent with the booking details and itinerary), and real-time request/response is not

Get a good handle on the 16 key areas of software engineering to open more doors

required (e.g. a long running report can be generated asynchronously and made available later via online or email).

Most conceptual architectures use a hybrid approach as shown above using a combination of different architectures based on the benefits of each approach and its pertinence to the situation. For example, the diagram below gives a simplified over view of an online trading system.

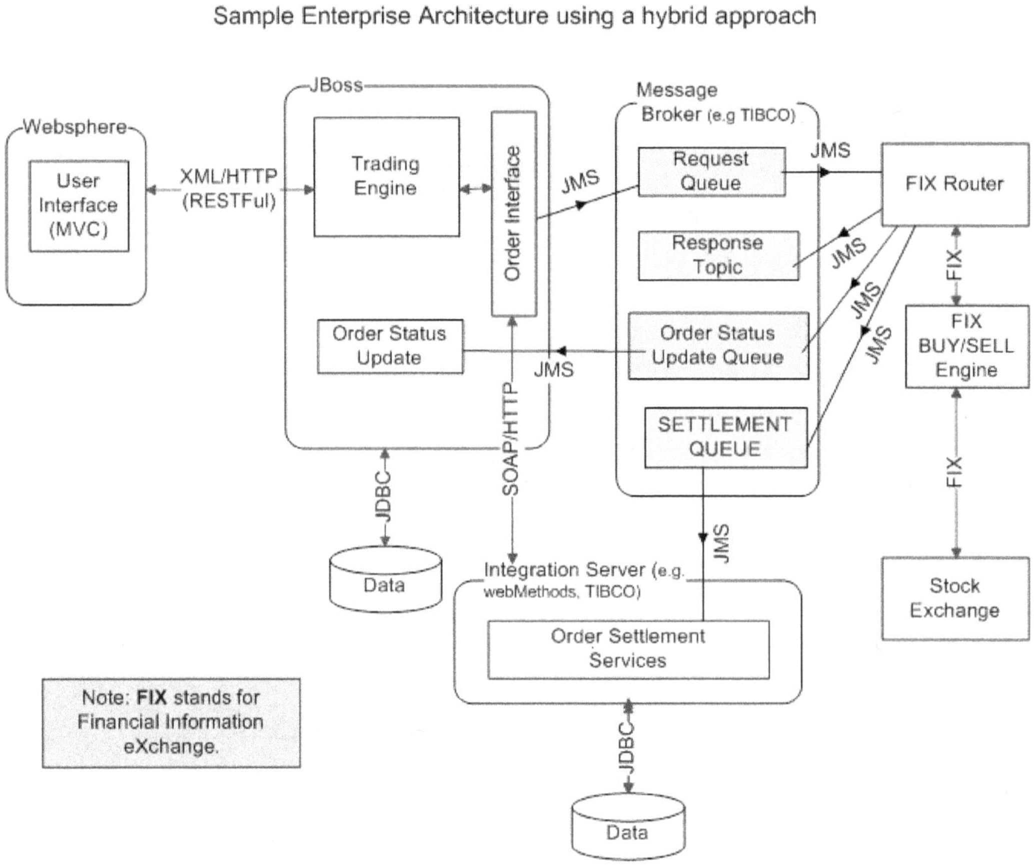

Sample Enterprise Architecture using a hybrid approach

JDBC → Java Data Base Connectivity and JMS → Java Messaging Service.

The above system uses a number of different architectural styles like MVC, EDA, Component architecture, RESTful data composition, etc. The above system is an

operational OLTP (i.e. On-Line Transaction Processing) system. These systems are also known as STP (i.e. Straight Through Processing) system. This leads to another question.

Q. What is the difference between **OLTP** and **OLAP**?
A. OLTP stands for On-Line Transaction Processing and OLAP stands for On-Line Analytical Processing. OLAP contains a multidimensional or relational data store designed to provide quick access to **pre-summarized** data & **multidimensional** analysis.

- **MOLAP**: Multidimensional OLAP – enabling OLAP by providing cubes.
- **ROLAP**: Relational OLAP – enabling OLAP using a relational database management system

OLTP	OLAP
Creates operational source data from transactional systems as shown in the above diagram. This data is the source of truth for many other systems.	Data comes from various OLTP data sources as shown in the below diagram.
Transactional and normalized data is used for daily operational business activities.	Historical, de-normalized and aggregated multidimensional data is used for analysis and decision making. This is also known as for BI (i.e. Business Intelligence).
Data is inserted via short inserts and updates. The data is normally captured via user actions.	Periodic (i.e. scheduled) and long running (i.e. during off-peak) batch jobs refresh the data. Also, known as ETL process as shown in the below diagram.
The database design involves highly normalized tables.	The database design involves de-normalized tables for speed. Also, requires more indexes for the aggregated data.
Regular backup of data is required to prevent any loss of data, monetary loss, and legal liability.	Data can be reloaded from the OLTP systems if required. Hence, stringent backup is not required.
Transactional data older than certain period can be archived and purged based on the compliance requirements.	Contains historical data. The volume of this data will be higher as well due to its requirement to maintain historical data.

The typical users are operational staff.	The typical users are management and executives to make business decisions.
The space requirement is relatively small if the historical data is regularly archived.	The space requirement is larger due to the existence of aggregation structures and historical data. Also requires more spaces for the indexes.

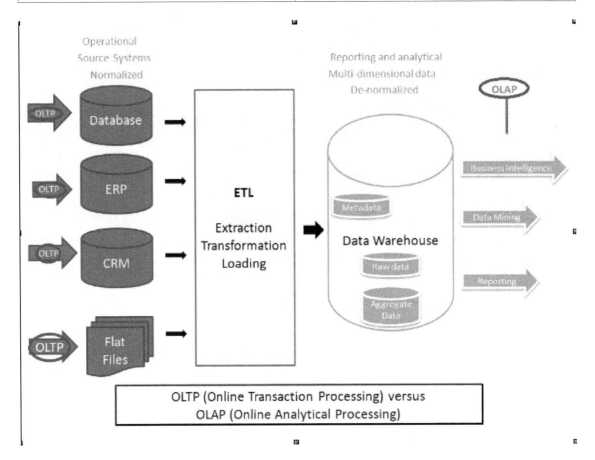

The enterprise systems need to integrate and exchange data with each other. There are a number of integration styles, and each style comes with its own pros and cons. The common integration styles are

- Shared database.
- Batch file transfer between databases using ETL (Extract Transform and Load operations).

- Invoking remote procedures (RPC) via RESTful and SOAP web services, CORBA, RMI, DCOM, etc.
- Exchanging synchronous (i.e. blocking) and asynchronous (i.e. non-blocking) messages over a message oriented middle-ware (MOM) like TIBCO, MQSeries, Oracle Service Bus, webMethods, etc.

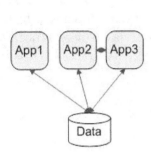

Applications share the same database

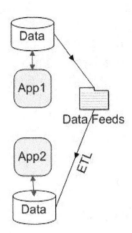

Scheduled batch jobs are run to extract data from
App1's database into feed files and then load
the data from the feed files into App2's database
via Extract Transform and Load (i.e. ETL) function.

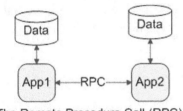

The Remote Procedure Call (RPC)
style calls can be achieved with
RMI, EJB, CORBA,
RESTful Web Service, and
SOAP based Web Service.

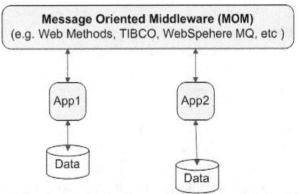

The App1 publishes the messages (i.e. xml, text, etc)
to a queue or topic on the MOM and the
App2 subscribes to the same queue or topic to
receive the messages and process them.

Get a good handle on the 16 key areas of software engineering to open more doors

Shared database:

PROS:
- The simplest solution.
- Real time data access.

CONS:
- All shared applications will be strongly coupled and cause maintenance issues. The maintenance issues can be mitigated to some extent by introducing a facade layer. For example, all applications need to communicate via a stored procedure layer.
- The changes to one application could affect the other applications and teams, hence changes need to be coordinated.
- The indexing, storage, materialized views, stored procedures, etc need to be optimized based on the usage patterns of all shared applications.

Batch file transfer between databases

Generally, the data is extracted from legacy systems, which are the source of truth via batch jobs, and transformed to the format that target systems can understand, and then loaded into the target systems. Basically, the data is copied from one storage to another. The source system is where the data is created, updated, and deleted and the target system may require the data for the reporting and analysis purpose only. This is also known as the data warehousing.

PROS:
- Once the data is copied over from the source of truth to the target system, the data retrieval is faster within the databases.
- Data inconsistencies can be identified and rectified prior to loading the data.

CONS:
- Initial data and script preparation can be time consuming, and also requires data compatibility and maintainability issues to be ironed out in an ongoing basis. For example, changes to target or source systems, incorrect transaction management leaving the data in an inconsistent state, data inconsistencies, etc.
- Data access is generally not real time. Generally the scripts are run periodically to synchronize the data. For example, every hour, once every night, etc via scheduled batch jobs to minimize any performance impact to the source and

target systems due to sheer volume of data that needs to be handled. Having said this, with the advent of real time data grids, which are generally memory based data storage where the data is constantly synchronized with the source systems and the target systems can fetch the data synchronously or asynchronously from the memory based data grids. For example, Oracle Coherence, GridGain, Hadoop, etc are in-memory distributed data grids.

Invoking remote procedures (RPC):

The pros and cons of RPC style depends on the type of protocols and the data formats used for communication.

Exchanging messages using a MOM

Messaging enables loosely coupled distributed communication. A component sends a message to a destination, and the recipient can retrieve the message from the destination. However, the sender and the receiver do not have to be available at the same time in order to communicate and also they are not aware of each other. In fact, the sender does not need to know anything about the receiver; nor does the receiver need to know anything about the sender. The sender and the receiver need to know only what message format and what destination to use. In this respect, messaging differs from tightly coupled RPC (Remote Procedure Call) style technologies, which require an application to know a remote application's methods.

Q. If two enterprise systems are using different platforms, how would you go about exchanging data between them?

Nowadays, the potential options are to use web services or messaging, depending on the scenario. In general, when a system needs to send data to another system as soon as it becomes available or to send data to several systems, then a messaging system might be the way to go. When a system has data to be processed by another system and needs back the result of this processing synchronously, then web service might be the way to go. Having said this, the answer depends more on the other key areas discussed below.

The design consideration key area is more closely related to other key areas. For example, a design decision to use a SOAP based web service or a RESTful web service will depend on the analysis of the following key areas.

Get a good handle on the 16 key areas of software engineering to open more doors

Key Area	SOAP based Web service	RESTful Web service
Specification/Platf orm Fundamentals (SF/PF)	Transport is platform & protocol neutral. Supports multiple protocols like HTTP(S), Messaging, TCP, UDP, SMTP, etc.	Transport is protocol specific. Supports only HTTP or HTTPS protocols.
	Permits only XML data format, hence language neutral.	Permits multiple data formats like XML, JSON data, text, HTML, atom, RSS, etc.
	You define operations, which tunnels through the **POST** or **GET**. The focus is on accessing the named operations and exposing the application logic as a service.	Any web browser or HTTP compliant clients like cURL can be used because the REST approach uses the standard **GET, PUT, POST,** and **DELETE** web operations. The focus is on accessing the named resources and exposing the data as a service.
	Defines the contract via **WSDL**.	Traditionally, the big drawback of REST was the lack of contract for the web service. This has changed with WSDL 2.0 defining non SOAP bindings and the emergence of **WADL**.
		Simpler to implement. REST has Ajax support. It can use the *XMLHttpRequest* object. Good for stateless CRUD (Create, Read, Update, and Delete) operations, which are mapped to HTTP methods POST, GET, PUT, and DELETE respectively.
Performance Consideration	SOAP based reads cannot be cached. The application that uses	REST based reads can be cached. Performs and scales better.

(PC)	SOAP needs to provide cacheing.	
Security (SE)	Supports both **SSL security** and **WS-security**, which adds some enterprise security features. Supports identity through intermediaries, not just point to point SSL. WS-Security maintains its encryption right up to the point where the request is being processed. WS-Security allows you to secure parts (e.g. only credit card details) of the message that needs to be secured. Given that encryption/decryption is not a cheap operation, this can be a performance boost for larger messages. It is also possible with WS-Security to secure different parts of the message using different keys or encryption algorithms. This allows separate parts of the message to be read by different people without exposing other, unneeded information. SSL security can only be used with HTTP. WS-Security can be used with other protocols like UDP, SMTP, etc.	Supports only point-to-point **SSL security**. The basic mechanism behind SSL is that the client encrypts all of the requests based on a key retrieved from a third party. When the request is received at the destination, it is decrypted and presented to the service. This means the request is only encrypted while it is traveling between the client and the server. Once it hits the server (or a proxy which has a valid certificate), it is decrypted from that moment on. The SSL encrypts the whole message, whether all of it is sensitive or not.
Transaction	Has comprehensive support for	REST supports transactions, but

Get a good handle on the 16 key areas of software engineering to open more doors

Management (TM)	both **ACID** based transaction management for short-lived transactions and **compensation** based transaction management for long-running transactions. It also supports two-phase commit across distributed resources.	it is neither ACID compliant nor can provide two phase commit across distributed transactional resources as it is limited by its HTTP protocol.
Quality of Service (QoS)	SOAP has success or retry logic built in and provides end-to-end reliability even through SOAP intermediaries.	REST does not have a standard messaging system, and expects clients invoking the service to deal with communication failures by retrying.
Best Practice (BP)	In general, a REST based web service is preferred due to its simplicity, performance, scalability, and support for multiple data formats. SOAP is favored where service requires comprehensive support for security, transactional reliability and stricter contract.	

HTTP is the most common web service protocol, but web services are currently built on multiple transports each with different communications, Quality of Service (QoS) and message semantics.

Key Area	XML or SOAP over HTTP	XML or SOAP over messaging protocols
Platform Fundamentals	Platform independent. Also, language neutral as both XML and SOAP can be used to exchange information between any distributed systems. The communication between the distributed systems are done using the famous **HTTP**(S) protocol. Easier to learn and implement.	Both platform and language neutral. The communication between the producers and the consumers use **proprietary protocols**. To mix providers to communicate externally or internally, you need to buy or build some sort of a bridge. The messaging APIs like AMQP and JMS are easy to learn, but implementing a messaging product across multiple systems

		is complex.
Specification Fundamentals	Point to point synchronous (i.e. blocking) call.	Asynchronous (i.e. non-blocking) call supporting point-to-point with queues and publish and subscribe with topics.
Design Considerations (DC)	The communicating applications are tightly coupled. Both applications need to be up and running.	The communicating applications no need to know each other. All they have to know is the destination to send the message to and agree on a format (or contract). The consuming application does not even have to be up and running.
Performance Considerations (PC)	XML over HTTP has lesser overheads than SOAP over HTTP.	Similar. Slightly better performance for larger payload sizes.
Transaction Management (TM)	SOAP has support for both ACID based and compensation based transaction management. XML over HTTP only has basic non ACID compliant transaction support.	ACID and XA (i.e. two-phase) compliant transactional boundaries can be defined for both SOAP and XML based messages.
Quality of Service (QoS)	Reliability depends on the SOAP providers. The XML over HTTP does not provide any reliability. It needs to be built by the developers in to the application with additional effort.	Reliability depends on the messaging providers. Generally has support for guaranteed once-only delivery, no duplicates, retries, etc.
Security (SE)	Firewall friendly. SOAP can use either SSL or WS-security. XML can use SSL.	Not firewall friendly. SOAP can use either SSL or WS-security. XML can use SSL.
Best Practice (BP)	In SOA architecture, the best practice is to use messaging when **reliability** is of highest priority, especially for **internal** producers and consumers that can easily connect to an ESB or MOM. Use	

	HTTP(S) for connecting to outside partners over the internet. The reliability of SOAP and messaging systems are vendor dependent. There are other reasons to choose messaging like asynchronous support or publish the same message to multiple subscribers using a topic as the destination as described in the EDA.

Note: Web services and messaging are very common integration technologies used in many conceptual architectures to integrate distributed systems together.

It is fairly common these days to go to a web site that generates content from different sites. For example, Google maps, RSS feeds, social bookmarking sites like del.icio.us, traffic tracker like Alexa, Omniture, etc. It is also common for sites to retrieve information from a content management system (aka CMS) like Vignette. The business or system admin staff can configure dynamic marketing promotional or system outage messages via CMS, which can be retrieved via web service calls and displayed on the web application or portal.

This merging of services and content from multiple web sites in an integrated and coherent way is called a **mashup**. The two primary mashup styles are server-side mashups and client side mashups. Each has its own pros and cons. A server-side mash-up integrates content in the server and pass it to the client. Hence this style of mash-up is also called a proxy-style mash up because the server acts as a proxy.

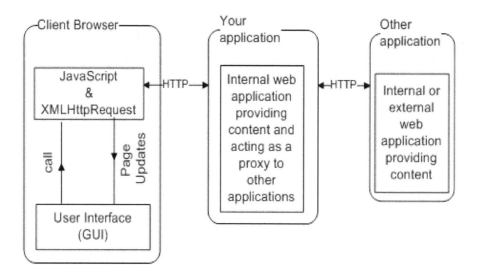

A client side mash-up integrate services and content on the client by mashing up directly with the other web applications' data or functionality. You also need to be aware of the cross domain restrictions imposed by JavaScript for ajax calls and you can overcome these restrictions with **JSONP** or **CORS** (Cross Origin Resource Sharing). The CORS is more industrial strength solution.

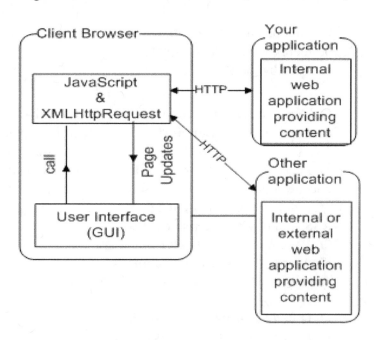

Key Area	Client side mash-up	Server side mash-up
Design Considerations (DC)	Easy to implement if the site you want to mash up with provides a JavaScript library. It reduces load on the server. The following questions need to be addressed. **Q.** Can the client directly access the service and content for the mashup?	The server acts as a buffer between the client and the other applications. This can shield clients from problems in other websites. For example, you can cache data, retry services, timeout services, construct appropriate error content, transform the data returned into a different format (e.g.

	Q. Is the other website stable and perform adequately? **Q.** Is there too much application logic on the client side? **Q.** Can the client handle the protocols and the data formats returned by the mashups	XML to JSON), manipulate the data to suit your requirements, etc.
Security (SE)	**Q. Can you trust the code and content from another site?** You need to assess the risks of these outside additions to your site. For example, bringing in an image or an RSS feed has limited risk because if the content is not available, the browser will handle it with a missing symbol. **Q. Is your client request restricted by the browser sandbox security, which is also known as the XMLHttpRequest sandbox?** Many mashups use ajax functionality, and to protect against possible security threats, most browsers allow JavaScript code that contains an XMLHttpRequest to communicate only with the site from which the browser loaded the code. This means, the cross domain calls are restricted. **Note:** This restriction may be circumvented by loading a JavaScript from your site, which	It is much easier to handle security requirements on the server through authentication, encryption, and data validation for any malicious characters.

	dynamically generates the script tag that interacts with other domains. But, this exposes your site to potential security threats. Research for **CORS** and **JSONP** to circumvent this cross domain restriction.	
Performance	The requests and responses are passed directly between the client and the mashup server. Hence receiving a response typically takes less time. Delays from other websites can frustrate the user and degrade the overall user experience. HTML 5 supports multi-threading with worker threads to improve performance.	The request and response go through additional hops to the proxy server, which can adversely impact performance. You can cache the data returned by the other applications. You can make concurrent asynchronous calls to many applications at the same time.
Best Practices (BP)	<ul><li>Provide adequate input validation to protect from security vulnerabilities like cross site scripting (XSS). Use vulnerability checking tools like Skipfish.</li><li>Perform cross browser compatibility test to ensure that it works across different browsers and operating systems. Some mashups may load more slowly on some browsers.</li><li>Take notice of the terms of use and legality. Each API typically carries terms of use that specify who can use the content and how it can be used.</li></ul>	

The most important concept in software design is an **interface**. Any good software is a model of a real (or imaginary) system. Understanding the contracts between two interfacing objects, components, layers, or systems to model a problem in terms of correct and simple interfaces is crucial. Apply the design concepts, especially the object oriented (**OO**) concepts abbreviated to "a pie", which stands for **a**bstraction, **p**olymorphism, **i**nheritance, and **e**ncapsulation, and the well proven **SOLID** design principles, which is an abbreviation for **S**ingle Responsibility Principle (SRP), **O**pen Closed Principle (OCP), **L**iskov's Substitution Principle (LSP), **I**nterface Segregation Principle (ISP), and **D**ependency Inversion Principle.

Lots of systems suffer from not having the right balance between the extremes of lengthy code with little abstractions and an overly designed system with unnecessary complexity and unused code. Apply these concepts and principles only where appropriate to achieve the design goals. Don't over design by speculating every possible future requirements. Also, don't under design by making your design rigid, fragile, and immobile. Strike a good balance by designing a loosely coupled system that is less complex, reusable, and scalable.

Tools: **Visio** for high-level architectural diagrams, Entity-Relationship (i.e. ER) diagrams, website wire frames and UML diagrams, **ArgoUML** for UML diagrams, **IBM Rational tools** for for full model driven tools to dictate the process that you use to design and develop applications, **SmartDraw** and **ConceptDraw** for non UML conceptual diagrams, Oracle SQL developer for ER diagrams, **Axure**, **mockingbird**, **Adobe Illustrator**, **Macromedia FreeHand,** etc to create, link, and share mockups for your website or application, and **ScreenHunter** or other similar screen scraping applications to capture screen shots. If you are new to programming, then UML and ER diagrams are best place to start.

Design Patterns (DP)

Design patterns and anti-patterns capture design experience from the past. Patterns reflect the experience and knowledge of developers who have successfully used these patterns in their own work. It lets you leverage the collective experience of the development community. For example, The **flyweight** pattern improves application performance through object reuse, which minimizes the overhead such as memory allocation and garbage collection. The patterns help applications to be loosely coupled. Patterns also provide software designers with a common vocabulary. Ideas can be conveyed to developers using this common vocabulary and format. For example, should we use a Data Access Object (DAO)?, how about using a Business Delegate to loosely couple the service from the client?, should we use a facade and value objects to reduce complexity and network overhead?, how about a **decorator** to impose security, thread-safety, or performance metrics recording?, etc.

There are a number of real life examples to use design patterns. One such example would be to use a **decorator** class to switch between an existing service that is used by many and a new and improved service used only by a handful of pilot users based on a flag read from a database. Some design patterns look similar, but the intent is different. For example, the **proxy** design pattern looks similar to the decorator, but the intents are different. The intent of a decorator is to enhance the behavior of the object it decorates. For example, decorate a third-party library class, which is not thread safe by enhancing its methods. The intent of a proxy is to act as a place holder or surrogate for another object. For example, the ORM (Object to Relational Mapping) frameworks make use of proxy classes to instantiate real objects that are more expensive to create. Create these real objects only when it is required by the client. This is also known as **lazy loading**. Another example would be RPC calls where a local representative object (aka a stub) acts as a **proxy** for a real object that resides in a different address space. The interceptors used by frameworks like Spring provide additional functionalities like logging and access control are based on dynamic proxying. For example, a "surrogate" object checks that the caller has the access permissions required prior to forwarding the request.

The design patterns promote good coding practices like code to interface, loose coupling, favoring composition over inheritance, recursion for composite objects, etc. In a **composite** pattern, you don't differentiate between a leaf and a composite. The client treats a leaf or a composite the same way. You can correlate this pattern with an organization. An organization consists of many departments. Each department consists of many projects. Recursion gives power to a composition. If you want to find the total number of employees in an organization, it is the sum of the root node plus all its children. The calculation goes recursively to calculate the total number of employees.

RSS feeds and messaging systems are real life examples of an **observer pattern**. When you want to get updates from a particular feed, you add that feed to your feed reader. Any time that the RSS feed has an update, it will appear in your reader automatically. This is the observer pattern in action, where a publisher/subscriber relationship with one source having many subscribers. This pattern **reduces coupling** like the other **Gang of Four (GoF) design patterns**. If you have an object that needs to share it's state with others, without knowing who those objects are, the observer is exactly what you need. The enterprise patterns like the **MVC** (Model-View-Controller) and **MVVM** (Model-View -ViewModel) are used in GUI applications to promote loose coupling between various components. Mission critical commercial applications need to be integrated to promote reuse and add value to the business. The **EIP** (Enterprise Integration Patterns) describes 65 integration patterns to solve many common integration challenges. Many frameworks have been developed based on these patterns to make development easier after the initial learning curve. These frameworks take care of 40+ protocols like making HTTP requests, sending emails, polling for a file to taking care of multi-threaded applications with internal and remote queues for asynchronous processing.

Memory is a constant bottleneck for large, busy applications. In some cases, effective caching strategies can both lower the memory footprint and speed up the application. Caching is a well known optimization technique because it keeps items that have been recently used in memory, anticipating that they will be needed again. **Caching** with the **flyweight** design pattern can improve performance.

The design patterns also favor the composition over implementation inheritance for code reuse. Inheritance can easily be used improperly. Some designs look like "is-a" situations, but aren't really an inheritance. Inheritance tends to create very coupled classes that are more fragile and harder to test in isolation. So, many patterns favor composition, but inheritance has its uses. One important pattern that requires inheritance is a **template method** pattern, and it is widely used in frameworks.

An anti-pattern is a design pattern that may be commonly used but is ineffective and/or counterproductive in practice. For example, there is an architectural anti-pattern known as "reinventing the wheel". When developing a service, you usually have two choices – either leveraging an existing service or developing a new service from scratch. While both approaches can be applied in different situations, it is always useful to analyze existing technology/service before reinventing the wheel to develop a service that already exists and can quite adequately meet the requirements. This not only saves money, but also reduces time to market, improves maintainability and supportability by leveraging knowledge that developers already might have. There are other common anti-patterns like:

- **Programming to concrete classes rather than interfaces**: Programming to an interface than a concrete class provides benefits like not being tied into using a specific implementation, and there will be a provision for changing behavior at runtime.

- **Excessive coupling**: One basic software concept to keep in mind is that less coupling is generally better. For example, cross cutting concerns like logging, security, and caching can be injected using Aspect Oriented Programming (AOP) at compile time or runtime, and dependency injection can be used as a technique to promote loose coupling with IoC (Inversion of Control) containers and interfaces. The event driven architectures loosely couple the source and the target systems.

- **Input kludge**: Failing to specify and implement the handling of possibly invalid input can not only break your code, but also make your application vulnerable to security threats.

- **Circular dependencie**s: Introducing unnecessary direct or indirect mutual dependencies between objects or software modules.

- **Anaemic domain model**: The use of domain model without any business logic. The domain model's objects cannot guarantee their correctness at any moment, because their validation and mutation logic is placed somewhere outside (most likely in multiple places).

There are other anti-patterns like singleton overuse, copy and paste coding (i.e. duplicated code), spaghetti coding (i.e. very long and twisted), a blob (i.e. a class with lots of attributes and methods), and many more. Do your research on software development, architectural, project management, and organizational anti-patterns.

Tools: **Sonar** can detect complex anti-patterns.

This technical key area would not be complete without covering the **Enterprise Integration Patterns** (EIP). Today's business applications rarely live in isolation. This requires disparate applications to be connected into a larger, integrated solution. This integration is usually achieved through the use of some form of "middleware". Middleware provides the "plumbing" such as data transport, data transformation, and routing. Architecting integration solutions is a complex task. There are many conflicting drivers and even more possible 'right' solutions. Enterprise Integration Patterns is a book by Gregor Hope and Bobby Wolf and describes a number of tested and proven design patterns for the use of enterprise application integration and message oriented middleware (MOM). The EIP patterns are divided into 7 sections – Messaging Systems, Messaging Channels, Message Constructions, Message Routing, Message Transformation, Messaging endpoints, and System management. For example, a sender and receiver applications are **messaging systems**, and a **message channel** is a logical channel used to connect the messaging systems. One messaging system writes messages to the channel and the other one (or others) reads that message from the channel. Message queue and message topic are examples of message channels. The **message constructor**s describe the intent, form and content of the messages that travel across the messaging system. **Message routing** consume messages from one channel and republish the message to another channel that is determined by a varying set of conditions using pipes and filter without modifying the message content. In many cases, a message format needs to be changed due to different data formats used by the sending and the receiving system, this is accomplished via **message transformation**. The **messaging endpoints** define different ways like point-to-point, publish and subscribe, etc in which applications can produce or consume messages. Finally, the **system management** deals with providing a robust solution that takes care of error conditions (e.g. with dead letter queues), performance bottlenecks and changes in the messaging systems. So, if you had worked on EIP, don't forget to add this to your resume along with the GoF design patterns, and bring it up in your next interview when asked to tell about yourself. You can read more about this at http://www.eaipatterns.com/eaipatterns.html.

Concurrency Considerations (CC)

Concurrency is very important in any modern system, and this is one topic many software engineers struggle to have a good grasp. The complexity in concurrency programming stems from the fact that the threads often need to operate on the common data. Each thread has its own sequence of execution, but accesses common data. A classic concurrency example is the producer/consumer, where the producer thread generates data or tasks, and places it for the consumer threads to work on them. The example below diagrammatically shows a Java program that uses two threads, one to print odd numbers and another to print even numbers. Both the threads share the same object instance numUtility. Both threads communicate with each other by acquiring and releasing locks on *numUtility* object. This will enable the threads to print numbers sequentially as in 1, 2, 3, 4, etc.

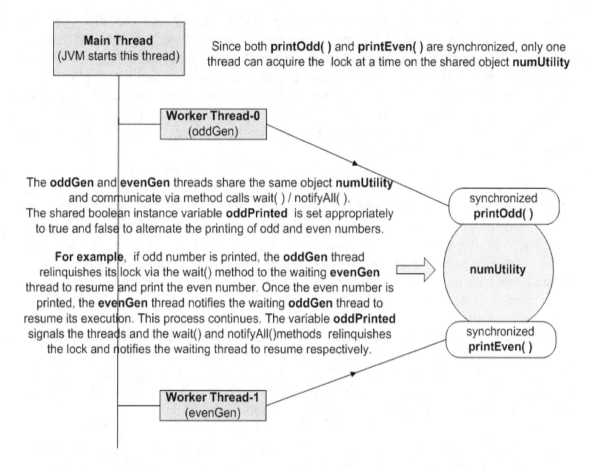

Many programming problems do not surface until you begin to execute the code associated with a class or object on multiple threads at once or under a certain load. For example, when multiple threads are executing methods concurrently on a single object, it opens up the possibility of one thread seeing data that's been left in an inconsistent or corrupted state by another thread. This is possible because of the way in which threads are scheduled by the underlying operating system. Writing thread-safe code requires additional analysis and more coding. It also requires a very thorough testing.

There are other types of concurrency issues like thread starvation, dead lock and contention issues. A thread is **starved** when one or more threads of execution are prevented from proceeding beyond a given point. Deadlock is a special form of starvation where threads of execution are prevented from making a progress due to conditions such as thread 1 holding on to shared resource A and thread 2 is holding on to shared resource B, and thread 1 needs resource B and thread 2 is waiting for thread 1 to release resource A. A deadlock never resolves itself. The deadlocks that occur on database servers are resolved by the server forcing one of the tasks to end with an exception. The onus is on the application to implement a deadlock retry service by catching the relevant exception or to redesign the application so that the deadlock does not occur in the first place. A thread **contention** issue occurs when a thread is waiting for a resource that is not readily available. It is simply the situation that two or more threads trying to use the same resource. A thread contention issue clears up over time, but it can severely impact application performance.

As an application designer or developer, it is your responsibility to design and code correct concurrent programs. When a concurrent program is not correctly written, the errors tend to fall into one of the three categories: *atomicity*, *visibility*, or *ordering*. Atomicity usually means using locking to enforce mutual exclusion. A less well understood issues are **visibility** and **ordering**. Ordinarily, writing a value to some variable from Thread 1 doesn't guarantee that the new value will be immediately visible from Thread 2, or even visible at all. Also, accessing multiple variables doesn't necessarily happen in "program order" for various reasons such as compiler optimizations and CPU memory cache behavior. A thread safe class is a class that guarantees the internal state of the class as well as returned values from methods are correct while invoked concurrently from multiple threads. In general, proper locking solves concurrency issues due to atomicity, visibility, and ordering. Here are some best practices to keep in mind relating to writing concurrent programs.

- Favor immutable objects as they are inherently thread-safe. Apply the **builder design pattern** to create immutable objects as opposed to using the constructor.
- If you need to use mutable objects, and share them among threads, then a key element of thread-safety is locking access to shared data while it is being operated on by a thread. For example, in Java you can use the synchronized keyword.
- Generally try to keep your locking for as shorter duration as possible to minimize any thread contention issues if you have many threads running. Putting a big, fat lock right at the start of the function and unlocking it at the end of the function is useful on functions that are rarely called, but can adversely impact performance on frequently called functions. Putting one or many smaller locks in the function around the data that actually need protection is a finer grained approach that works better than the coarse grained approach, especially when there are only a few places in the function that actually need protection and there are larger areas that are thread-safe and can be carried out concurrently.

- Use proven concurrency libraries (e.g. *java.util.concurrency*) as opposed to writing your own. Well written concurrency libraries provide concurrent access to reads, while restricting concurrent writes.

Debugging concurrency issues and fixing any thread starvation, dead lock, and contention require skills and experience to identify and reproduce these hard to resolve issues. Here are some techniques to detect concurrency issues.

- Manually reviewing the code for any obvious thread-safety issues. There are static analysis tools like Sonar, *ThreadCheck*, etc for catching concurrency bugs at compile-time by analyzing their byte code.
- List all possible causes and add extensive log statements and write test cases to prove or disprove your theories.
- Thread dumps are very useful for diagnosing synchronization problems such as deadlocks. The trick is to take 5 or 6 sets of thread dumps at an interval of 5 seconds between each to have a log file that has 25 to 30 seconds worth of runtime action. For thread dumps, use kill -3 <pid> in Unix and CTRL+BREAK in Windows. There are tools like *Thread Dump Analyzer (TDA), Samurai, etc.* to derive useful information from the thread dumps to find where the problem is. For example, Samurai colors idle threads in grey, blocked threads in red, and running threads in green. You must pay more attention to those red threads.
- There are tools like JDB (i.e. Java DeBugger) where a "watch" can be set up on the suspected variable. When ever the application is modifying that variable, a thread dump will be printed.
- There are dynamic analysis tools like jstack and JConsole, which is a JMX compliant GUI tool to get a thread dump on the fly. The JConsole GUI tool does have handy features like "detect deadlock" button to perform deadlock detection operations and ability to inspect the threads and objects in error states. Similar tools are available for other languages as well.

Q. Lock, mutex, and semaphore – what is the difference?
A. A **lock** allows only one thread to enter the part that's locked and the lock is not shared with any other processes, a **mutex** is the same as a lock but across processes (i.e. system wide) and a **semaphore** does the same as a lock but allows x number of threads to enter.

Performance Considerations (PC)

When somebody says an application is running "very slow," he/she is generally referring to one of two performance attributes – **latency** or **scalability**. Latency describes how long it takes for a given task to complete, whereas scalability describes how a program's performance gets impacted under increasing load. Building high performance applications require

- Low latency – for example, low page loading times.
- High scalability – for example, serving increasing number of users without adversely impacting performance.
- High availability – for example, staying up 24x7, without going down due to memory leak or running out of connections to the database or LDAP server.

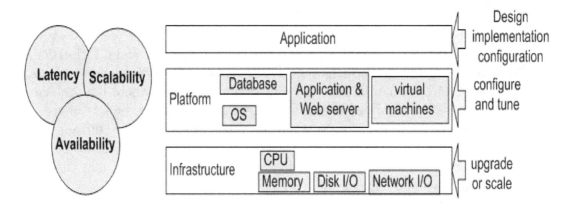

Performance issues can occur due to a variety of reasons. It can vary from a bad application, database, or infrastructure design that does not scale well due to lack of proper capacity planning to poorly tuned load balancer, virtual machine, application server, and from badly constructed SQL statements (e.g. a Cartesian join) and frequently back tracking regular expressions to thread contention issues caused by multiple threads simultaneously waiting for a long running locked method, block of code, or database records. Memory and non-memory (e.g. sockets, connections, etc) leaks can also degrade performance by depriving your application of these scarce resources by either consuming more CPU cycles due to over working the garbage collection or by running out of memory or connections.

Building real time STP (Straight Through Processing) applications can be quite complex. Real-time and low-latency are distinctly separate subjects although often related. Real-time is about being more predictable than fast.

No modern web system runs without a cache, which is an in-memory store that holds subset of information typically stored in a database, LDAP server, CMS server like Vignette, or any other external data that are accessed via a web service. Static files such as property files should also be cached to prevent excessive disk access. **Good caching strategies are vital for low latency applications**. Think about the caching strategies like when to cache and when to clear them, what to cache and what not to cache, choice of the caching framework, etc. Caching comes with a cost. Only some subsets of information can be stored in memory. The most common data pruning strategy is to evict items that are least recently used (LRU). The pruning needs to be efficient, not to slow down the application. Too much caching or caching the wrong data could adversely impact performance. If you attempt to cache too much data then you run the risk of excessive garbage collection and running out of memory.

Modern applications are distributed and integrates with many internal and external systems. Poor integration with internal and external systems can cause performance issues. For example, not properly testing the non-happy path to internal or external systems for scenarios like the system being unavailable, failure conditions and heavy load conditions. Proper service retries and timeouts needs to be configured to prevent increased thread utilization due to an internal or external system outage or its poor response times.

Excessive or inconsistent logging can trigger high I/O on your server and consequently increase CPU utilization. Use appropriate logging frameworks that allow you to configure logging levels like trace, debug, info, warning, and error, and has support for both synchronous and asynchronous logging.

Think about the **algorithmic complexities**. Think in terms of big O notation. Low latency applications need to aim for O(1) or O(log n) complexity. If something takes O(n), it's linear in the size of data. O(n^2) is quadratic. Using this notation, you should know that search through a list is O(n) and binary search (through a sorted list) is log(n). And sorting of n items would take n*log(n) time. Due to abundance of excellent libraries, we are not as focused on efficiency these days. Your code should never have multiple nested loops (a loop inside a loop inside a loop). Most of the code written today should use hash-maps, simple lists, singly nested **iterations**, and **recursions** for tree structures. Think about **hashing algorithms**, but modern libraries should have good default functions. The idea behind hashing is fast access to the data. If the data is stored sequentially in a list, the time to find the item is proportional to the size of the list. If you use a hash-map, for each element, a hash function calculates a number, which is used as an index into the table. Given a good hash function that uniformly spreads data along the table, the look-up time is constant (i.e. 1).

Reduce the number of objects you create. Apply the flyweight design pattern where applicable. Favor stateless objects. In garbage collected languages like Java, you should avoid GC pauses. Specialist GC collectors like the Azul collector can in many cases solve this problem for you out of the box, but for many of you who use the Oracle's GC, you need to understand how GC works and tune it to minimize the pauses. GC tuning is very application specific. So, turn on the GC debugging and tune your GC.

It is important to set performance requirements in the technical specifications by including a performance focus in the analysis and design and also creating a production like performance testing environment. But one should not compromise on architectural principles for just performance. One should take the effort to write architecturally sound programs as opposed to writing only fast programs. If your architecture is sound enough, then it would allow your program not only to scale better, but also allows it to be optimized for performance if it is not fast enough. If you write applications with poor architecture, but performs well for the current requirements, what will happen if the requirements grow and your architecture is not flexible enough to extend, and creates a maintenance nightmare where fixing a code in one area would break your code in another area. This will cause your application to be re-written rather than to be tuned.

Use **lock free algorithms and I/O**. For example, in Java the *java.util.concurrent* package and the Java NIO (New I/O using non-blocking multiplexers) respectively. Even the most well designed concurrent application that uses locks is at risk of blocking. Blocking is not good for low latency applications.

Most software projects face problems relating to performance bottlenecks, and the root cause(s) can be very subtle, and can be hard to understand, reproduce and solve without the adequate technical skills. Many performance problems do not surface until the application is running in production mode, 24 hours a day, 7 days a week with 10+ concurrent users and gets pushed to its limits during some unexpected peak period. Hence, it is a very bad idea to deploy your application without load testing. One key aspect of capacity planning is load and performance testing. There are a number of open-source (e.g. *JMeter*) and commercial (e.g. *HP LoadRunner*, *NeoLoad Web Load and Stress Testing*, etc) performance testing tools to simulate these production like conditions. There are functional testing automation tools like *BadBoy,* which can be used to auto generate scripts while using the website and then export the script in *JMeter* format to be opened in *JMeter* for load testing. Once your application is running in a simulated production mode, you can determine if an application is running more slowly than it should by verifying the results against the SLAs (aka Service Level Agreement) defined in the non-functional specification or running more slowly than it did previously by comparing the new results against the previously obtained results. This is known as **benchmarking**. You could also identify any other catastrophic failures like the application being unresponsive or hangs due to memory/resource leaks, deadlocks, etc. Performance and scalability problems typically fall into the following 5 major categories:

- **Inefficient use of CPU resources:** For example, heavily backtracking regular expressions, bad SQL queries, algorithmic complexities, etc.
- **Inefficient use of memory resources:** For example, memory leaks, spending too much time on garbage collection, allocating insufficient heap or perm gen space, etc.
- **Inefficient use of non-memory resources** like database connections, LDAP connections, sockets, file handles, etc. For example, not using connection pools, not freeing connections back to the pool, improper connection or socket timeouts, etc.
- **Inefficient use of threads:** For example, 2 or more threads requiring access to a specific resource to perform a unit of work, and are required to wait for a period of time to acquire the resources because another thread has control of the resource.
- **Inefficient use of the networked resources:** For example, too many round trips to and from the database, web service calls, and other remoting. There could be other environmental factors like the load balancers not opening enough sockets or sending requests to the same server, etc. The **netstat** is a handy command to identify network issues. There are other system monitoring tools and they can be used in combination with each other in order to get an accurate picture of your system. For example, iostat, vmstat, nfsstat, uptime, ps, top, sar, etc.

The performance testing can be categorized into following 3 groups:

- **Load testing** for daily peak (e.g. 100+ concurrent users) and off peak (e.g 40 concurrent users) conditions to ensure that the application meets the service level agreements (i.e. SLAs).

Get a good handle on the 16 key areas of software engineering to open more doors

- **Stress testing** for extreme conditions (e.g. 200+ concurrent users) to ensure that the application can handle unexpected loads. For example, a stock trading application must be able to handle panic selling during a global financial crisis.

- **Soak** (aka endurance) testing to ensure that the application does not have to be restarted every 2nd or 3rd day due to potential memory and resource leaks. This can be achieved by letting the stress testing run continuously for 24 to 48 hours.

Hence, it really pays to have the right people who have the experience and the know how to identify, reproduce, and resolve these problems by using the right tools and the know how. Some of the tools listed below can profile and monitor CPU, memory, threads, and sockets.

Tools: For troubleshooting Java applications, there are **basic tools** like vmstat, hprof, *JConsole*, *JAMon*, *PerfAnal*, etc to **more feature packed profiling tools** like *VisualVM*, *Netbeans* profiler, *eclipse TPTP* (i.e. Test & Performance Tools Platform), etc to **tools that can be used in production** environment like *YourKit* for Java & .Net, *JProfiler* for Java, etc to **tools for larger distributed and clustered systems with large number of nodes** like *CA Wiley Introscope* for Java and .Net and *ClearStone* for Java.

Memory/resource Considerations (MC)

Memory and resource leaks are possible in any robust application. While free and third-party tools exist to detect such leaks, it is usually difficult to reproduce these issues as they can surface only under certain load or user behavior. The load testing scripts need to properly emulate the scenarios that cause resource or memory leaks. Memory leaks are generally caused by coding errors like not explicitly freeing the allocated memory, cyclic references, and global variables or singleton classes holding on to large amount of data. A typical tell tale sign of a memory or a non-memory (e.g. database connections) leak is having to restart the application often.

In managed languages such as Java and C#, the developers do not have to worry too much about memory management as the garbage collector (GC) will do this job for you. The garbage collectors can be tuned with different algorithms and hints depending on the behavior of the application. This does not mean that the garbage collected languages are immuned from memory leaks.

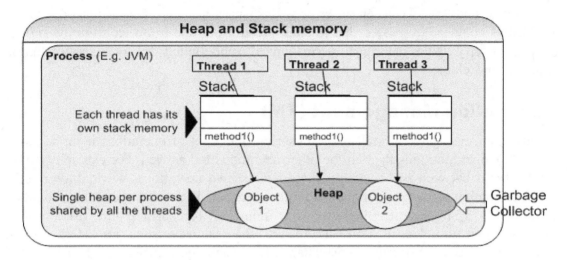

Memory leaks can occur in managed languages when objects of longer life cycle (e.g. static or global variables, singleton classes, etc) hold on to objects of a shorter life cycle. This prevents the objects with short life cycle being garbage collected. The developer must remember to remove the references to the short-lived objects from the long-lived objects. Objects with the same life cycle generally do not cause any issues because the garbage collector is smart enough to deal with the circular references. Memory leaks can also occur when a GC managed code call native system resources that are typically written in native code (not managed by GC) like C or C++. For example, in Java, Java Native Interface (JNI) APIs are used to embed native libraries/code into Java code. Finally, there could be memory leaks in a third party library or a particular version of the language API library itself.

The **Flyweight design pattern** is all about managing memory more efficiently by sharing objects. It's a useful pattern to have under your belt to prevent memory issues. It is a best practice to favor immutable objects where possible in your application, and you might try creating flyweights, or shared instances, of them and then reference those flyweights in your application requests rather than create them on a per request basis. The flyweight pattern can help reduce memory consumption, decrease the frequency of garbage collection, and improve the response time of your application.

Non memory resource leaks are generally caused by not properly closing database connections, LDAP server connections, and sockets. These are scarce resources, and must be immediately returned to a pool once finished using them or when it times out. Quite often these resources are either not closed properly in an application under exceptional condition like when an error is thrown as the line of code responsible for closing this could be by passed due to sloppy coding or due to not configuring proper time out or retry values causing these resources to indefinitely try for a service that is currently unavailable.

Transaction Management (TM)

A transaction management is all about ensuring that a set of operations complete as a unit. If one operation fails then all the other operations fail as well. For example, if you transfer funds between two accounts, there will be two operations – withdraw money from one account, and deposit money into other account. These two operations should be completed as a single unit. Otherwise your money will get lost if the withdrawal is successful and the deposit fails. There are four characteristics for a transaction abbreviated as ACID properties, which stands for **A**tomicity, **C**onsistency, **I**solation, and **D**urability. The transaction management makes use of different levels of optimistic or pessimistic locking to achieve these characteristics. A transaction could be a simple local (e.g. within the same database) transaction or a distributed (e.g. across a database and a messaging queue) transaction using a concept known as the **2-phase commit**.

ACID based **two phase commit** transaction

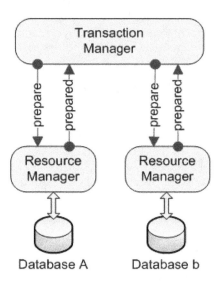

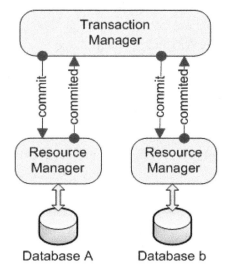

For example, booking an online airline ticket where actions are required to reserve a seat and pay for the ticket. Both of these actions must either succeed or if one fails, both actions should be rolled back. Isolation is one of the basic tenets of the ACID model to prevent any anomalies relating to dirty reads, non-repeatable reads, and phantom reads. These anomalies can leave a database in inconsistent state when accessed concurrently. Improper isolation levels could end up double booking a seat in an airline booking system. **Dirty Reads** occur when one transaction reads data written by another, uncommitted, transaction. The danger with dirty reads is that the other transaction might never commit, leaving the original transaction with "dirty" data. **Non Repeatable Reads** occur when one transaction attempts to access the same data twice and a second transaction modifies the data between the first transaction's read attempts. This may cause the first transaction to read two different values for the same data, causing the original read to be non-repeatable.

The isolation levels lock database records at different granularity. For example, a single row, set of rows or the whole table. This type of locking is known as the "**pessimistic locking**" and you need to apply this type of locking judiciously as it can adversely impact performance. The "pessimistic locking" doesn't work well in a web application, as you don't want to hold on to the locks during the user think time or if a user locks a record and then forgets that s/he locked it, you will have a record that is locked forever.

The best way to handle this problem is to assume that you aren't going to have two people trying to update the same data at the same time too often. You do this by making only one person responsible for updating each data item. You're still going to have the occasional race condition, for example when two or more users update the same record, but you can deal with those on an ad-hoc basis with the help of a version or timestamp column in the database to detect if the record is dirty without needing to lock the record. This approach is known as the "**optimistic locking**". The optimistic locking is more scalable and the ORM tools do support the "**dirty checking**" feature with version numbers or timestamp columns in the database table. Here is how you can implement optimistic locking in a web application:

If you want to implement optimistic locking, add a version number or timestamp column to the table. When you insert a new record set the version number to say 1. When you get a record to show to the user on the GUI, get the version number and store in a hidden form field. When the user submits the form, the version number should be submitted in the update request. When updating the request, get the latest version number for the record from the database, and see if it is different from the version number that is already in the update request. If they are different, show error to user as someone has changed the data. If they are the same, increment the version number and save.

If you use a timestamp, the timestamp column will be automatically updated by the database management system during updates and inserts. You need to compare the timestamps in your application to detect if a record is dirty to prevent any concurrent updates of the same record.

Increasingly, web services are used in business applications for third-party integration. For example, an online travel application calls a number of different external third party applications like an airline ticketing system, a hotel reservation, and a rental car reservation system. All of these services need to succeed, and if one of the services fail, then all the other services must be rolled back. If you use a traditional ACID based transaction management, you would run into the scenario where the third-party resources used by the web services would be locked for an indefinite period of time, until all the other participating services have executed. So, the ACID based transactions are not suited for the long running transactions, and **compensation based transactions** need to be used.

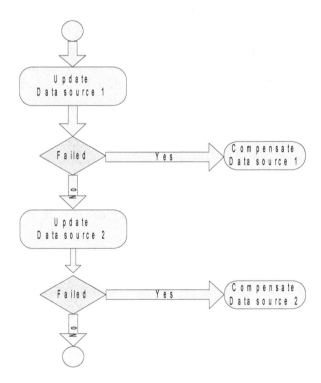

The **compensation based transaction management** has features such as

- Managing data consistency without locking the resources. The coordinator (WS-C) is responsible for sending messages back and forth between the transaction participants. The participants register themselves with the coordinator to receive messages. The coordinator is also responsible for propagating transactional context information between participants.
- Unlike ACID based transactions where the complete authority is given to a single transaction manager, the transactions are coordinated among the various participants without giving complete authority to a single transaction manager. The coordinators and compensating tasks replace the transaction managers.
- Works well in scenarios where participants' availability or response is not guaranteed.
- The participants are notified via the life cycle methods to take the appropriate course of action. The participants do have life cycle methods like compensate( ) to be executed when a transaction fails and a close( ) method to indicate successful transaction completion.

Q. How will you write atomically some data from your code to a file? In other words, Either all of your writes have to make it to the disk, or none of them.
A. File writes are not atomic, but meta operations like rename, copy, creating a new file, etc are atomic. So, you need to write to a temp file, and once everything is written successfully, **rename** the file to actual name.

Q. How will you handle producer-consumer scenario where a consumer polls for availability of a file, whilst the producer is responsible for producing a file?
A. The key consideration here is that the consumer needs to read the file only once it is fully written and not read a partially read file while it is being written by the producer. This can be achieved as described below.

1. The producer writing to a file say **customer.csv** should create a new empty file named cusomer.csv**.end** file at the completion. This is an empty flag file that signals the file completion.
2. The consumer should be polling for presence of a file named **customer.csv.end** to trigger reading from a file named customer.csv by dropping ".**end**", which is used only as a signal file.

Security (SE)

Software is increasingly used for mission critical systems, hence it is important to weigh up amount of effort expended in security against significance of damage in terms of dollars and reputation. Security may delay the time to market. At the same time, insecure systems can earn a bad reputation and lose user confidence, and consequently adversely impact the profitability of the business. One needs to strike a good balance by asking the right questions like what am I trying to hide? What can they do with it? How much will it hurt if someone find out? How much effort is required to hide in terms of time, money, and pain?

Security is all about having policies, procedures, and systems in place. It also includes coding defensively to prevent any vulnerabilities like SQL injection attack, cross site scripting, exposing detailed error messages, access control bypass, and missing "HTTPonly" cookie attribute. It is also really important to understand the following security concepts:

- **Authentication** is basically an identification process. Do I know who you are? A basic authentication can be carried out by challenging the user to provide one of the following to authenticate his/her identity – password/PIN (Personal Identification Number); A physical token, passport, driver's license, or an ID card; or biometric data like fingerprint, face geometry, or iris recognition. A two-factor authentication takes this a step further by requiring any two forms of the above authentication. Organizations do use Single Sign-On (SSO) with softwares like SiteMinder or Tivoli Access Manager (TAM) to permit a user to enter one name and password in order to access multiple applications.

- **Authorization** is the process by which a program determines whether a given identity is permitted to access a resource such as a file or an application component. Now that you are authenticated, I know who you are? But are you allowed to access the resource or component you are requesting? LDAP servers or database tables are used to map users to groups and roles. In order to determine who can do what, the roles are mapped to web resources and methods to control access.

- **Data Integrity** helps to make sure if something is intact and not tampered with during transmission or under exceptional conditions. For example, message digests and Secured Hash Algorithms (SHA) are used to ensure that the data

90

has not been modified. A message digest is a digitally created hash (fingerprint) created from a plain text block. All the information of the message is used to construct the message digest hash, but the message cannot be recovered from the hash. For this reason, message digests are also known as *one way hash functions.*

- **Confidentiality and privacy** can be accomplished through encryption. There are two basic techniques for encrypting information: **symmetric encryption** (aka secret key encryption) and **asymmetric encryption** (aka public key encryption). The symmetric encryption uses a secret key, which is a string of random letters, and is applied to the text of a message to change the content in a particular way. This might be as simple as shifting each letter by a number of places in the alphabet. As long as both sender and recipient know the secret key, they can encrypt and decrypt all messages that use this key. The problem with a secret key is that exchanging them over the Internet or a large network while preventing them from falling into the wrong hands. Anyone who knows the secret key can decrypt the message. One answer to this problem is asymmetric encryption, in which there are two related keys--a key pair. A public key is made freely available to anyone who might want to send you a message. A second, private key is kept secret, so that only you know it. Any message (text, binary files, or documents) that are encrypted by using the public key can only be decrypted by applying the same algorithm, but by using the matching private key. Any message that is encrypted by using the private key can only be decrypted by using the matching public key. This means that you do not have to worry about passing public keys over the Internet. A problem with asymmetric encryption is that it is slower than symmetric encryption. It requires far more processing power to both encrypt and decrypt the content of the message.

Q. What is a salt in cryptography?
A. Salt is a random number that is needed to access the encrypted data, along with the password. If an attacker does not know the password, and is trying to guess it with a brute-force attack, then every password the attacker tries has to be tried with each salt value. So, for a one-bit salt (0 or 1), this makes the encryption twice as hard to break in this way. A two bit salt makes it four times as hard and so on. Can you imagine how difficult it is to crack passwords with encryption that uses a 32-bit salt?

Get a good handle on the 16 key areas of software engineering to open more doors

- **Non-repudiation and auditing**: Proof that the sender actually sent the message. It also prohibits the author of the message from falsely denying that he/she sent the message. This is achieved by record keeping the exact time of the message transmission, the public key used to decrypt the message, and the encrypted message itself. Record keeping can be complicated but critical for non-repudiation.

- **Secure Socket Layer (SSL)** uses a combination of symmetric and asymmetric (public-key) encryption to accomplish confidentiality, integrity, authentication and non-repudiation for Internet communication. Asymmetric encryption is used for the initial once of handshake between the client and the server, and during this handshake, a secret known as a session key is established for ongoing symmetric encryption and decryption.

- **Digital certificates**: In order to use asymmetric encryption, there must be a way for people to discover other public keys. The prevalent technique is to use digital certificates. A certificate is a package of information that identifies a user or a server, and contains information such as the organization name, the organization that issued the certificate, the user's e-mail address and country, and the user's public key. When a server and client require a secured handshake, they send a query over the network to the other party, which sends back a copy of the certificate. The other party's public key can be extracted from the certificate. A certificate can also be used to uniquely identify the holder.

Scalability (SC)

Q. What is the difference between performance and scalability?
A. The performance and scalability are two different things.

For example, if you are in the business of transporting people in a horse carriage, the performance is all about utilizing more powerful horses to transporting your people quicker to their destination. Scalability is all about catering for increase in demand for such transportation as your business grows by either increasing the capacity of individual actors (e.g. carriage capacity) or adding more actors (e.g. horses and carriages).

Scalability is a desirable property of a system, a network, or a process, which indicates its ability to either handle growing amounts of work in a graceful manner, or to be readily enlarged. For example, in the diagram below the response time starts to degrade when 1000 users hit the the system.

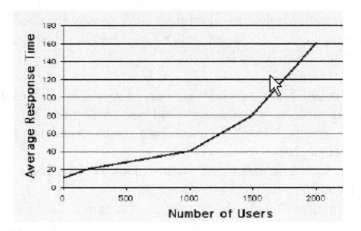

The key aspect is to architect the application with the vision of scalability. Applications can be scaled either **horizontally** by adding a new physical server to the load balancer or cluster that is already serving requests to 3 servers or **vertically** by adding more CPU, memory, or virtual servers to the existing physical servers. A single-threaded application or batch process can be parallelized with multi-threading on a multi-core CPU machine to scale.

If your application/system is multi-threaded or multi-processed and is running out of CPU resources, then your application will most likely scale well when more CPUs are added. Before adding more CPUs, check for one of the following reasons for scalability problems.

- Firstly, the high CPU usage. If the allocated heap memory size is not enough, then the garbage collector (GC) will run more frequently to clear the unused objects by consuming majority of the CPU cycles. This can be fixed by allocating more memory and tuning the GC fewer pauses.

- Secondly, if the application maximizes the use of the CPUs through multi-threading, see if the multi-threaded code can be tuned by keeping the synchronization blocks as short as possible. For example, reducing the locking granularity by locking a block of code instead of the whole instance method can improve CPU utilization. It is even worse to lock a static method. It is better to use APIs that allow concurrent reads and apply locks only for concurrent write operations. Where possible make your objects immutable so that they can be accessed concurrently without any need for locking.

Multi-threaded applications need to coordinate tasks with each other by using locks to avoid any concurrency issues discussed earlier. Good **locking practices** listed below can make your application more scalable.

- Keep the locked block of code as short as possible. For example, instead of putting a big fat lock to a whole method, use smaller locks to relevant blocks of code within a method. Don't put a lock on a static method as it will lock the whole instances of that class.
- Reduce the time a thread hangs on to a lock. This reduces the probability of another thread competing for the same lock.
- Use more efficient thread-safe data structure libraries. For example, in Java, lock free and wait free algorithms were introduced as part of the *java.util.concurrent* package from version 5 onwards.

If you create a thread dump as discussed earlier, and in Java, if you see lots of lines as shown below, then you have a potential scalability problem due to locking.

```
Thread-1" prio=10 tid=0x08223eb0 nid=0x7 waiting for monitor entry
[0xf928b000..0xf927bde
```

A server's ability to handle several client requests effectively depends on how it uses I/O streams. When a server has to handle hundreds of clients simultaneously, it must be able to use I/O services concurrently. One way to cater for this scenario is to use threads, but having almost one-to-one ratio of threads (i.e. 100 clients will have 100 threads) is prone to enormous thread overhead and can result in performance and scalability problems due to consumption of memory stacks (i.e. each thread has its own stack.) and CPU context switching (i.e. switching between threads as opposed to doing real computation.). This problem can be overcome by using **non-blocking I/O** and events driven development. For example, the Apache MINA framework in Java, JavaScript based server node.js, etc.

Q. What is **SEDA**? Where will you use it?
A. SEDA stands for Staged Event Driven Architecture, and it decomposes a complex, event-driven application into a set of *stages* connected by *queues*. This design avoids the high overhead associated with thread-based concurrency models, and decouples event

and thread scheduling from application logic. This architecture improves performance and latency because SEDA based services are constructed as a network of stages, and each stage with an associated incoming event queue. Each stage consists of a thread pool with a finite number of threads and an application-supplied event handler. The stage's operation is managed by the controller, which adjusts resource allocations and scheduling dynamically. Each stage can be individually conditioned to load by thresholding or filtering its event queue. SEDA is good for horizontally scaling out large sophisticated services by decoupling them with stages and queues.

Q. How will you scale your data store?
A. The scalability of database is critical because data is often a shared resource, and it becomes the main contact point for nearly every web request. The most important question you have to ask when considering the scalability of your database is, "What kind of system am I working with?" Are you working with a read-heavy or a write-heavy system?

Scaling Reads: If your website is primarily a read-centric system, vertically scale your data store with a caching strategy that uses memory cache (e.g. ehcache) or a CDN (Content Delivery Newtork). You can also add more CPU/RAM/Disk to scale vertically.

Scaling Writes: If your website is primarily a write-heavy system, you want to think about using a horizontally scalable datastore such as **MongoDB (NoSQL database)**, Riak, Cassandra or HBase. MongoDB is a NoSQL database with great features like replication and sharding built in. This allows you to scale your database to as many servers as you would like by distributing content among them. A database shard ("sharding") is the phrase used to describe a horizontal partition in a database or search engine. The idea behind sharding is to split data among multiple machines while ensuring that the data is always accessed from the correct place. Since sharding spreads the database across multiple machines, the database programmer specifies explicit sharding rules to determine which machines any piece of data will be stored on. Sharding may also be referred to as horizontal scaling or horizontal partitioning. Oracle uses (**RAC** - Real Application Cluster) where small server blades are genned-in to an Oracle RAC cluster over a high-speed interconnect.

Q. What is BigData?
A. Big data is the term for a collection of data sets so large and complex that becomes very difficult to work with using most relational database management systems and desktop statistics and visualization packages, requiring instead "massively parallel

software running on tens, hundreds, or even thousands of servers". Apache™ Hadoop® is an open source software project that enables the distributed processing of large data sets across clusters of commodity servers. It is designed to scale up from a single server to thousands of machines, with a very high degree of fault tolerance.

Hadoop uses **MapReduce** to understand and assign work to nodes in the cluster and **HDFS**(Hadoop Distributed File System), which is file system that spans all the nodes in a Hadoop cluster for data storage.

As discussed earlier under performance consideration, there are a number of other factors that can impact scalability.

- Bad database or application design, heavy use of stored procedures putting more load on database servers, SQL query performing full table scan, heavily back tracking regex, producing complex online reports without opting for off-peak scheduled reports, etc.
- Synchronous logging. When there is a stringent requirement on adequate logging, asynchronous logging might be a better option.

Now a days cloud computing is changing the way we deliver large scale web applications. It is all about delivering Software as a Service (SaaS), Platform as a Service (PaaS), and Infrastructure as a Service (IaaS). The application server virtualization is an idea where the applications are run on demand to minimize under utilization of valuable resources. So, cloud computing provides on-demand scalability, fixed cost reduction, pay per use, and lower cost. These benefits are realized at the cost of increased architecture complexity, security implications, and less control on cloud resources. Amazon Elastic Compute Cloud (i.e. EC2) presents a true virtual computing environment, allowing you to use web service interfaces to launch instances with a variety of operating systems, load them with your custom application environment, manage your network's access permissions, and run your image using as many or few systems as you desire.

Best Practices (BP)

Understanding some of the nuances and best practices can help you write less error-prone and more robust code. It is a best practice to reuse proven, well-tested, and robust libraries and frameworks as opposed to reinventing the wheel or writing sub-standard functions, libraries, or frameworks. There are best practices to just about every key area listed here and every new technology, framework or tool you intend to learn or use.

During the design phase, ensure that the applications are neither over designed nor under designed. Apply UML and proven patterns. Strive for code reuse and loose coupling. Build a full end-to-end vertical slice as a proof of concept for a typical use case to validate the choice of technologies, frameworks, and tools. This will help you iron out any potential issues.

During the coding phase, you will need to apply the best practices relating to language, specification, and platform fundamentals. Follow best practices relating to software development like test driven development (TDD), behavior driven development (BDD), daily builds, and continuous integration. Even if you use the waterfall approach for your development process, you still can cherry pick some of the best practices like daily stand ups, iterative development, test driven development, etc from the agile development methodologies. During the testing phase, include performance testing and penetration testing to the functional testing to detect issues that only surface under certain load or malicious use of the system respectively.

Understanding some of the nuances, pitfalls, and best practices can help you write less error-prone and more robust code. You will find plethora of information online when you search for key words like "Technology-X pitfalls", "Framework-Y best practices.", "Technology-X tips", "Framework-Y caveats" or "Technology-X do's and don'ts".

Coding (CO)

Writing maintainable, supportable, readable, and testable code will increase the overall software quality. Software engineering is not only a science, it is an art as well.

> "Any fool can write code that a computer can understand.
> Good programmers write code that humans can understand."
> –   by Martin Fowler

Here are a few things to keep in mind to ensure code quality:

- Write unit tests and re-factor your code where necessary to make it more maintainable, testable, and readable
- Think of all possible inputs your test should pass for it to be correct. This means test for negative scenarios like service timeouts, negative or null inputs,

exceptions, etc.
- Code for better testability by loosely coupling your classes using the principle of dependency injection.
- Make your code more maintainable by applying the DRY (Don't Repeat Yourself) principle.
- Write fail-fast code, which immediately report any failure or conditions rather than attempting to continue a possibly flawed process.
- Business logic must be written in a protocol agnostic manner to increase reuse.
- Know your OO concepts and apply them.
- Have good understanding of the data structures and algorithms.
- Be aware of the SOLID design principles that allow your code to be more flexible to extend, reuse, and understand.
- Use the right tool to get the job done. For example, don't use string operations to parse or write XML documents.
- When coding, think about thread-safety and atomicity. Issues arising from these are harder to detect and test.
- Always write readable code. Don't rely too much on comments. Make your code self-explanatory with meaningful variable, method and class names.
- Handle exceptions properly. Don't sweep them under a carpet.
- Reduce state with local variables and make your code inherently thread-safe with immutable objects where possible.
- Be aware of the common gotchas, pitfalls, anti patterns, and caveats.
- Code defensively to prevent any security holes with proper input validation and failing fast.
- Watch-out and test for thread safety and transactional issues.
- Apply proven design patterns where it makes sense.

Exception Handling (EH)

Exception handling is the method of building a system to detect and recover from exceptional conditions. Exceptional conditions are any unexpected occurrences that are not accounted for in a system's normal operation. Improper exception handling can make your system less secured by exposing lower level details to the users under exceptional conditions, hide problems by ignoring the exceptions, make debugging harder by losing the stack trace, and possibly leak resources or handle transactions incorrectly by taking a different flow by skipping the close or release calls of those resources or not rolling back a transaction respectively. Things to keep in mind while handling exceptions are

- Throw an exception early because the exception stack trace helps you pinpoint where an exception occurred by showing you the exact sequence of method calls that lead to the exception.

- Catch an exception late. You should not try to catch an exception before your program can handle it in an appropriate manner. The natural tendency when a compiler complains about a checked exception is to catch it so that the compiler stops reporting errors. It is a bad practice to sweep the exceptions under the carpet by catching it and not doing anything with it to make the compiler happy.

- Don't lose your stack trace. Throwing a new exception from a catch block without passing the original exception into the new exception can cause some part of the stack trace to be lost, and can make debugging less effective.

Software Development Process (SDP)

Since software development can be very difficult and complex, having the right tools and people alone not enough. You need to have proper processes (aka SDLC) in place to guide the development to make it more systematic and efficient. There are a number of approaches to software development from "agile" to classic "water fall". My experience is that the best method is one that works for your environment. The SDLC process pans from conception to completion of any software project. More and more firms are using either agile or a hybrid development model that combines some elements of agile with waterfall approach. It is worth understanding the agile principles, and try practicing some of the principles for a while and then decide what will work and not work for the team. Some advanced agile practices should be tried only after more basic agile practices, such as daily stand-ups, iterative development, continuous integration, etc are successful. Adopting an agile process is a process in itself, and requires full support and commitment from the management.

Build automation tools that include continuous integration (CI), build-scripting, code-quality metrics, version-control (e.g. SCM – Source Control Management) and dependency management are important to get the software development into the rhythm of build, deploy, test, and manage. The automated testing tools are essential for both functional and non-functional testing. The defect and task management systems are critical to manage defects and tasks like system testing, performance testing, penetration testing, outage testing, data preparation, and releasing to various environments like system testing, user acceptance testing, staging, and production. It also acts as a dashboard for reporting purpose to the stakeholders, peers and superiors.

The SDLC process also involves producing relevant documentation and acquiring sign-offs from the relevant stake holders. The relevant documentations involve business requirements, functional requirements, non-functional requirements, solution designs, technical designs, performance, penetration, and cross-browser compatibility testing plans, results and summary, implementation plans, support hand-over, etc. These tasks need to be managed via task management systems like JIRA. The cross functional teams like the business users, release management, infrastructure, application support, etc need to review and sign-off the relevant documents.

In a nutshell, all the relevant boxes need to be ticked before an application becomes live. This requires good soft-skills, and personal traits to get things done. You can build up a reputation as someone who gets things done by complementing your technical skills in these key areas with good understanding of the full SDLC to contribute process improvements to better manage complexities.

Quality of Service (QoS)

The term 'Quality of Service' also means taking care of the 'non-functional requirements'. Adequate monitoring, gathering performance metrics, auditing, security, raising system alerts, clustering and fail over capabilities, etc improve the quality of service provided by the application. The virtualization tools like vmware and application severs that execute the application provides quality of services like reliability, high availability, and clustering. Innovative products like Terracotta, a JVM clustering solution can turn single-node, multi-threaded applications into distributed, multi-node applications with no code changes. HP NonStop technology provides 24/7 application availability out of the box, enabling the most critical and complex environments to run continuously in a straightforward manner. It is also vital to have a good disaster recovery plan to ensure the continuity of the business for the mission critical applications. This includes regular back up of data, uninterrupted power supply, off site back up of data, and a back up infrastructure at a different location.

The system **outage tests** need to be carried out to ensure that the clustering and load balancing works as expected. This can be tested by bringing a node down in a cluster, and checking if the requests are sent to a different node. Some of the key considerations include sticky versus non-sticky (i.e. stateless) sessions, active/active versus active/passive clusters, and application level fail overs like deadlock retry, service timeout retry, etc. In active/passive mode, all business logic runs on one node and the "passive" node just waits for a fail-over. In Active/Active mode both nodes are running business logic and should one node fail, the other node will start the failed resources. Different configurations are possible in a multi-node environment.

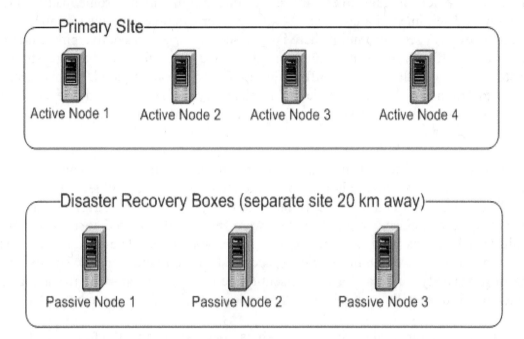

Sticky sessions mean stateful sessions where the requests from the same user will go to the same node/server. Your load balancer should be able to look at IP addresses and HTTP cookies to determine stickiness. With sticky sessions

- the initial requests will be distributed evenly, but you might end up with a significant number of users spending more time than others. If all of these users are initially set to a single server, that server will have much more load. This can be mitigated by having more servers in your cluster.

- You will also lose the ability to take one or more nodes down for maintenance in the event of any system failures. If you are using a sticky session, then you will have to wait until the number of existing sticky connections to drop to an acceptable level.

So, generally favor non-sticky sessions and stateless services where possible. But, if you must maintain session state, sticky sessions are definitely the way to go and even if you don't use session state, stickiness has benefits when it comes to cache utilization.

When you are performing outage testing, there could be instances where your application may have to implement a fail-over retry service due to limitations in some load-balancers as to how it determines as a node being "offline". For example, the load balancer pings each node every 5 seconds, and if there is no response for 3 consecutive pings, it marks the node as 'offline'. With this limitation, there is a possibility of the requests to be directed to the node that is going offline during this 15 second interval. In this scenario, your application will be responsible for implementing a fail-over retry service using interceptors to catch the exception and retry the service 3 times at an interval of 5 seconds.

The applications need to be constantly monitored for availability, performance and other potential issues. There are monitoring tools like HP SiteScope, CA Wiley Introscope and IBM Tivoli to monitor and raise alerts/alarms to notify the support staff. For example, if you are using a message oriented middle-ware, proper alerts need to be installed to monitor queue depths (i.e. total number of messages in a queue). The log directories need to be monitored for availability of disk spaces. When the queues or disk spaces reach 80% of its capacity, notifications can be sent to the first-level support staff. The logs can be monitored for specific errors like "database deadlocks" and alerts can be raised.

The penetration testing, which is also known as "**pentest**" is a method of evaluating the security of an application by simulating an attack from malicious outsiders. There are tools such as Tamper Data plug-in for Firefox and Skipfish from Google to simulate malicious attacks. The applications and systems need to be properly audited for any potential security holes and breaches.

The performance or load testing verifies application performance and functionality under heavy load. As discussed earlier, many issues can only be detected under heavy load and also the system must meet the SLAs (i.e. Service Level agreements) in the business requirements. For example, the business and the relevant stake holders need to sign-off on the performance metrics under different scenarios like normal load, peak load, crisis load (e.g. global financial crisis), peak load in 2 years time, peak load in 5 years, etc. The response times monitored include min, max, average, median, standard deviation and percentiles like 80%, 85%, 90%, and 95%. The 90% percentile line gets rid of the best

5% and worst 5% to give a normal distribution. For example, the round trip response time is 2.2 seconds for 90% of the orders placed. This is also known as the confidence interval. The table below can be used to calculate the confidence level on the standard deviation.

Confidence Interval	Probability (+ or - Z)
0.8	1.2815
0.9	1.6444
0.95	1.9599
0.99	2.5758

The following formula can be used to determine the lower and upper limit in a normal distribution curve.

UPPER = Avg + Prob * Deviation/ SQRT of **Sample size**
LOWER = Avg - Prob * Deviation/ SQRT of **Sample size**

For example, a sample size of 7500, with average response time of 1.136 seconds and deviation of 5.396 seconds will take an upper limit of 1.215 seconds 80% of the time.

At **80% confidence**: 1.136 + 1.2815*5.396/ SQRT 7500
1.1136 + 1.2815*5.396/86.60254
1.2815 + 0.079847 = 1.215 seconds

Another performance testing indicator is the **throughput**. For example, the application can handle a throughput of 210 orders a minute before the performance starts to degrade. It is also imperative that while the performance tests are being performed, the CPU usage, memory usage, and application logs are monitored. The response data also need to be validated and asserted to ensure that the application is functioning correctly under load. The logs and assertions can pinpoint any potential issues due to thread-safety, deadlock, transaction management, application level fail-over retry failures, etc under heavy load.

Finally, the data and logs need to be properly archived. Some critical information needs to be archived for up to 10 years. Some transactional data needs to be adequately audited and archived. Database triggers can be used to audit CRUD (Create, Read, Update, and Delete) operations by storing individual activities to a separate audit log table. Any heavy logging mechanism can also be asynchronously performed by publishing the log events to a queue and letting a separate process to process those events to a database. The audited data can be viewed via a web based user interface or direct SQL.

How do you acquire or enhance your skills in these key areas?

Don't be overwhelmed by the number of key areas. The software development is a team sport requiring a collaborative effort by bringing in a group of people with varying strengths and responsibilities. Depending on your role, responsibilities, and seniority, there are some key areas you must know well, and other key areas you must have a good understanding and how to go about get it done by engaging the right people. In this case, you will take on the role as a facilitator to manage and get things moving. But you should always strive to get a good handle on these key areas to better manage complexities and get things done, and consequently fast track your career.

Nothing beats hands-on experience. Experience can be gained by proactively applying these key areas in your paid professional work, unpaid professional work, open-source projects, and self-taught projects. Businesses do not like to hire people without experience, and many businesses are not willing to train.

If you want to get ahead, you have to think and do things differently. Most of you won't be handed opportunities on a silver platter. So, to gain the real know how in these key areas, there is no magic formula other than to acquire more hands-on experience. Even if you have a paid job, there would be times in your career where you may feel stagnated or not have much to do at work. This will be a great opportunity for you to challenge yourself with self-taught or open-source projects to increase your awareness and enhance your skills on these key areas to become a great contributor in your future projects.

Good developers learn to analyze negative scenarios by asking the right questions like "what could possibly go wrong here?", "what if an exception is thrown here?", "what if the service is unavailable?", etc. Once you get a good handle on these key areas, you will think it through from critical viewpoint than to assume that everything is going to work alright. Good developers know that by being a pessimist in the short-term, they can gain long term success by building quality systems and self-promoting their key technical know-how to take their careers to a new level. This is where you can differentiate yourself from someone who has been in the industry for the same duration or longer than you have been. How you think and what questions you ask will become evident in job interviews, brain storming sessions, code review sessions, crisis meetings, workshops, regular team meetings/catch ups, technical/design presentations and project retrospectives (i.e. What went well? What didn't go well? How could we improve next time?, etc).

If you just rely on your experience alone, it can take ages to get a good handle on these key areas. So, you can fast-track your learning process by tapping into others' experience by investing in self-taught projects, tutorials, subscribing to good blogs, reading relevant articles and white papers, having good mentors who can guide you, becoming a member of an industry forum, and volunteering to help others solve their problems. No matter where you learn these key areas from, you need to **proactively apply them** to identify and fix any existing issues or prevent any potential problems from occurring in your projects.

Even though the above mentioned approaches are the most effective ones that can be carried out together, some of you, especially the beginners may lack motivation to kick start your careers using the above approaches. If you are in this category, you may look at gaining a certification as a short term goal to give you an incentive to study. The certification must not be the real goal. The real goal must be to gain some hands-on experience with good technical know how in these key areas to do a better job. The most of the good and successful software professionals are self-taught, and take pride in their craftsmanship and on the job accomplishments than the number of certificates they hold. They continuously motivate themselves to learn and acquire new skills.

Here is my thought on how you can achieve this by a process I call it **Learn → Experience → Let the world know**, which can motivate you to not only learn and experience, but also to open more doors for you.

Learn, experience, and let the world know

Learn: Pick a key area, technology, or a sought-after framework to learn. If you are a beginner, the obvious choice would be to learn the language fundamentals and platform fundamentals followed by the specification fundamentals. If you are an experienced professional, pick a key area, technology, or a framework that will have immediate use in your current project. If you are contemplating of changing jobs, pick an area that is conducive to market yourself in a better light. Pick a sought-after technology/framework by checking your local online advertisements to see what is in demand. Validate your finding against http://www.google.com/trends and industry specific sites like infoq.com, theserverside.com, dzone.com, etc. Identify the resources you would like to use like good books, online resources like tutorials, white papers, articles, blogs, and guidance from your mentors.

Experience: Once you learn the basics, find a way to apply it on a project you are currently working on or think of a new project to apply it on. This can be a paid, unpaid, open-source, or a self-taught project. If your self-taught project is unique and good enough, you have the option to open-source it. Check your past projects you had worked on and the current projects you are working with, to see how this particular key area is or can be applied. Critically review the projects you are working on to see if there are any potential issues relating to these key areas like thread-safety issues, security vulnerabilities, anti-patterns, design flaws, bad exception handling, code duplication, etc. While you are learning how to use this key area, **don't hesitate to ask yourself lots of questions**. Good caliber professionals are paid well to think, ask the right questions, and provide most suitable solution.

Let the world know: Once you experience it, don't keep it to yourself. Let the world know about it by adding this experience to your resume/CV, online profiles like http://www.LinkedIn.com, and most importantly blogging about it and creating an online portfolio. When you blog about it, you are not only helping others learn from your experience, but also increasing your understanding of this key area by doing more research, thinking more creatively to make your blog stand-out, and inviting your readers to provide constructive criticisms, and of course appreciation for your work. You could even build up your network of subscribers and followers. Blog comments are an excellent way to build your network with key people in your field. A good blog is more likely to invite more comments on your blog. Also, be prepared to have the right attitude and courage to withstand criticisms and harsh language on blog comments.

If your blog is professional enough, you could provide a link to your blog from your resume/CV and LinkedIn.com profile. Your potential employers who would like to learn more about your passion, thinking, communication skills, values, and capabilities will be encouraged to visit your blog. Good blogs can open up other possibilities like invites for book reviews, joint ventures, attracting customers to sell your software products (e.g. games), ideas, and your development talent. Your blog contents could also become an inspiration to self publish your book via lulu.com or createspace.com.

It is easy enough to get started with a blog by visiting http://www.wordpress.com or http://www.blogger.com. But promoting your blog can be a bit more challenging. Do your online research to learn more about techniques to attract more people to leave comments on blogs and getting search engines to rank your keywords high. Firstly, you need to think of creating a brand for yourself.

Initially, you can promote your blogs through technical forums by helping others and providing a link to your blog as your signature. You can also promote it by contributing daily doses, articles, tips, and know-hows via industry specific sites like http://dzone.com/. Make it a point to provide a link to your blog at the bottom of your contributions. Think about other avenues to attract your target audience.

Once you start to get enough hits, you can think about monetizing your blogs by signing up for Google adsense http://www.google.com/adsense, which will display advertisements on your blog. Don't over do it, and the income you generate from adsense is generally trivial, unless you have very large visits or selling some products and books to get a better income. Publishing a book is much easier with the advent of print on demand publishers like http://www.lulu.com and http://www.createspace.com. Your priority must be getting some quality contents, products, and books that will be useful to others, and building your own brand to collaborate with the like minded professionals. You are only limited by your imagination, passion, and drive to open more possibilities. If your income is reasonable, you could further promote your offerings and services with Google adwords program. So, don't under estimate the power of online presence while learning to open more doors.

Always think of doing things differently and taking the road less traveled. Overall it is not a bad plan to build your online persona to open more doors for you while learning, helping others, and gaining much needed experience. Your blog does not have to always be related to these key areas. The experience you gained here can be applied to an idea specific to other business domains. So, promote yourself as a change agent, consultant, or a facilitator of these key areas.

"A journey of a thousand miles begins with a single step." -- Confucius

Get a good handle on the 16 key areas of software engineering to open more doors

Section-3:

Become a change agent, facilitator, and a problem solver to open more doors

Just knowing the key areas won't open more doors. You need to apply these key areas to solve problems and add value to the business. Regardless of the job specification, every organization needs a good change agent or a facilitator. Being a change agent is someone who alters system or human capability to achieve a higher degree of output. This is all about identifying any opportunities to change or improve system, application, or development process. In most cases, smaller changes can yield much greater benefits. Take the lead with the help of your immediate boss on a number of initiates where possible. You don't have to be an architect, technical lead, team lead or a lead developer to be a facilitator of these key areas. Any passionate software engineer can do this, and it will not go unnoticed by your superiors and peers. Here are a few real life examples and suggestions.

Action is the real measure of intelligence -- Napoleon Hill

Become a change agent, facilitator, and a problem solver to open more doors

Initiate QuickWins projects

One of such initiates is called "*QuickWins*" project. The focus is to improve the overall effectiveness and usefulness of a system through small changes in a collaborative effort with the business. Workshops and customer surveys are conducted to list the top 10 or 20 things that can add real value to a particular system. This could be the look and feel of the system, ease of use of the system, responsiveness of the system, etc. A few items are prioritized based on its cost-benefit analysis, and improvements are made to the system. One of such projects that I had been involved in, which stood out was improving the ranking of a web based financial application for a large insurance company. The financial service websites are ranked by an independent body, and this particular company's website that I was the technical lead for was ranked 23rd out of 31 possible companies that took part. I took the initiative with the collaboration of the business and technical leaders to launch a "*QuickWins*" project to improve the overall ranking of the website. An independent user experience consultant was hired to analyze and produce a report with 18 most important things that can potentially improve the user friendliness, look and feel, and ease of use of the overall website. Out of those 18 recommendations, 4 of them needed major design and development changes, and did not stack up well in the cost-benefit analysis. The remaining 14 recommendations were implemented within 3 months. The implementation was fast-tracked by adopting some of the agile development practices like iterative development, daily stand-up meetings, and regular catch-ups with the business. This initiative was a major success and the website ranking was improved from being 23rd to 12th. The management was very impressed, and the contributions were well noticed and rewarded. That was also one of my longest and rewarding contracts.

Fix security holes

Security is of paramount importance to any application or website. Applications with security vulnerabilities can not only tarnish the reputation of a company, but also can adversely impact the bottom-line of that organization. So, it really pays for the organizations to have the right people who can identity potential security vulnerabilities, which is one of the key areas discussed earlier. Security is a specialized field, and most large companies do have dedicated teams, but most of the basic security vulnerabilities can be easily identified if you have the basic know how. For example,

- HTTP/Get query strings exposing an adviser code or an account number of a logged on financial adviser can be manipulated by substituting the original adviser's code with another adviser's code to ascertain if the system suffers from any access control vulnerabilities. If it does, it can be a serious security threat as one adviser can potentially view sensitive information like account balance of another adviser by manipulating the query string. A more sophisticated tool like Burp Proxy, skipfish, or Firefox add-on like *tamperdata* can be used to tamper HTTP/HTTPS post parameters to take advantage of any access control vulnerabilities.

Example: Access control vulnerabilities can be detected by substituting "0188' in the following query string

https://www.myapp.com/MyContext/MyServlet?adviser_code=0188

with 9999 as shown below

https://www.myapp.com/MyContext/MyServlet?adviser_code=9999

These access control issues need to be fixed by closing any holes in the authorization logic.

- SQL injection attack is another common security threat and the database calls in your code must be parametrized to prevent the risk of SQL injection attack. In Java, this is achieved by using prepared or callable statements instead of ordinary statements.

Example: The above URL can also be exploited for SQL injection attack by manipulating the query string as shown below by appending "wait for delay".

https://www.myapp.com/MyContext/MyServlet?
adviser_code='0188'if(1=1)**waitfor%20delay%20**'0:0:20'--

Which can be translated into an SQL query as shown below if the parameters are passed directly to the SQL statement causing the query to wait for 20 seconds. The example below shows that the query string is not parametrized.

```
SELECT * FROM ADV_TABLE WHERE adv_code='0188'if(1=1)waitfor
                                         delay'0:0:20'--
```

The parametrized query string will look like
```
String sqlString = "SELECT * FROM ADV_TABLE WHERE adv_code = ?";
```

Become a change agent, facilitator, and a problem solver to open more doors

```
PreparedStatement st = MyConnection.prepareStatement(sqlString);
st.setString(1, adviserCode);
```

- Sensitive information needs to be properly encrypted and password protected.

https://ww.myapp.com/cash/accountDetails-create.do?
                    accountNum=HnGoGRvmCQ26LVigIzHtMA~~

It is also imperative to store passwords hashed, encrypted or salted and encrypted. Encrypted plain-text can be decrypted, but a hashing is a one-way function that creates a fixed length string based on a plain-text. It's one-way because you can go from a plain-text to a hash, but you cannot recreate the original plain-text from the hash. Password salting is a way of making passwords more secure by adding a random string of characters to passwords before their md5 hash is calculated, which makes them harder to reverse. The longer the random string, the harder you make it for the hackers.

For example, if your application is sending reports containing sensitive information to clients, it is imperative that the reports are adequately protected. This can be achieved by sending the reports as password protected zip files. This involves additional considerations listed below to minimize security issues.

- The generated report and the password to unzip the report(s) need to be sent out in separate emails.
- Individual (i.e. per client) passwords need to be used and regularly (say every 3 months) recycled.
- These individual passwords need to be stored encrypted in a database or a file system.
- A master password needs to be used to encrypt and decrypt the individual passwords.
- The master password itself needs to be securely stored.

- Improper exception handling can leak sensitive or irrelevant information like database name, table name, user name, etc to potential hackers. Lower level exception details should not be exposed to the end users. They must be caught at the higher layer, and only generic information like "Please contact support … " should be made available to the end user.

- Applying output sanitization to all untrusted data (preferably all data values) before rendering within application output can minimize cross site scripting vulnerabilities (i.e. XSS). You may have an application with the following URL that uses the parameter "productCode" to display the appropriate details on a web page.

https://ww.myapp.com/cash/accountDetails.do?**productCode=CHI**

The productCode parameter may be tweaked using the cross-site scripting (XSS) to cause arbitrary JavaScript to run on page load as shown below:

to display a pop up:

https://ww.myapp.com/cash/accountDetails.do?**productCode=CHI";**
onerror=alert(1);//

to redirect to any other page:

https://ww.myapp.com/cash/accountDetails.do?**productCode=CHIXSS";**
onerror=window.location='http://www.google.com';//

A regular expression based validation of the parameter productCode to reject input with meta-characters like &, <, :, /, ', ",\, and ; will prevent the potential XSS attack.

- Buffer overflow vulnerabilities are also common in web applications. By sending in a large number of bytes to web applications that are not geared to deal with them can have unexpected consequences. During penetration testing assignments, it is possible to disclose the path of the functions being used by sending in a very large value in the input fields. As the sanitized example below shows, when 6000 or more bytes were fed into a particular input field, the server side script was unable to process them and the error that was displayed revealed the location of these functions.

"Error:maximum execution time of 20 seconds exceeded in
/var/www/html/func/admin/accountDetails.php"

Validate input data on both client and server side and use correctly typed data to

Become a change agent, facilitator, and a problem solver to open more doors

mitigate buffer overflow vulnerabilities.

- Web applications are also susceptible to application level denial of service attacks (DoS), because it is hard to detect the difference between ordinary traffic and an attack. The infrastructure level denial of service can be prevented via firewall rules. So, test your application under load for the application level DoS. Think carefully about password change or lockout mechanisms. Make use of the cacheing strategies to restrict access to database servers and other internal services and systems, especially the web services that can result in heavy loads. Web services are the most attractive target for hackers because even a novice hacker can bring down a server by repeatedly calling a web service which does expensive work. Avoid requests that result in heavy system load, especially for anonymous users. Avoid large HTTP POSTs, storing large amount of data in HTTP session objects, and keeping a database connection open for a long time due to bad coding or heavy queries. Home pages are the best target for such DoS attack because if you just visit the homepage repeatedly without preserving the user in a cookie, every hit is producing a brand new user, new page setup, new widgets and what not. The first visit experience is the most expensive one. Nonetheless, it's the easiest one to exploit and bring down the site. You can also make use of inexpensive tricks to remember how many requests are coming from a particular IP address. When the number of requests exceed the threshold, deny further request for some duration or provide a verification screen requesting for manual human intervention. This is known as a **CAPTCHA**, which is an acronym for "**C**ompletely **A**utomated **P**ublic **T**uring test to tell **C**omputers and **H**umans **A**part"). Using an ACID based transaction management instead of a compensation based transaction management for web service calls is more susceptible to DoS attack by getting a rogue process to start a transaction involving various web services, and then keeping the web services waiting for a task to finish, which might never happen.

- Session hijacking is another type of attack, where someone steals a session cookie and uses it to gain access to the system. Use SSL to secure all session-cookie/server communications and set "HTTPOnly" on the cookie to prevent JavaScript from being able to read the session cookie in XSS attacks, but it is still vulnerable to ajax based attacks. You could also include a security token or a nonce in the session cookie that gets updated on each request. You store the token in a server-side data store and in the cookie, and on each request you compare that the token in the cookie matches the token in the data store. If the tokens don't

114

match that could be an indicator that someone stole the session and is trying to use it so you can either ignore the request or invalidate the session and request the user to re-authenticate. Alternatively, you could time-stamp each session and check if the timestamps are within some short, specified range, say 20 seconds. If the user's session cookie time stamp is within 20 seconds of the server's stored session time-stamp, then the session is deemed authentic.

- Ajax is mostly driven by JavaScript. JavaScript can not access the local file system without the user's permission. An ajax interaction can only be made with the server-side component from which the page was loaded, makes ajax pretty safe. In other words, the *XMLHttpRequest* object is prevented from calling web services from outside its own domain (i.e. <host>:<port>). This is sensible given that if you called a script in one place and it, in turn, called a script on another server, it could leave an application open to all sorts of malicious scripts, hacks and exploits. Understandably, the reason behind this is security. However, there are legitimate reasons why you would need to call out to other domains from the *XMLHttpRequest* object. One way to get around this issue is to let the server-side perform the HTTP request to the external site on behalf of the client browser. Instead of making your XMLHttpRequest calls directly to an external web service, you make your calls to your web server proxy. The proxy then passes the call onto the web service and in return passes the data back to your client application. Because the connection is made to your server, and the data comes back from your server, the browser has nothing to complain about. The other alternatives to make cross domain ajax calls are CORS, which is industrial strength solution and JSONP.

Isolate and reproduce intermittent issues

You may have come across intermittent issues that are hard to reproduce and debug. A novice developer will promptly mark those defects in the bug tracking system as "cannot be reproduced" without having the skill to isolate, reproduce and then fix the issue. An experienced developer with good grasp on the key areas will not only have the skill to identify these potential issues by analyzing the code, but also will have the competency to isolate, reproduce, and fix these issues.

- Not adhering to language basics and contracts can lead to non-deterministic behaviors. For example, in Java, incorrect implementation of *hashCode()*, *equals(..)*, and *compareTo(..)* method contracts can lead to unpredictable

Become a change agent, facilitator, and a problem solver to open more doors

behaviors. Servlets, Struts action classes, *SimpleDateFormat*, etc are not inherently thread-safe and can be accessed by multiple threads. Hence not using them in a thread-safe manner can cause intermittent issues. The APIs clearly specify these contracts, and it is imperative to keep the API documentation handy when coding.

- Some operations not only need to be thread-safe, but also must be atomic. Issues arising from incorrect transaction management can cause intermittent issues by corrupting some records in the database tables. The database operations need to be atomic. If you are transferring money from one account to another, the both operations of subtracting from one account and adding to another account must succeed or fail as a unit. If one operation succeeds and the other one fails, the money will be lost and the records will be corrupted. If the transactions are carried across two distributed systems, then the 2-phase commit transaction management needs to be used. If proper transaction isolation levels are not used, the flight seats can be double booked due to dirty reads, phantom updates, or phantom inserts. Be aware of the ACID (Atomic, Consistent, Isolation, and Durability) properties to ensure that the database transactions are processed reliably. The web services based transactions need to be using compensation based transaction management as opposed to the ACID based transaction management.

- You could also have intermittent issues due to proxy server or load balancer timeouts or connection leaks. Your application might not be coded with appropriate connection retries or appropriate time out values. You could simulate connectivity issues by creating SSH tunnels to the actual destination server.

For example, your application may have connectivity to a Vignette *ServerB* running on port 9111. To simulate connectivity issues, you may create a local SSH tunnel to a UNIX *ServerA*, which connects to Vignette application running on *ServerB:9111*. Once you log on to *ServerA* via *PuTTY* (i.e. a Unix client on Windows) as shown below, a tunnel will be opened to *ServerB:9111*. Any calls to *localhost:4000* will be forwarded to *ServerB:9111* via *ServerA*. In your application, you could use the *localhost:4000* instead of using *ServerB:9111* to connect to the Vignette application. This will enable you to simulate the scenario of the Vignette server on *ServerB* being down by just destroying the tunnel, and not the actual server, which might be used by others. By destroying the tunnel, you could improve your application code to graciously handle connectivity issues, timeouts, and retries. The exception handling logic also needs to be verified so that that it does not expose any internal server details.

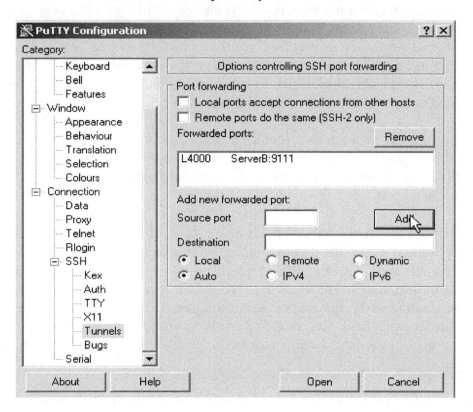

- There could be general runtime production issues that either slow down or make a system to hang. In these situations, the general approach for troubleshooting would be to analyze the thread dumps to isolate the threads which are causing the the system to slow-down or hang. For example, a Java thread dump gives you a snapshot of all threads running inside a Java Virtual Machine. There are graphical tools like *Samurai* to help you analyze the thread dumps more effectively.

Application seems to consume 100% CPU and throughput has drastically reduced – Get a series of thread dumps, say 7 to 10 at a particular interval, say 5 to 8 seconds and analyze these thread dumps by inspecting closely the "**runnable**" threads to ensure that if a particular thread is progressing well. If a particular thread is executing the same method through all the thread dumps, then that particular method could be the root cause. You can now continue your

Become a change agent, facilitator, and a problem solver to open more doors

investigation by inspecting the code.

Application consumes very less CPU and response times are very poor due to heavy I/O operations like file or database read/write operations – Get a series of thread dumps and inspect for threads that are in "**blocked**" status. This analysis can also be used for situations where the application server hangs due to running out of all runnable threads due to a deadlock or a thread is holding a lock on an object and never returns it while other threads are waiting for the same lock.

The solution to the above problems could vastly vary from fixing the thread safety issue(s) to reducing the size of synchronization granularity, and from implementing appropriate caching strategies to setting the appropriate connection timeouts.

- Intermittent issues could also arise due to environmental complexities. Your application might be running under an uncontrolled environment. Lack of communication among multiple projects using the same environment could cause intermittent issues. For example, security certificates or passwords could have been modified by the system administrators. Database table or LDAP server schemas could have been modified by the other developers. Messages published to a queue may have been consumed by another process listening on the same queue.

Speaking of intermittent issues, database deadlock issues are very common. Whenever you have competing DML (Data Manipulation Language) running against the same data, you run the risk of a deadlock. When this happens, the database server identifies the problem and ends the deadlock by automatically choosing one process and aborting the other process, allowing the unaborted process to continue. The aborted transaction is rolled back and an error message is sent to the user of the aborted process. For example, in Sybase database

Your server command (family id #%d, process id #%d) encountered a deadlock situation. Please re-run your command.

Generally, the transaction that requires the least amount of overhead to rollback is the transaction that is aborted. You can deal with database deadlock situations in two ways. The first option is to redesign the application so that the deadlock does not take place in the first place. This is the preferred option, but at times not practical to redesign an existing application without significant effort. The second option is to retry the aborted task after receiving a deadlock message, and it will most likely succeed during 2-5 additional retries. If the retry happens very frequently, the performance of the application can be adversely impacted. Here are some general tips on how to avoid deadlocking

- Aim for properly normalized database designs
- Avoid or minimize the use of cursors.
- Keep transactions as short as possible, use lower isolation levels and minimize the number of round trips between your application and the database server.
- Reduce lock time. Try to develop your application so that it grabs locks at the latest possible time, and then releases them at the very earliest time.
- Make relevant design or coding changes like single-threading related updates, and re-scheduling batch update jobs to low-update time period can often remove deadlocks.

Identify performance issues and bench mark them with the view to improve

I have never been in a project or organization that is yet to have any performance or scalability issues. It is a safe bet to talk up your achievements in fixing performance or resource leak issues in job interviews. Unlike web security testing, performance testing is very prevalent in many applications. Premature optimization of your code is bad as it can compromise on good design or writing maintainable and testable code. But one needs to be aware of potential causes for performance issues that can occur due to major bottlenecks in a handful of places or minor inefficiencies in thousands of places (i.e. death by thousand cuts). Let's look at some of the common causes of performance issues.

- Too many database calls and inefficient SQL queries performing full table scan can cause performance issues. SQL statements need to be carefully constructed and prepared statements need to be favored over ordinary statements, as it improves performance by pre-compiling the execution plan for repeated calls. In some scenarios, more data is requested than actually is required by the current page. Eagerly fetching data from an ORM tool can bring in more data than actually required. In other scenarios, too many fine grained calls are made to the database instead of eagerly fetching the required data in 1 or fewer calls. At times, not using proper pagination strategies to divide and conquer how data is accessed or not carefully thinking through ways to improve re-usability of the same data requested multiple times through caching strategies can lead to bad performance. Excessive or wrong caching strategies to minimize remote calls could adversely impact performance due to increased garbage collection activity to make the memory available.

- A frequently back tracking regular expression can adversely impact performance. Care should be taken to not run a web service or a web application that allows users to supply their own regular expressions. People with little regular expression experience can come up with an exponentially complex regular expressions.

- Lack of understanding between local and remote calls. Remote calls do have the overhead of latency, serialization, network traffic, and memory usage under the hood. Too many remote calls can cause performance and scalability issues.

- Memory leaks and connection leaks (e.g. database connections, LDAP connections, sockets) can cause performance and scalability issues. Wasteful handling of these finite resources can adversely impact performance. These resources must be judiciously used for a request and promptly returned to the pool to be reused by other users or requests. It should not be kept open for the whole session for a particular user because a user session can span multiple clicks interleaved with long pauses and user think times.

- Third party rich web frameworks can make your front end HTML source code bloated. For example, overuse of some libraries or rich widgets can not only make the HTML code bloated, but also its aggressive use of ajax/JavaScript can result in performance problems on the browser. This might not be a problem for an internal application, but can be a problem for all external customer facing applications as some users may not have super fast internet access. Some older versions of some browsers may also take longer time to render the bloated HTML code.

- Finally, the application server or database server may not have been adequately tuned with proper heap space, perm gen space, tempdb space, etc. Also, not having appropriate configuration values for various service timeouts, connection pool, or thread pool sizes can adversely impact performance. The database tables or LDAP serer schemas may not have been properly indexed or designed. It is imperative to test the application under full size data as many performance issues will only surface under sheer volume of data. Some scenarios (e.g. reporting) require de-normalized tables to store a large volume of aggregated historic data. The performance tests must also need to factor worst case scenarios into consideration. For example, a trading platform might handle 150 trades per minute under normal peak conditions, but it may have to handle 400 trades per minute in the event of a stock market crash.

Once you identify a performance issue, proper test scripts need to be written and run to benchmark a particular application. Open source tools like *BadBoy* or *JMeter proxy server* can be used to record the web actions, and the recorded scripts can be converted to *JMeter* scripts to perform stress/load tests to benchmark the application. The initial test conditions and results need to be properly documented so that the results can be compared after improving or fixing the performance issues. The load/stress tests can also be used to reproduce and fix intermittent issues like thread-safety, memory leak, connection leak, and database contention issues that mostly occur above certain load.

The earlier discussions in the "Key Areas" section highlighted some of the handy profiling tools to gather performance metrics, but there are scenarios in real life where a custom solution would be required to compliment the profiling tool(s).

For example, a trading application may have a number of synchronous and asynchronous moving parts and metrics needs to be recorded for various operations like placing a trade on to a queue, receiving asynchronous responses from the stock market, correlating order ids, linking similar order ids, etc. A custom metrics gathering solution can be accomplished by logging the relevant metrics to a database and then running relevant aggregate queries or writing to a file system and then running PERL based text searches to aggregate the results to a "csv" based file to be opened and analyzed in a spreadsheet with graphs. Alternatively, use Splunk, which is a powerful search and analysis engine. In my view, writing to a database provides a greater flexibility. For example, in Java, the following approach can be used.

Step 1: Use log4j JMS appender or a custom JMS appender to send log messages to a queue. This ensures that your application's performance is not adversely impacted by logging activities by decoupling it.

Become a change agent, facilitator, and a problem solver to open more doors

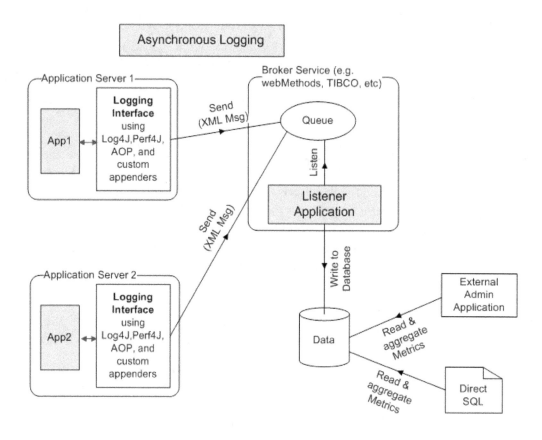

Step 2: Use this appender in your application via Aspect Oriented Programming (AOP – e.g Spring AOP, AspectJ, etc) or dynamic proxy classes to non-intrusively log relevant metrics to a queue. It is worth looking at Perf4j and context based logging with MDC (Mapped Diagnostic Contexts) or NDC (Nested Diagnostic Contexts) to log on a per thread basis to correlate or link relevant operations. Perf4J is a great framework for performance logging. It's non-intrusive and really fills the need for accurate performance logging. The Perf4j provides features like a command line tool to generate aggregated results and graphs from raw log files, ability to expose performance statistics as JMX attributes and to send notifications when statistics exceed specified thresholds, custom log4j appenders, and AOP aspects that allow non obtrusive statements when used with Spring AOP. The Perf4J is for

System.currentTimeMillis( );

as Log4J is for

```
System.out.println(.....);
```

Step 3: A stand-alone listener application needs to be developed to dequeue the performance metrics messages from the queue and write to a database or a file system for further analysis and reporting purpose. This listener could be written in Java as a JMX service using JMS or via broker service like webMethods, TIBCO, etc. This service needs to correlate related messages using a correlation id to determine the elapsed time at the various points in the system.

Step 4: Finally, relevant SQL (for database) or Splunk/regular expression (for flat files) based queries can be written to aggregate and report relevant metrics in a customized way.
The context based data captured could contain the following attributes

```
private final String environment;        // source environment
private final Long timestamp;            // source timestamp
private final Long duration;             // sample duration
private final String thread;             // Log4j ThreadName
private final String component;          // component name
private final Stage stage;               // enum BEGIN | END | NONE
private final String source;             // Log4j LoggerName
private final String context;            // Log4j NDC
private final String process;            // work process
private final String item;               // work item identity (e.g. correlation id)
private final String level;              // Log4j Level
private final String message;            // Log4j RenderedMessage
private final String exceptionMessage;   // Log4j Throwable Message
private final String exceptionStacktrace; // Log4j Throwable Stacktrace
```

Q. What is **Splunk** and where will you use it?
A. Splunk is an enterprise-grade software tool for collecting and analyzing "machine data" like log files, feed files, and other big data in terra bytes. You can upload logs from your websites and let Splunk index them, and produce reports with graphs to analyze the reports. This is very useful in capturing start and finish times from asynchronous processes to calculate elapsed times. If you have Splunk, you can use its search language along with your contextual logging to gather metrics.

Use the right tools to be more productive

- Tools like **regexpal.com** is very handy to quickly verify your regular expressions while working on a project. The regex keywords and the results are highlighted in color for better clarity.
- Notepad++ is a powerful text editor with many handy features like regex based find and replace. Here is a quick example of how you can take an un quoted CSV file, and add quotes to each entry in Notepad++.

BA555,04-May-2013,04-04-2013,12358
becomes
"BA555","04-May-2013","04-04-2013","12358"

Another typical industrial example would be to convert comma separated entries to "new line" separated entries. Each line will have a single entry.

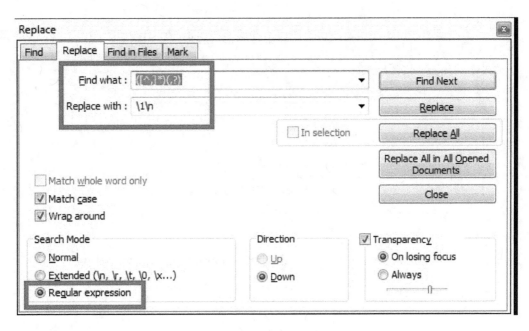

BA555,04-May-2013,04-04-2013,12358

becomes

BA555
04-May-2013
04-04-2013
12358

- Spreadsheets like MS Excel is handy to construct SQL queries with static and dynamic data. Here is an example as to how to construct insert statements. The Excel concatenate character "&" can be used to construct insert statements from tabular data as demonstrated below. The formula is constructed for the initial row 2 data, and then copied down for the rows 3 and 4. The "$" symbols are used to fix row, column or both. The static data is captured within quotes.

Become a change agent, facilitator, and a problem solver to open more doors

	A	B	C	D	E	F	G	H	I	J
1	first_name	surname	age							
2	Peter	Smith	35							
3	John	Smith	12							
4	Eddy	Wayne	32							
5										
6										
7										
8	insert into person (first_name, surname, age) values ('Peter','Smith',35)									
9	insert into person (first_name, surname, age) values ('John','Smith ',12)									
10	insert into person (first_name, surname, age) values ('Eddy','Wayne',32)									
11										

A8 — fx ="insert into person ("&A1&", "&B1&", "&C1&") values ('"&$A2&"','"&$B2&"',"&$C2&")"

The above formula is easily understood when separated as shown below.

```
"insert into person ("
&
$A$1
&
" ,"
&
$B$1
&
" ,"
$C$1
&
") values ('"
&
$A2
&
"' ,'"
&
$B2
&
"' ,"
&
$C2
&
" ) "
```

126

So, use the right tools to get things done more efficiently.

Enforce standards and processes

A change agent not only changes a system's or application's behavior but also people's behavior, attitude, and culture towards writing quality software. People's behavior can be changed by enforcing good coding standards. One way to enforce these standards is through regular peer code reviews. Code review sessions can catch more bugs earlier on in the software development life cycle. It gives junior developers to learn from more experienced professionals. It motivates developers to avoid common mistakes, sloppy code, and inadequate unit test coverage. Automated code review tools like sonar can also be used to enforce consistency in code, identify potential bugs and redundant code snippets. The peer code reviews can be better managed through tools like Crucible.

Substandard software development processes can also demotivate developers and adversely impact their behavior and attitude. The development processes need to be continuously improved by adopting good tools and practices. A build and deploy process that you can repeat consistently across team members, across environments, and across different versions of the software is critical to successfully shipping your software or deploying it into production. This can make developers' life a lot easier by allowing them to concentrate more on what they do best rather than wasting time on fixing bad processes or performing administrative tasks.

Finally, a framework needs to be put in place for adequate documentation. Most software professionals don't like to write documentation. Proper guidelines and templates need to be created to encourage developers to write simple enough, but not too simple documentation. No body is going to read complex documentation. Documentation needs to be written with the target audience in mind. All the documents should be easily accessible. Good document management systems/repositories allow developers to find documents quickly by project, contents, date, author, etc and saves lots of frustrations.

Champion continuous improvement programs

Organizations must develop a culture of continuous improvement in order to flourish. I am yet to work for an organization that did not have any environmental or process related issues and challenges. Many of these tasks can be simplified, automated, and integrated to avoid monotonous and error prone human intervention. So, experience with the agile practices, continuous integration and build, environmental improvements, etc will be of

Become a change agent, facilitator, and a problem solver to open more doors

great asset to any organization. A software must be architected for deployability. Deployability is a non-functional requirement that addresses how reliably and easily a software can be deployed from development into the production environment. Firstly, for a software to be deployable, there must be minimal differences between environments. The more similar the environments, the simpler and more reliable it is to deploy the software. It is not possible to completely eliminate any differences between various environments, but certainly can be minimized. The continuous improvement programs can be championed as described below:

Describe the Issue → Determine the Cause → Resolve the Issue → Follow-Up

Example 1:

Describe the Issue :   Frequent intermittent database errors in DEV environment.

Determine the Cause: Multiple project teams are using the same database.

Resolve the issue: Refresh the database weekly from the test environment, and
get the DEV teams sharing the same database to submit the scripts
to a central utility program that will run the delta scripts to make
the relevant project specific schema changes and the data load.
Create a dash-board that will enable project teams to book
and share relevant databases. It will also increase communication
across project teams sharing the same database. This will create
a more controlled environment.

Follow-Up: The intermittent issues were minimized due to better coordinated
and disciplined database changes, improved visibility of who is
using what, and better communication across project teams.

Example 2:

Describe the Issue :   New errors surface in non DEV environments.

Determine the Cause: The DEV databases are cut-down version of the PROD
databases having much less data.

Resolve the issue: Use full size database for the DEV environment. If this is not

128

practical, deploy to a production like staging environment as part of the continuous integration process and test.

Follow-Up: Data related issues are minimized.

Example 3:

Describe the Issue: Builds are constantly broken.

Determine the Cause: Individual developers built changes locally and isolated from the changes made by the other developers until they checkout others' changes. The unit test coverage was bad as well.

Resolve the issue: Have a better test coverage and monitor test coverage with the tools like sonar. Implement a continuous integration and build server that continuously builds the code that are checked-in to the version control repository and also execute the unit test cases to ensure that nothing is broken. If the build or unit tests fail, the team members are notified via emails. This will also ensure that the developers will be more disciplined to test their code locally before checking them into the version control repository.

Follow-Up: Developers get into the rhythm of code, build, test, and integrate to minimize any down time caused by broken builds.

Some organizations are very passionate about hiring professionals with experience in agile practices. If you had experience in facilitating agile practices, it will be looked upon very favorably by those organizations.

It is a best practice to have **project retrospective** meetings after each major mile stones of a project to see what worked well, what did not work well, lessons learned, and how could you improve on things that did not work well for the next milestone release.

Making technical changes are easier than changing human behavior. So, to champion continuous improvement processes, one needs to have good technical skills complemented with great soft skills.

Assess non-functional requirements

Like deployability, many non-functional requirements like security, performance, transaction management, thread-safety, quality of service, etc are often neglected or overlooked during application development. Inexperienced or rushed developers can create systems that work great in development, but have many problems in the test or production environments due to sheer load, concurrent access, locale or timezone settings, portability issues due to operating system specific file separator or new line character, hard coded values requiring externalization, etc. If you identify any gaps in these non-functional requirements, take the initiative to close the gap as you would do with any functional requirements.

Most software projects face problems relating to non-functional requirements, and the root cause(s) can be very subtle, and can be hard to understand, reproduce and solve without the adequate technical skills. Hence, it really pays to have the right people who have the experience and the know how to identify, reproduce, and resolve these problems by using the right tools and know how. You can earn the appreciation of your superiors and peers by pro-actively and retroactively solving problems relating to performance, thread-safety, memory/resource leaks, and security vulnerabilities by understanding the relevant key areas. These are highly visible issues because the end users will start to complain and get frustrated with the applications that are too slow, frequently crashing, and intermittently not doing the right thing. Issues relating to these key areas often bring together the senior management with the people with the technical know how for brain storming sessions and crisis talks. These situations can provide you with great opportunities to make your mark.

Be pragmatic, and know what works for your environment without all the hype

When designing or developing systems, be pragmatic without all the buzz words and hype. Pick the proven technology and framework stacks that will get the job done. Ensure that you have the right people with the relevant skills in those technology stacks. Evaluate the architecture and choice of technology/framework/tool with a proof of concept. Determine if a particular architecture, process, or methodology will work for your environment and culture. For example, SOA is an enterprise architecture strategy where business logic is organized into services, and business processes are realized through the invocation of these services. SOA has benefits such as bridging the divide between the I.T. and the business, loose coupling, reuse of business logic, etc. But to successfully implement a SOA based architecture, a number of organizational boundaries need to be bridged. This typically requires a change in organizational culture, which is very difficult to achieve in some organizations that are siloed and have different business teams looking after different products. There are also other inherent challenges like changing a service implementation can break one or more of the consumers, overall reliability of the system when one service is down, rolling back other services when a service fails, propagating security and transactional contexts between the services, deployability of those services and performance considerations in devising services as too many remote calls can adversely impact performance. At times you need to come up with a hybrid approach to attack a problem. The software development is full of trade-offs and be pragmatic about getting things done by looking at the big picture and having attention to detail. For example, an organization using a waterfall approach to software development could adopt some of the agile practices to suit their environment.

Good caliber professionals are promoted or hired to solve business problems by not only having the grasp on these key areas, but as a facilitator or a change agent, you need to have a good understanding of how the business is structured and works, and apply what works best to achieve the short-term and long-term business goals. If the business is committed to change to become more competitive, as a **change agent** you can redesign existing business processes and design new processes and then try to get people to buy into these ideas. Change stirs up a lot of resistance in people. A change agent or a facilitator has to get past this resistance and convince others to embrace new ways of doing things. But first, he or she needs to get people to listen to what he/she has to say. The best way to convince people is by doing things – proof of concepts, demos, wireframe models, proven case studies, etc.

So, if you want to get ahead in your career, you need to use your head. Come up with creative solutions and present them in an easy to understand language without too much technical jargon. When talking to the business, put yourself in their shoes. The key question to ask is – How can I do things differently?

Be aware of the embarrassing mistakes

Here are some examples of the embarrassing mistakes that software professionals need to be aware of.

- Inadvertently spamming your clients with unintended emails during development or testing phases. Avoid these types of issues with proper configuration files using

Become a change agent, facilitator, and a problem solver to open more doors

internal email exchange servers and mocked up data using your email address to receive and send emails.

- Hard coding production URLs directly or indirectly in your code base or performance test scripts. Avoid these issues by always externalizing server, URL, and other environment specific details to relevant configuration files.

- Security holes that allow URL parameters to be manipulated to view others' personal details and sensitive information. Test your application by modifying the URL parameters to identify any obvious security holes. For example, if you are using a URL like http://myapp.com/accountId=123 , try replacing the *accountId* to some other accountId. Also, be aware of the other common security threats discussed earlier.

- Input search boxes break when special characters like '%', &, etc are entered. Test your input boxes for special characters and implement proper client side and server side input validation.

- Other environmental issues like testing the application against a cut-down database to later find that the application does not perform or scale well with the production size data. Avoid these issues with proper performance testing in a production like environment.

- It is a known fact that the software artifacts need to be properly versioned. This is a mostly adhered standard practice. But when designing an application with dynamic application configuration values or validation rules via database, some designers overlook the importance of versioning. In larger applications, at any point in time there will be multiple streams of parallel development work going on. Many development streams will be sharing the same database. So, if you don't have proper versioning, any changes to the configuration values or validation rules can break other development streams. With proper versioning, multiple streams can use the relevant version numbers.

- Some designers and developers fail to understand the difference between a local call and a remote call. The remote calls have more performance overheads due to network round trips and serialization/deserialization of data. So, avoid making remote calls (via RPC or web services) from a loop on the client side. This will end up in many remote calls. It is better to have the loop on the service side and get the client to make a single remote call by passing a collection of data. This collection of data can be looped through on the server side by making local calls within the same process.

- Never hard code system error or warning messages, config parameters like host name, web service URLs, service timeouts, etc and application specific business data like max account count, bulk data load threshold, feature on/off choices, etc. The error/warning messages and UI labels need to be stored in internationalizable files. Additional files can be added relevant to the locale. The system configuration parameters need to be configured via environment specific properties files and stored separately from the deployable artifacts. The business specific configuration data can be stored either in a config table in a database or in a configuration file stored outside the deployable artifact.

Stay visible and add value

- Don't just get glued to your keyboard. Make yourself and your contributions visible. Get involved in the full development life cycle of the project, team meetings, and technical sessions.

- Pro-actively provide either verbal or written recommendations and suggestions on improving the quality of the software, business process, development process, deployment process, and system design.

- Accept compliments without putting yourself down.

- Be prepared for the daily stand-ups, team meetings and code review sessions, so that you can add value.

- When asked, "How are things…" by your peer or superior, grab this opportunity to mention your accomplishments.

- Weave your accomplishments into conversations when appropriate.

- Don't mention the same accomplishments over and over again like a parrot. This will make you sound like a braggart.

- Speak well of others. You will only put yourself down by bad-mouthing others.

Become a change agent, facilitator, and a problem solver to open more doors

- Don't wait for your superior to check up on your progress. Provide regular updates to your superiors as to your progress, key problems faced, how you resolved it, and any potential recommendations to avoid it in the future. The issues may include gaps in the business requirements or solution design. Take the initiative by organizing a meeting or brain storming session to get things clarified. Your pro-activeness will be appreciated.

- If you identify any potential issues relating to the 16 key areas discussed earlier, bring it to your superior's attention with a possible solution and take the initiative to fix it. For example, test for concurrent update issue by opening 2 browser windows to submit 2 update requests at the same time. One update should succeed and the other update should display a concurrent update error, and prompt the other user to resubmit after refreshing the page to reflect the changes made by the first user. Developers with good grasp of identifying non-functional issues are a minority and it really pays to be in that group.

- Make recommendations in regards to anything that could ease developers' life, speed up new starters' learning curve, reduce cost of new development, improve deployment and release management phases, and facilitates easier maintenance. For example, proposing a coding standard template for your IDE so that consistency in line length, braces, tabs, etc can be enforced. This will result in making developers' life easier in terms of merging code.

Don't be a "yes person"

You can never rise in an organization by not having an **independent opinion**. The "yes person" will never be recognized. Good software engineers do have an opinion about what works and what doesn't based on their experience. Look at things critically by asking questions like what can go wrong here? This does not mean that you are a pessimist, but a realist. If you are working with a legacy application, make a list of 10 most annoying things like messy application configuration in database or path to a configuration file is hard coded. One of the main reasons you were hired was to solve problems. Don't take a problem to your superior without a suggested solution. Even when you require a decision to be made at a higher level, before you take it, make sure that you have done enough preparatory work and have some sort of a solution. Your superior may reject your solution, and propose an alternative solution as he/she may see a bigger picture. You will still be recognized for (a) identifying the problem (b) taking the effort to come up with a potential solution.

You are paid to add value and not to make waves

Not being an "yes person" does not mean that you have to be a rebel or make waves. As a software professional, you need to work within some boundaries and constraints. Things won't be perfect. Some environments are easy to function in, especially when the processes, rules and values are similar to what you would like to be. But often you find environments that are not ideal. You have three tips.

- **Tip 1**: Accept the rules and conditions as they are and make recommendations or changes where feasible and within your control, and put up with things when they are beyond your direct control. Don't become a whinger or bad mouth others or the organization. I have seen frustrations getting into some passionate programmers, which resulting in inappropriate comments like "I am ashamed to be working with this code base ..." made in the code base or circulated via emails. Some even vent their frustrations inappropriately in team meetings. You can get sacked or overlooked for potential promotions over these behaviors. It is not easy to put up with things that you are passionate about, but look at things this way – If you are paid 60K to do a job, think of it as you are paid 30K to add value and the other 30k to put up with some crap from time to time. In other words, 30k to be a team player and putting up with a peer, superior, bad process, horrible code, etc. This does not mean that you should not take initiatives, but do it patiently and tactfully without making waves.

- **Tip 2**: Vent your frustrations and learning in a professional way through blogs, forums, and tweets without giving anything away about your organization or an individual.

- **Tip 3**: Change the environment by changing teams, jobs or starting your own company. When you do this, don't burn bridges. Your current employer may become your client or a key referee in the future. You can also direct your energy and creativity through other channels discussed in the big picture diagram. Remember this – if you are in others' ballpark, you need to work by others' rules.

Solve problems by getting a good grip on domain knowledge

For example, to answer the following question, you need to apply the domain knowledge. The examples are not related to programming, but general problem solving. When you are applying problem solving in real life, you have an opportunity to perform your own research and talk to the relevant team members to gather relevant information.

Q. If a clock is showing 3.15 pm, what is the angle between the hour and the minute hands?
A. Firstly, list the domain knowledge

- A clock has 12 major divisions representing hours 1-12 and 60 minor divisions representing 60 minutes. Each major division has 5 minor divisions, hence 12 major * 5 minor = 60 minor divisions.

- When the minute hand goes through its 60 minor divisions, the hour hand completes a single major division (or 5 minor divisions).

- The full circle is 360 degrees. So, each minor division will be 360/60, which is 6 degrees.

Now, apply the problem solving to your domain knowledge. Often, graphical representation or pseudo code can help you solve a problem.

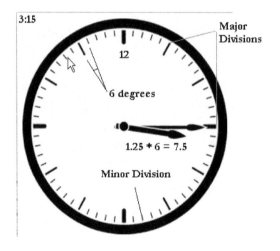

- When it is 3:15, the minute hand will be on 3, and the hour hand would be somewhere between 3 and 4. We know that when the minute hand goes through 60 divisions, the hour hand completes 5 minor (or 1 major) divisions. If the minute hand is on 3, it has gone through ¼ of its revolution, which means the hour hand would have done ¼ of 5 minor divisions (or 1 major division), which is **1.25 minor divisions**.

- We know that each minor division is 6 degrees. Hence, 1.25 minor division is equal 6 * 1.25, which is **7.5 degrees.**

The pseudo code will be something like

- 1 division = 360/60 degrees = 6 degrees
- 60 minor div minute hand move = 5 minor div hour hand move.
- 15 minor div minute hand move = ¼ * 5 = 1.25 minor div hour hand move.
- 1.25 minor division = 1.25 * 6 degrees = 7.5 degrees.

As you could see, listing the known facts, the diagram, and the pseudo code not only help you with solving the problem, but also in communicating the solution to others. The analytical, problem solving, and communication skills are key to your career success.

The example below illustrates that knowing the key area of the problem can help you solve a problem.

Q. If there is a hot and a cold tap, and the hot tap fills a bucket in 2 minutes and the cold tap fills the same bucket in 3 minutes, how long will take to fill the same bucket if both the taps are turned on?

A. The mathematical key area to above question is **ratios**. The hot and cold taps fill at **2:3 ratio**. The ratio of the portions of the buckets they fill is the reverse – 3:2 because the tap that takes lesser time should fill more. This means when both the taps are turned on, the hot tap fills $3/5^{th}$ portion of the bucket (as the hot tap flows faster) and the cold tap fills $2/5^{th}$ portion of the bucket. The hot tap takes 2 minutes to fill the entire bucket, hence to fill $3/5^{th}$ of the bucket it takes 3/5 of 2 minutes, which is 6/5 = **1.2 minutes**. Same is true for the cold tap as well. It takes 3 minutes to fill the whole bucket, hence to fill $2/5^{th}$ of the bucket it takes $2/5^{th}$ of 3 minutes, which is 6/5 = **1.2 minutes**. So, it will take 1.2 minutes to fill the bucket when both taps are running simultaneously.

Become a change agent, facilitator, and a problem solver to open more doors

It is easier to understand when represented as shown below

	Hot Tap	Cold Tap
Time it takes to fill a bucket	2 minutes	3 minutes
The ratio of the parts it fills	3 parts	2 parts
When both are turned on, the portion of the bucket it fills.	$3/5^{th}$	$2/5^{th}$
Time it takes when both are turned on	$3/5^{th} * 2 = \textbf{1.2 minutes}$	$2/5^{th} * 3 = \textbf{1.2 minutes}$

The key aspect of problem solving is to **break a complex problem into smaller manageable chunks**. It also involves making valid assumptions, asking the right questions and looking at things in different angles. Good researching skills, investing in books, lots of coding and asking the right questions will help you improve your problem solving skills in software engineering.

Section 4:

Write effective resumes to open doors

If you want to win an interview, you must write a resume that captures the following 7 aspects

- Results oriented.
- Key areas driven.
- Soft skills & personal traits are captured.
- Sought after technologies, frameworks, and tools are mentioned.
- Strengths are highlighted.
- Credible.
- Concise and well formatted without spelling errors.

Knowing and applying the key areas alone not enough. You need to effectively let others know of your accomplishments via resumes, online portfolios, job interviews, blogs, and written articles.

Note: Bold faces and underlines are used in this section to highlight the importance and relevance to the reader, and this should not be construed as to be reflected in the real resume. Names and numbers are used for illustrative purpose only, and use your own data by reflecting back on your own experience if using similar examples on your resume.

Why is your resume an important tool in marketing your Services?

Prospective employers don't have the time to go through your resume line by line. Reading others' resume is a boring task. This means, you need to have the "know how" to make your resume interesting to read by concisely and effectively selling your achievements, capabilities, and suitability.

Boring resumes sound a lot like job descriptions. If your resume is simply a list of tasks that you performed at each job, then you probably have a boring resume. The prospective employers are more interested in the **impact you made**. Another factor that can make a resume boring is its tone. If you find it a chore to write your resume, that sense of tedium will probably come through in the tone of your document. If you can't communicate your career highlights in a simplest manner, your prospective employer may have concerns about your ability to communicate your thoughts.

Think of your resume as a short story about your career. A good story would present focused, quantifiable and credible facts of your career in an easy-to-follow fashion while keeping the reader interested throughout. Use a language that is expressive, action-oriented, and demonstrates your enthusiasm for your chosen field and the pride you take in your work.

How would you go about comparing ordinary versus outstanding resumes?

There are no clear cut definitions in separating an ordinary resume from a resume that stands out. This is always subjective based on the prospective employer. The important point to remember is that as long as your resume looks neat, has no "typos", and includes **"relevant"** and **"significant"** information your resume will be fine. Pay close attention to the terms **"relevant"** and **"significant"**. Writing a resume is an ongoing process where you will be updating and changing information. Some guidelines can be drawn to compare an ordinary resume with a one that is more effective.

Ordinary Resume	*Outstanding Resume*
Markets you just as a techie. • What really is the big deal in being a Java or .Net guru if you cannot understand how the business works and how you can contribute to add value? • What really is the big deal in being a superstar developer if you are perceived as being difficult, unfriendly, and no one is willing to work with you? • What value are your PHP skills going to add if you do not have the ability to translate business requirements into technical design and convey your ideas to the masses in the simplest possible manner?	Markets you as a well-rounded professional with both technical and non-technical skills. Technical skills alone can be easily replaced, but not good technical skills complemented with great soft skills and right attitude. This is a very important point not only from your resume perspective to impress your prospective employer, but more importantly, from your career progression, and surviving layoffs and probation period perspective. This becomes even more essential if you want to find your next job via networking or referrals.
Uses ordinary phrases without being results oriented and credible. Example:	Uses perfect phrases in a clear and concise manner that emphasize your skills and highlight your accomplishments for potential employers.

Write effective resumes to open doors

• Performance tuned a .Net based application. Uses pretty bland phrases without quantifying the information. Example: • Led a team of PHP developers.	Example: • Re-architected, refactored and performance tuned a .Net based online insurance application, which previously came down almost daily, became a true 24x7 application. **Note**: Be prepared to explain how in the job interview. You can see the difference quantifying makes as shown below: • Provided leadership by managing a team of 15, for a mission critical PHP based project budgeted at $9.0 million. **Note**: Your prospective employers will see this. They would like to know that you have worked on large and mission critical projects.
One size fits all resume. The same resume is emailed or reprinted as required. This is wasting an opportunity to present you in the best possible way.	Resume is made relevant to the position you are applying for e.g. senior developer, architect, team lead, etc. Resume can also be tailored to industry or domain specific like finance, insurance, retail, telecommunications, software house, etc. It does not take much long to produce customized resumes based on the job specification.
Important information is scattered	Important information is in the first page.

throughout the pages in the resume.	Unless you impress the prospective employer in the first page, he or she may not read your remaining pages. If you are a seasoned professional, then draw on your hands on experience. If you have little or no experience, then draw on your academic qualifications, certifications, contribution to open-source projects, self-taught projects, part-time jobs, community projects, university projects, assignments, etc.
No professional online presence. We are living in the digital media age, and many employers perform additional screening via your online presence.	Provides links to professional online presence. For example, blog, online portfolio, and linked in profile.

It seems unfair that you have to take your entire experience and fit into a document that is 2 to 4 pages long. That is why it is very important to write catchy-phrases. Outstanding phrases can put your resume on the top of the stack and put you ahead of the pack in today's competitive job market. Some phrases are overused and fail to make an impact. For example, avoid blanket phrases like "team player", "excellent communication skills", "hard worker", "solid work ethic", etc. These phrases do not mean much because everyone uses them. Apparently everyone in the world is a hard worker, team player and excellent communicator.

Ordinary Phrase	*Outstanding Phrase*
• Designed and developed a Java/JEE based online system for the XYZ Ltd.	• Designed and developed a Java/JEE based online insurance system, which serves 400 concurrent users using Spring, Hibernate, JSF, ajax, and jQuery. **Standout factor:** Shows that you have experience in building large and complex production systems using sought after

	technologies like Spring, Hibernate, ajax, and jQuery.
• I am an excellent leader and a communicator. Any one can say this. How do you know that you are an excellent leader? Where did you apply your leadership skills? What did you accomplish?	• Led resolution of customer inquiries concerning policies, procedures, and programs through active listening and standard coaching methods at XYZ Retail Services. • On taking up the position as a .NET technical lead, I set up a team of 8 developers to successfully complete the project on time and within budget.
• Wrote stored procedures with inner and outer joins. Don't include trivial information. The above statement is an easy give away that you are a beginner. It even implicitly mean that you just learned inner and outer SQL joins.	• Wrote complex stored procedures to load ~3.5 million records into 14 different tables. • Reduced the over-night batch job runtime from 3 hours to 40 minutes by optimizing the SQL and fixing the intermittent deadlock issues. Always quantify your statements and leave out the details to be discussed at the interview. This will arouse the curiosity to learn more about your accomplishments.
• Acquired team work and problem solving skills while collaborating on a university assignment with other students.	• Applied strong interpersonal and communication capabilities in working with a wide range of personnel at all levels to gain valuable insight, solve potential problems, and facilitate the timely completion of tasks at AAA hospitality industries.

So, remember that you need to phrase your sentences and write your resume such a way that the employer or recruiter wants to interview YOU and not the other person who has done exactly the same thing or little more, but did not phrase it correctly in the resume. So, it really matters how you phrase your sentences.

What are the 7 aspects of an effective resume?

To write an effective resume, you do not have to hard sell or make any false claims, but you need to get over your shyness and unwillingness to toot your own horn. If you cannot, who can? If you are willing to take some extra effort to learn and apply some of the guidelines discussed here and be more creative in preparing your resume, then you will definitely get a better response from prospective employers. So, to win an interview, you should write a resume that is:

1. Results oriented
2. Key areas driven
3. Soft skills and personal attributes are captured
4. Sought after technologies and frameworks are mentioned

5. Strengths are highlighted
6. Credible
7. Concise and well-formatted without spelling errors.

Some accomplish great results in their career, but fail to communicate that effectively in their resumes (i.e. so called quiet achievers), whilst others have accomplished ordinary results, but make an effort to communicate that more effectively to standout from their competition. Also bear in mind that marketing skills without real substance (i.e. technical skills) can bring about short lived success and disappointment. So you need to build your substance based on these examples to gain real success. For example, if you can't clearly explain how you went about reducing the batch runs from 3 hours to 40 minutes in your interview, then you are not likely to succeed. The examples I have shown below are for illustrative purpose only based on my own experience to help you reflect back on your own past experiences and achievements if you are a seasoned professional or proactively look for opportunities to build these types of experiences in your current or future jobs if you are a novice.

No matter how great your technical skills are, when job hunting, your marketing skills should be first-class. Let's look at the 7 key aspects of an effective resume.

Results oriented

Your resume should give your recruiter the confidence that you could do the job based on your past results i.e. achievements, skills, experience, and capabilities. Most resumes only describe the tasks and activities as shown below instead of results.

- My responsibility included design and development of the payment and claims module.

- Involved in the design and development of the payment and claims module.

You can re-write the above lines in a results oriented way as shown below:

- Designed and developed the payment and claims module, which is capable of handling 120 requests per second and runs as a true 24 x 7 system module.

- Designed and developed the payment and claims module, which is a mission critical module that currently handles in excess of 120 concurrent requests.

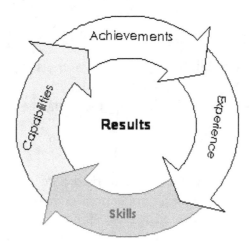

What the recruiters are looking for is the **impact** of your tasks or activities on the organization. Quantify your information as much as possible by including dollar amount, time frames, how many, how big, how much, how often, and so on. Just like a picture is worth thousands words, quantifying by using numbers in your resume can make a huge difference. For job seekers with little or no experience, put the emphasis on your academic achievements like certifications, any test scores, etc along with the experience gained from self-taught project(s), university project(s), open-source community project(s), and non-industry specific part-time jobs (i.e. paid or unpaid). With each new job and experience, you need to work towards improving this with industry specific experience.

Example(s):

- Reduced the monthly Java based commission batch runs from **18 hours to 7 hours** at XYZ ltd.

- Championed the iterative and test driven development (TDD) with regular code reviews, bamboo based continuous integration, and sonar based code coverage, which resulted in not only more maintainable and extensible code, but also roughly **30% drop in bugs**.

- Spearheaded the design and development of a Spring MVC, Spring, and Hibernate based mission critical system that **earned high accolades** in the code and design reviews conducted by an independent consultancy.

Standout factor(s):

- The above examples highlight the impact of your tasks.
- It shows that you are passionate about code quality.
- It also shows that you take pride in your achievements.

Example(s):

- Motivated the fellow developers and worked hard to successfully complete the task of enhancing a PHP based application in **8 weeks** to meet the deadline as opposed to **10 weeks** as it was originally estimated.

- Spearheaded the "Quick Wins" project by working very closely with the business and end users to **improve the current website's ranking from being 23rd to 6th in just 3 months.**

Standout factor(s):

- Shows that you are not only technical, but also a people oriented person with interpersonal skills like mentoring and collaborating.
- Shows that you strive to meet the deadlines.
- Highlights your customer driven approach.

Example(s):

- Received an initial 3 month contract with a multinational Fortune 500 company to upgrade a poorly performing .Net based application and integrated it with 3 other systems. My contract was further extended **6 times** on a six monthly basis.

Standout factor(s):

- Gives an overall credibility to your technical ability, work ethics, and interpersonal skills. No one will extend your contract 6 times unless they are happy with your performance.

Key areas driven

In my view, good software engineers need to have good handle on the 16 key areas that were discussed earlier, not only to build a robust system, but also to open more doors to their career advancement. As a software engineer, one needs to be skilled in certain areas, and have good awareness in the other areas to engage the right teams like an infrastructure team, quality assurance team, integration team, etc to meet the business needs.

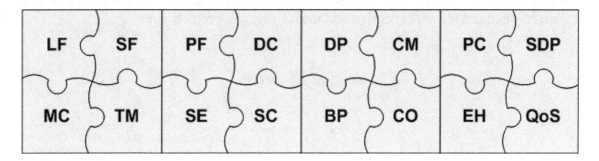

Example(s):

- Identified and fixed **transactional** issues due to incorrect **exception handling** and **concurrency** issues due to not properly synchronized block of code in a Java/JEE based Web application for ABC limited.

- Applied **design patterns** and OO design concepts to improve the existing C# based code base for PQR limited by refactoring it with test driven development (TDD) and behavior driven development (BDD) principles.

- Proactively identified and addressed issues relating to **performance**, **scalability**, and **security** vulnerabilities in a number of consulting assignments, and impressed my peers and superiors.

Standout factor(s):

- It shows that you have hands-on experience with various key areas that are critical to any software project.
- It shows that you are passionate about building quality software.

- It also shows that you have the ability to take initiatives and be pro-active.

Soft skills and personal attributes are captured

Just being a superstar developer alone isn't enough to advance in your career or to survive layoffs. Technical professionals are increasingly required to broaden their skill sets to master the so-called soft skills. The increased global competition and the changing nature of most technical jobs have made soft skills more than simply "nice to have". These skills are "must have". Your prospective employer would prefer to employ someone who has adequate technical skills combined with the necessary soft skills (i.e. a balanced candidate) to get expensive and mission critical projects done.

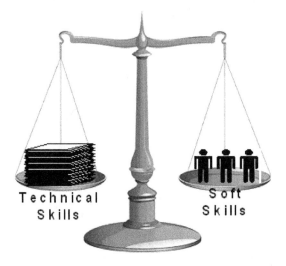

So, if you are an experienced professional and deciding, which professional skill to improve, picking up another certification may be the wrong choice. Learning soft skills can make you not only more employable, but also can make you a more valuable and hard to replace team member. Why is this so? Let's have a look at with some examples.

Mr. X is technically brilliant in UNIX, SQL, and Database administration, and most active member of a project team, but he has some concerns:

- Why do his team mates not prefer to come to him, for solutions and recommendations, and go to less capable team members instead?
- Does he have the ability to convey his ideas, solutions, and design alternatives to the cross functional teams in the simplest possible manner?

- Will he be able to communicate the detailed design to his client in an impressive manner, so that the client is convinced?
- Has he got leadership and motivational skills? Does he speak up in team meetings and make contributions?
- Is he perceived as a contributor or just another techie by his project manager?
- Can he convey his ideas to the business users without getting too technical?

Mr. Y is a very technically capable professional with lots of attention to details, but he has a few areas to work on:

- Does he complain frequently? Does he focus more on possible negative outcomes than the positive ones? Does he easily get frustrated and give up on things too easily?
- Can he look at the big picture and prioritize tasks based on that matter most to the business as opposed to just getting too much fixated with minor technical details?
- Is he rigid in his goals and how things are to be done? Is it possible to dissuade him once he is fixated on something? Why is he not flexible and adaptable?
- Does he blame others more often than accepting his own mistakes?
- Has he got a good work ethic? Does he occasionally and especially when really needed work past his usual hours? Does he strike a good balance between work and personal life?

Ms. Z is a very technically competent Java/JEE professional, but she has some areas to improve on.

- Why is she pinned to her seat and keyboard all the time? Does she interact with the cross-functional teams?
- Why does she just perform as told and not question the solution or requirement and propose alternative solutions? Can she identify potential technical and non-technical issues?
- Does she ask the right questions to identify gaps in the requirements? Does she take the initiative to organize meetings and follow up with the right people to get the doubts and concerns clarified?
- Can she get things done with minimal supervision and follow ups?

If you know .NET and C# inside and out, you are just a coder and you can be replaced by any other coder. Your technical skills will have more value when complemented with good soft skills and domain knowledge. IT projects fail mainly due to:

- Not clearly defined business needs and project scope and lack of strategy and vision.
- Wrong, incomplete, inconsistent, or inaccurate specifications.
- Staff lacking motivation, dedication, qualification, and experience to pro-actively identify potential issues, both technical and non-technical and propose alternative solutions.
- No formal project management and development methodologies and best practices to align with the company's specific needs. Lack of communication, team work, proper documentation, and document sign-offs.
- Insufficient funding, incorrect budgets, and economic down turns.

Most soft skills like communication, interpersonal, leadership, team work, etc are regarded as transferable skills because they are needed in nearly all aspects of life, not just for your career alone. New technical skills can be acquired in days and new frameworks can be learned in weeks, but improving on soft skills can take months if not years.

You need to grow not just as a "techie" but as a well-rounded person with good technical skills. The soft skill requirements vary from company to company, but there are some core soft skills that are common to most companies. I have identified the following 10 key soft skills:

> Top notch **interpersonal skills** to deliver results with your colleagues in IT and non-IT areas you must work with.

Interpersonal skills are must-have foundation for your career growth. In most fields winners need to be people oriented and software development is no exception. In software development, one needs to work **with** and **through** and **for** other people, which is always not easy. Without the ability to get along with people, many other talents may be of little value.

Friendliness and helpfulness cost little but mean a lot. Interpersonal skills are all about approachability, ability to build rapport with other people, understanding cultural differences and acting accordingly, self-awareness, and emotional maturity (e.g. not losing your temper, handling criticisms well, etc).

Excellent written and oral **communication** skills.

This is the ability to convey information in both verbal and written formats as appropriate for the needs of target audience like technical staff, business users, stake holders, etc. Good eye contact and body language are essential for effective communication. A skilful communicator draws on a number of different means like graphical, visual (e.g. screen-shots, conceptual, and UML diagrams), statistical, audio-visual, and most importantly analogical to get the point across. Using analogies and visual representations are very powerful to take something complex, which is obvious to you and turn it into something easily graspable by others. Good analogies and diagrams stick in peoples' minds. For example, driving a car is an analogy to interfaces and implementation. The steering wheel and other controls that are used by a driver to drive a car are interfaces. No matter what make or model of a car you drive, the interfaces are similar. But the actual implementation under the covers can vary among different makes and models. It is the responsibility of the car manufacturers to adhere to the standard interfaces, but the actual implementations can be improved from one model to another. An order going through a number of state changes like filled, partially filled, rejected, on-hold, etc can be better communicated via a state-chart diagram.

Many believe that an effective communication is all about giving information clearly or explaining something so that people understand you. This is only partly correct. The other two key aspects of effective communication are **active listening** and **human motivation**.

We were given two ears and one mouth to appreciate active listening. Most of us like to talk but hardly like to listen. A good communicator needs to actively listen and put himself or herself in the shoes of others and look at things from others' point of view. If you are writing a resume, put your self in your prospective employers' or recruiters' shoes. If you are talking to your business or application users, look at things from their perspective. It is also imperative to engage your stakeholders in active listening by using effective communication techniques discussed above without too much technical jargon.

"I only wish I could find an institute that teaches people how to listen. Business people need to listen at least as much as they need to talk. Too many people fail to realize that real communication goes in both directions." — Lee Iacocca

> Well developed **research** and **analytical skills** with good **problem solving** and **lateral thinking** ability to challenge, conceptualize, and recommend simpler, improved, and alternative solution(s).

- Ability to conceptualize problems. Do you analyze "What if" scenarios? e.g. What if an exception is thrown? Will the scarce resources like sockets, file handles, database connections, etc get closed properly? What if the customer cancels the transaction, will the transaction be rolled back properly? What if a catastrophic failure occurs?

- Ability to brainstorm ideas in a group. How many items need to be shown on the screen at a time? Can we conserve memory and improve response times by implementing true pagination? Can the long running report be generated asynchronously and emailed to the customer? Should we put any restrictions on the size of the reports produced? What if the producer and consumer of the web services are in different time zones? Are these historical tables needed to be partitioned?

- Ability to break down and understand complex content. Can you break down complex work flow logic and business processes into more manageable steps? You can apply visual UML diagrams such as use case diagrams, state chart diagrams, collaboration diagrams, and activity diagrams to help you analyze the content.

- Ability to combine and integrate information from disparate sources. Can you gather requirements from the business users, business analysts, and system analysts to put together the functional and technical specifications? Can you research for information on the internet with the right key words and produce a summary document?

- Ability to generate multiple and creative solutions and arrive at a conclusion. Can you carry out a feasibility study documenting all the pros and cons? Can you document alternative solutions listing possible pros and cons for each approach and the reasoning for recommending a particular option?

- Ability to use troubleshooting skills. Can you list all possible causes and isolate the more likely causes? Can you research on the internet with the right key words to identify any possible causes?

- Ability to express problems or solutions quantitatively, interpret irregular results and invalid data. For example, 30% of the requests are timed out, 25% improvement in response times, inconsistent results due to potential concurrency issues, database in inconsistent state due to transactional issues, etc.

Exceptional **leadership skills**. Being a good leader, listener, and **mentor** with ability to provide advice and feedback, share knowledge, face challenges, handle pressure, and admit mistakes.

Leadership skills and techniques can be learned. You don't have to be a natural leader. Very few people are. Don't confuse the word managers with leaders. Managers are thought to be the budgeters, the organizers, the controllers, the policy makers, etc whereas the leaders are the agile and charismatic big-picture visionaries, the ones who can proactively make a visible difference. Not all mangers are good leaders. Effective leaders continually devise strategies to improve things, they try to analyze what is working and what is not, they set directions and align people, they motivate and inspire people, they are proactive, and they communicate continually and effectively with the target audience. So, not all managers are good leaders. To become a good leader, you need to have

- a very good knowledge of the business. This includes the domain knowledge, business drivers and risks, and high level understanding of the various systems.
- technical skills to be able to translate business requirements into high level technical specifications and to guide team members.
- good communication and interpersonal skills to share information with your team and earn the respect and corporation of the team members to work towards the same goal and objectives.
- strategic thinking ability to plan, organize, allocate, and prioritize resources and tasks. Good leaders drive changes without resorting to "this is how we always did it" mentality and always open to good ideas. For example, ask your team members to list 10 most annoying problems.

"The key to success is to get out into the store and listen to what the associates have to say. It's terribly important for everyone to get involved. Our best ideas come from clerks and stock boys." — Sam Walton

Knowing your business well enough with good **work ethics**.

What is the big deal in being a Java or .Net guru if you can't understand how the business works and how you can enhance value? The more you know about your business the more you will be able to contribute in project and team meetings, and consequently make an impression.

You must understand the short and long term goals of the business, so that you can devise tactical and strategical solutions. Also, technical people need to understand the company's products and services, who the target customers are, and how these products and services are used. Having a good understanding of "whys" behind a project can help you figure out the "hows" much easier. In tough times, technical skills alone can be easily replaced, but not technical skills coupled with good business knowledge.

Being a **team player** as well as ability to work independently with reliability and integrity.

A successful team is a group of many hands, but one objective. Be reliable by cultivating the trust of your boss in you. So, how do you impress your boss?

- Get things done as promised in a timely fashion.
- When you are in doubt, don't assume things. Seek clarifications from your boss or relevant people. Ask the right questions to gather requirements. Identify gaps in the requirements.
- Where ever possible, take on more responsibilities as if you were the boss. Conduct meetings when your boss is away on leave.
- When things do not turn up as planned, you come up with an alternative solution instead of asking your boss for help.
- Finally, love the job you are performing. When you are happy at what you are doing, you will work smarter and harder with enthusiasm. Your superiors will

definitely notice this.

> Ability to establish and maintain productive working relationships in **multidisciplinary** teams with good **adaptability**, **flexibility**, and **negotiation** skills.

Flexibility and adaptability are qualities many employers seek. We are living in a very competitive global economy where companies and organizations must respond to changes quickly and easily. Why do you think the agile development practices have moved into the mainstream? Agile development practices help minimize the overall risk, and allow the project adapt to changes more quickly.

There is often a pretty big gap in thinking and communication between a company's business units and technical teams. The business people are perceived as demanding and impatient (i.e. everything is due today), and technical people are seen as lazy and sometimes arrogant. The agile development methodology, if properly implemented, can improve this situation.

Very often the technical people find the business requirements to be vague or incomplete, but as a member of the team, it is the responsibility of the technical people to do what is best for the project by getting it clarified or properly documented in a tactful manner. At times technical people can offer to make the necessary changes themselves to the business requirements to move forward without having to wait for the business people who can be very busy.

> **Quick learner** with ability to learn new skills/technology from scratch.

An experienced programmer with good grasp of fundamentals can quickly learn new frameworks/technologies. There are more than 20 web frameworks for Java, but if you understand some of the core concepts and paradigms relating to web development and well versed in one or two frameworks with hands on experience, then learning a new framework can be much easier.

> Behavioral traits such as **right attitude** (i.e. positive can-do, can-bounce-back without "I know it all" mindset), **motivation**, **taking initiatives**, **enthusiasm**, **passion**, **organizational** skills, and effective **time management**.

Have the right attitude. Stay away from attitudes like "I know it all", "I am just paid to do a specific role or task", and "it is not my problem". If you think you do not get noticed, you are wrong. Your employers do notice and hear. So,

- Show a lot of enthusiasm for the job. Take pride in the end products or results that shape up nicely with all the key areas in place, and presenting your achievements to the relevant stake holders and prospective employers, and listing it as an accomplishment in your resume and online portfolio.

- Be willing to do more than you are being paid to do. Help others whenever you can and learn from their challenges and experiences.

- Treat the business as if it were your own, as if you had stock in the company, and never bad mouth your present and past companies.

- Always try to leave a company on good terms, so that you can not only use them as a reference, but also can make them part of your network. In difficult economic times, you will at least have a few numbers to call.

Learn to look at the **big picture** in addition to paying **attention to the details**.

Anyone who has ever attempted to piece together a complex jigsaw puzzle likely will tell you that they get through the painstaking process by focusing on the big picture — and the software development is no exception. When you build a software, the 16 key areas mentioned above should fit together nicely like a puzzle to build a robust application. As a software engineer, you must learn to break down a large project or a pressing problem into manageable chunks, and delegate the relevant chunks to the right people to get things done. Even though the ability to look at the big picture is a must have trait for the architects and managers, the developers must also learn to look at the big picture from time to time, without getting too bogged down with only details. Software development is all about managing complexities and making trade-offs to get the best possible outcome. The table below shows looking at the big picture for a solution to a problem by depicting the pros and cons from different perspectives.

For example, consider a scenario of building a main customer facing portal application and a number of independent (or plug-in) web applications accessed via the main portal. This will require a number of shared services, components, mashups, and single sign on

(SSO) to provide a holistic end-user experience. As far as the user is concerned, it is a single website as everything looks the same and function the same way. This divide and conquer approach has a number of pros and cons from business, design, development, testing, release, and support perspective.

Perspective	Pros	Cons
Business	Seamless and well integrated user experience. Reduced initial and potentially ongoing outlay as efforts in terms of infrastructure, design, development, and support can be greatly shared and reused.	Extra effort is required in terms of testing and release management. Any changes to a shared service or component may require testing of a number of dependent applications that use this service/component. The testing efforts can be minimized by having a good coverage of automated regression testing scripts. Other governance issues due to the way the businesses are structured. For example, when the business is structured by products as in insurance, cash management, portfolios, mortgages, etc.
Design	Architecturally sound due to clear separation of functionalities without any duplication of efforts. Easier to maintain and adapt to future growth and requirements. No workarounds are required to achieve the end goal. This approach is more inline with what the other industries are doing and more conducive to adoption of the Service Oriented Architecture	Potential risk of bloating the UI layer with badly designed UI component or mash-up. Services and components need to be designed with other applications in mind.

	(SOA) in the future.	
Development	Each team can learn from each other. The divide and conquer approach will make the code more manageable and maintainable.	Combined effort is required from the main portal and the plug-in application development teams. Code duplication is possible if the individual teams are not talking to each other. Proper service timeouts and exception handling needs to be properly analyzed. For example, what if the main portal is down? None of the dependent applications can be accessed. What if one of the dependent applications is down?
Testing	Testing teams will have diverse knowledge in terms of functionalities relating to the main portal application and the plug-in applications.	More testing effort is required. Change to either the main portal or plug-in application will require some level of regression testing of the dependent applications. This can be kept to a minimum by writing automated regression testing suites.
Release management		Coordinated upgrades and impact analysis are required.
Support	Much easier to support with this divide and conquer approach.	
Infrastructure & operations.	Existing infrastructure can be leveraged or extended. This means reduced cost.	Changes need to be properly coordinated among relevant teams.

How do you improve on these soft skills?

- Identifying your weaknesses based on your performance appraisals at work or asking a friend/colleague, and most importantly, consciously taking the time and effort to self-assess.

- Learning from your role models, superiors, and peers, and most importantly, consciously and constantly applying what you learn by observing them.

- Taking up relevant training courses.

Here are some examples that highlights your soft skills. You need to add "where you did this?".

Example(s):

- **Guided** and **mentored** new recruits within the development team with setting up of their environments, performing automated builds, unit and integration testing, which ensured smoother transition and improved productivity.

- **Worked closely** with the business users, analysts, infrastructure, testing, and project management teams to come up with the detailed design.

- **Communicated** the detailed design and solution architecture to cross-functional teams like developers, business users, testers, external vendors, and management.

- **Documented** and delivered RUP light artifacts such as software architecture documents, deployment model, and system use cases.

- Fostered better communication and centralization of team knowledge by introducing and implementing a Wiki site.

- **Analyzed** "what if" scenarios and exceptional conditions and made recommendations to fill the gaps identified in the functional specs and detailed design.

- Contributed immensely to brain storming and design sessions with creative ideas and alternative solutions to simplify over engineered solutions.

- Identified the root cause and fixed a hard to reproduce production issue where the server had to be restarted every second day.

- Resolved product complications at customer sites and funneled the insights to the development and deployment teams to adopt long term product development strategy with minimal roadblocks.

- **Convinced** business users and analysts with alternative solutions that are more robust and simpler to implement from technical perspective, while satisfying the functional requirements from the business perspective.

- Held job titles such as senior developer (4+ yrs), technical lead (2+ yrs), senior designer (3+ yrs), systems analyst (6m+), mentor (5+ yrs), and consultant (3+ yrs) to understand well enough technical, **human**, and **business** side of IT.

- Worked in insurance and financial services sectors, and gained **domain knowledge** in field commission calculations, trading systems, and cash, mortgage, and insurance products.

- **Solved** a number of small technical issues, which were huge roadblocks from a business standpoint by coming up with solutions in my spare time.

- Learned on the fly new and home grown frameworks and difficult concepts, and hit the ground running as a key contributor.

- Spearheaded the agile development methodology initiative, which improved the communication and cooperation between business owners and the developers.

- Awarded outstanding achievement for coming in just 2 months before the deadline in a development effort that was going on for 18 months to contribute significantly to fast track development, where some home grown Java based frameworks/technologies had to be **quickly learned**.

- Initial contract was further extended 7 times with **increased responsibilities**.

- **Led** and **mentored** a team of 10 developers on best practices, full SDLC processes, solving business and technical issues, and clarifying the business requirements.

- **Convinced** the management to agree on open-source tools and encouraged the development team to use them.

162

- **Trained** clients on best practices and common pitfalls, so that they could continue and extend the project on their own.

- Took on the acting project manager role and led a multidisciplinary team of 20.

- **Headed** the development of a pure Java based work flow engine, which is successfully used in over 4 production systems. Continuously **adapted** the designs and implementations based on user feedback and changing requirements.

- Set clear goals, responsibilities, and communicated effectively, so that tasks can be completed with high quality and in a timely manner.

Standout factor(s):

- The above examples illustrate various soft skills.

"Software isn't an artifact that someone buys; it's a relationship between a customer and the provider of a service." - **Tim O'Reilly**

Sought after technologies, frameworks, and tools are mentioned

A resume, which fails to describe the sought-after technologies, is a resume that is doomed to fail. You always need to include the technology in your work experience section and be repetitive in regard to technology. Technology (i.e. relevant to the position) used should be mentioned at the end of each project, so that the prospective employer or recruiter can see that you have a lot of Java, JEE, Spring, JSF, etc. If you just only mention it once then you only have some experience in Java, JEE, Spring, JSF, etc. It is amazing that many candidates who have the skills and technology the recruiter or employer is looking for, but fail to mention them on their resumes.

Write effective resumes to open doors

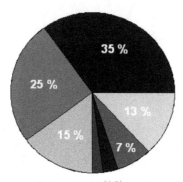

Technologies in demand

Professional Experience:

Dec 2006 – Present   **XYZ Ltd**

Position: Senior Java/JEE Consultant - Design & development focus

Achievements: • Designed and developed a Java NIO, multi-threaded, Spring 2.0, and Hibernate 3.0 based application to serve up to 400 concurrent socket connections.

                            • Designed and developed a JSF, Websphere, Oracle, Spring, and Hibernate based web application.

Technologies used: Java 1.5, JSF Sun RI, Facelets, Ajax4JSF, Richfaces, Spring, XML, XSL, XSD, XHTML, Hibernate, MINA, JiBX, Spring-ws, SOAP Web service, Websphere, Oracle, Maven, SVN, etc

Many hi-tech-companies and recruitment agencies use databases to quickly and efficiently match job openings with qualified job seekers. Searches are done using technologies used and phrases that describe the skills and education required for the position, thus when writing a resume it is extremely important to use terms and familiar Java/JEE specific acronyms that describes your skills and experience. Include every sought after technology even if something is implicitly understood like HTML & CSS are required for web development because you know this, but the recruitment agencies may not know this.

Technical Summary:

Core Java   Java 1.4, 1.5, Swing, Applet, JMX, JDBC, and RMI.

JEE Technologies   JSP, Servlet, JSF, EJB, JMS, JSTL, EL, JNDI, JTA, and LDAP.

Frameworks/Libraries Spring, Hibernate, Acegi, Spring-ws, Tapestry, Struts, JSF Sun RI, MyFaces, Facelets, Ajax4JSF, JAXB, JiBX, MINA, JBoss Seam, JBoss RESTEasy, Apache CXF, etc.

Tools: Ant, Maven, CVS, SVN, Eclipse, Rational Software Architect, SoapUI, JMeter, Selenium, FirFox plugins like Firebug, Modify Headers, Live HTTP headers, etc and Internet Explorer plugins like Fiddler2.

Platforms: **Databases** (Oracle, MySQL, DB2) , **OS** (Linux, Windows) , **Application Servers** (Tomcat, JBoss, Websphere, Weblogic, etc), **Message Oriented Middleware** (Websphere MQ), **Enterprise Service Bus** (webMethods, Oracle Service Bus), **Business Process Management** (Lombardi BPM, Pega BPM), **Business Rules Engine** (Drools).

Design skills: OOA (Object Oriented Analysis) & OOD (Object Oriented Design), AOP (Aspect Oriented Programming), Design by contract, GoF design patterns, JEE design patterns and UML.

Software Development Agile methodology, RUP (Rational Unified Process),
Methodology: SCRUM, TDD (Test Driven Development), and XP (eXtreme Programming).

Other: SOAP Web services, HTML, CSS, ajax, JavaScript, XML, XSD, XSL, XSLT, XSL-FO, WSDL, JAXP,

Xalan, Xerces, SQL, etc.

If you are a seasoned professional then include number of years of experience and last used version. For example:

Core Java (7+ years):   Java 1.4, 1.5, Swing, Applet, JMX, JDBC, and RMI.

JEE Technologies   JSP, Servlet, JSF, EJB, JMS, JSTL, EL, JNDI, JTA, and
(6+ years):   LDAP.

Frameworks/Libraries   Spring, Hibernate, Acegi, Spring-ws, Tapestry, JSF Sun
(3+ years)   RI, MyFaces, Facelets, Ajax4JSF, JiBX, MINA, etc

Note: Don't clutter your resume with technologies such as Word, Excel, Microsoft Project, PowerPoint, and irrelevant legacy or proprietary technologies unless specifically mentioned in the job specification. If you really want to include them, do it towards the end of your resume under "Other Skills". The skills summary section will also help you identify the next technical skills you might like to learn.

Keep up with the market trends and acquire the skills in the sought after technologies and frameworks.

Example(s):

- Designed and developed a web based application that has over 3 million registered users using Spring, Hibernate, JSF, and ajax for ABC retail limited.

- Developed various data-processing and back office processing applications for a telecommunication industry using Spring 2.0, Hibernate 3.0, JSF, EJB3, JMS, JMX, Websphere MQ and JavaScript.

Standout factor(s):

- Since June 2005, Spring Framework has grown in popularity, and has become the defacto standard for enterprise Java development. The IT job advertisements citing Spring framework has also been rising since June 2005.

- Many Java/JEE based job vacancies are Web development based. Struts, Spring MVC and JSF are sought after frameworks for web development in Java/JEE.

Do your research by looking at the job posting sites in your country. Do your research by googling for the technology names e.g. "Java JSF", "JSF Jobs", etc for trend analysis. Check your local online job advertisements to see what technologies and frameworks are on the rise. Some of the sites shown below analyze the job and technology trends:

- http://www.google.com/trends.
- http://www.indeed.com/jobtrends.
- Industry specific websites like
  http://www.infoq.com,
  http://www.theserverside.com
  http://www.dzone.com

For job seekers with little or no experience: (e.g. graduates, career changers, etc)

Example(s):

- 3 month hands-on experience with Spring 2.0, Hibernate 3.0, and JSF due to self-taught projects and keen to apply this knowledge in a commercial project.

- Familiar with Spring 2.0, Hibernate 3.0 and JSF 1.2 due to self-education (e.g. tutorials, learning of high level concepts, etc) and keen to apply this knowledge in a commercial project.

Standout factor(s):

- Puts more credibility and shows that you are a pro-active learner.
- Shows that you are keen to use sought after technologies like Spring, Hibernate, etc.
- Prospective employer/recruiter will be more interested in someone who is familiar with these sought after technologies than having no awareness or basic knowledge. I landed in most of my jobs in the beginning of my career with the small self-taught projects and learning the fundamentals followed by succeeding in the interviews and then gaining the commercial experience.

"The good news is that better hiring managers won't care about whether or not you know the flavor of the month. The bad news is that the better hiring managers are a small percentage of the total". Mark Hershberg at http://www.javaranch.com forum.

Strengths are highlighted

You need to know what would make someone a superior candidate in your field. What technologies are popular and widely used? What are the immediate needs or requirements of the prospective employer? If you are not sure, then do your research by surfing the internet, asking your recruitment agent, calling the prospective employer, asking other people who work in the same company, etc. Do not make guesses and it is important that you do this step so that you can tailor your resume and interview preparation to address the real needs of your prospective employer as opposed to just stating what you can offer. This will enable you to accentuate your strengths and de-emphasize your weakness.

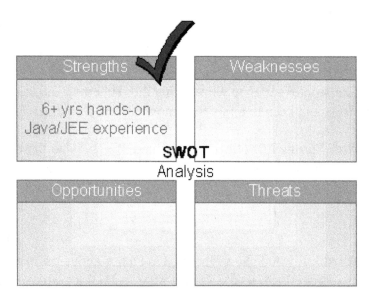

You need to highlight not only your technical strengths but also non-technical strength like domain knowledge, interpersonal skills, good understanding of full software development life cycle (aka. SDLC), analytical skills, problem solving skills, and documentation and presentation skills. Remember what I said before, technical skills and knowledge alone can be easily replaced, but not the well-rounded ability with both technical & non-technical skills.

Knowing your strengths will help you present yourself in a better light. Your resume, job interviews, code review sessions, daily stand-ups, project retrospective meetings, etc give you a great opportunity to sell your strengths.

Example(s):

- Over **9 years of programming experience** with numerous technologies of which 5+ **years in .NET** based applications, and integrating them with the distributed systems like Vignette (CMS), Salesforce (CRM), data warehouse, and many other internal legacy and non-legacy systems.

- Proven track record of delivering quality PHP based systems and solutions in the Investment, Insurance, Finance, and Telecom industries with over 6 years of experience at the **Brand-name** consultancy.

- Experienced in design and development of 3 to n-tier architectures to integration of legacy and non-legacy applications via daily feeds, proprietary protocols, Service Oriented Architectures (SOA), message oriented middle-wares and BPM products.

- Managed a Java/JEE based project with both on site and off-shore development and delivery effort of a team consisting of ~25 developers resulting in successful delivery of the end product both within budget ($12 million) and on time.

- Received an award for exceptional performance in the project for building several custom components and delivery frameworks to save time, cost, and development effort in addition to promoting code reuse and easier maintenance.

- Increased the number of JUnit tests from **30+ to 800+ in my watchful eye** to improve the overall quality of the application.

- Performed 10-12 hour shifts as and when required to get the project over the line.

- Conceptualized and implemented a large scale multi-threaded socket server to communicate with 450 retail stores and seamlessly integrated it with 3 other back end systems via Web services and asynchronous messaging..

- Served on the 3 person core technical team to analyze process improvements,

169

develop training systems, define design goals and directions, and fulfill resource requirements.

- Instrumental in coordinating development activities among a multidisciplinary team of 3 business analysts, 22 developers, 2 project managers, 1 infrastructure analyst, and 8 testers at GHF Ltd.

- Took on the acting project manager role with added responsibilities.

Standout factor(s):

- Highlights your wealth of experience.

- Exemplifies your expertise in specific domains like Finance, Insurance, etc.

- Demonstrates your architectural skills in 3-tier architecture, integration, etc. Also highlights the next big thing for many companies like SOA, BPM, and Cloud computing.

- Demonstrates your ability to manage and lead large development teams and also illustrates that you have a good understanding of full software development life cycle.

- Shows that you have experience in designing large mission critical (e.g. $9.0 million) systems.

- Illustrates that you are a quality conscious developer.

- Illustrates your ability to adapt well within the team.

- Demonstrates your ability to work in a dynamic and fast paced development environments.

- Implies that you are a self-starter, can work under pressure, can adopt new technologies, frameworks, and processes quickly and a team player with a "can do" attitude.

- Highlights your skills and experience in the integration space. All large scale enterprise applications require some form of integration with other disparate systems.

- Developing frameworks requires good understanding of the fundamentals and strong technical skills. Hence this highlights your technical strength.

- Shows that you can take on extra responsibilities.

For job seekers with little or no experience: (e.g. graduates, career changers, etc)

Example(s):

- BSc in Computer Science with First Class Honors.

- 3 months hands-on experience with Spring 2.0, Hibernate 3.0, and JSF due to self-taught project on a library management system, for which URL is <myapp URL>. Other artifacts are available on request, and keen to apply this knowledge and exposure in a commercial project.

- Completed my university thesis with a Java 1.5, Servlet, JSP, OOA, OOD, OOP, design patterns, and SQL based online library management system using MySQL database.

- Self-starter and a quick learner, which are evident from my self-taught project at <URL> and also have blogged my thoughts and experience at <link to my blog>.

- Demonstrated my interpersonal skills, adaptability, and ability to work as a team through university group assignments, 2 year part-time and casual employment, raising funds for the charity, and organizing cultural events. References are available on request.

Standout factor(s):

- Puts more credibility and shows that you are a pro-active learner. Also highlights your impressive score. If your score is not that impressive, then do not include it.

- Shows that you are keen to use sought after technologies like Spring, Hibernate, etc.

- Highlights some of the key software development and Java related technologies like Servlets, SQL, OOA, etc and your familiarity with it.

- Illustrates your ability to learn things quickly and be a self-starter. This can be a big plus for projects on tight schedules, limited budget, and resources.

- When you are competing with candidates who have the same qualification, it is absolutely vital that you have just more than formal education. So, you can distinguish yourself from your competition by illustrating your additional technical skills and hands-on experience gained through other means like self-taught tutorials and projects, open-source contribution, volunteer work, non-technical skills gained through part-time, casual and voluntary employment, charity work, organizing cultural events, taking part in sports and scouts, tutoring, public speaking, contribution to news letters, preparing marketing plans, writing reports, creating flyers or posters, handling difficult customers, and so on.

Credible

Make sure that information you provide in the resume is credible by mentioning the name of the company and if possible the URL of the web application you built. Also, be honest. I have seen resumes where candidates claim that they have 4+ years of experience when a particular technology or framework that had been there for only 2 years.

Example(s):

- Mentored junior developers by providing technical guidance and motivating them to meet the tight deadlines at **MQR Investment banking**.

- Developed a Struts, EJB, and Oracle database based online trading system for BB Trading systems. **URL**: http://sample.trading.systems.

Standout factor(s):

- Makes your claims more credible by mentioning the company name and URL of the Web application you built.

- You can also mention that "source code is available on request", for self-taught projects and "references are available on request" to make your claims more credible, but try not to over do it. If you have an online portfolio, upload your work and provide a link to it on your resume.

Concise and well formatted without spelling errors

Keep your resume as short as possible (i.e. 2 to 4 pages) unless you can write a resume that is 10 page long and you can keep the reader's undivided attention and interest that long. Unless you have a wide list of extra ordinary achievements, make it shorter. It is a mistake to think of your resume as the history of the past. If you have 15 years of experience and out of which first 8 years in some other field then you can summarize those eight years in a few lines as opposed to describing every job you held or task you performed in that period. Also, remember to put the most important information in the first line of the writing block or paragraph because the first line is read the most.

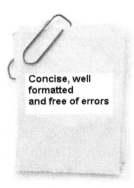

Concise, well
formatted
and free of errors

Example(s):

- Increased the number of JUnit tests from 30+ to 800+ in my watchful eye to improve the overall quality of the Java based application.

- Improved the overall web site performance by 40% at XYZ ltd.

Standout factor(s):

- Concise and easy to read with bare minimum required information.

- Concise and leave the prospective employer with a bit of mystery that how you achieved such a significant performance gain. Be prepared to explain, how you went about improving performance in your interview.

Resume formats

This is open to debate, but try to keep it simple.

- Font style should be 11 point Times New Roman or Arial. Headings could be up to 14 points.
- Avoid any kind of irrelevant graphics.
- If your resume is more than 1 page, place your name and phone number on every page as a header. At times pages can get separated.
- Make sure that your layout does not waste lot of space and is easy on the eyes.
- Use bold fonts very judiciously.

What not to put on your resume?

- Any thing that could turn off prospective employer. e.g. political or controversial.
- Salary information.
- Names of managers or supervisors.
- References.
- Reasons for leaving jobs.
- Fluffy statements, especially in the "Objective" section.
- Too much information in the "Contact Details" section.
- Improper or invalid e-mail addresses. **Tip:** Have a hotmail, gmail or yahoo email

address with your name. e.g. john.e@hotmail.com. Mention your blogs and websites.

No spelling or grammatical errors!! This is a must if you do not want your resume sent to the trash can.

Finally, it is not a good idea to have spelling errors in a resume or covering letter. Use the spell checker and also have several people read your resume to ensure that it is free of spelling and grammatical errors. You need to pay particular attention to technology because if you cannot spell it, do you really have enough experience of it to add it to your resume.

Would the first page stand on its own?

In reality, only first page of your resume is read and the remaining pages are scanned. So, you need to make sure that your resume's first page can stand on its own by capturing various key aspects described below. If the prospective employer or recruiter is motivated by the first page and interested in learning a bit more about you and your capabilities, he or she would scan through the additional pages.

Check points	Comments (example only, do your own review based on real job specifications)
Is the objective clearly defined?	The objective section is concise and it clearly states my career objective without any fluffy statements.
Does it clearly summarize my experience?	Yes it does. 3 years in Java/JEE, 8 months with sought-after technology A, and 1 year in finance domain.
Does it clearly summarize my technical skills?	Yes it does. The key required technologies like Java, Servlet, JSP, SQL, JDBC, etc and sought after frameworks like Spring, Hibernate, and JSF are captured not only in the technical summary section, but also emphasized in the objective and profile sections.
What are my selling points?	• Shows that I am committed to my chosen profession via open source contribution, part-time volunteer work, and self-taught projects. • Shows my awareness and passion for current

	trends. • Technical strengths like identifying and fixing issues that are hard to identify and reproduce are highlighted and quantified. • Promotes me as a well balanced professional with good soft skills and right attitude, which are evident from my promotion as a lead developer within 3 years.
Does it satisfy the prospective employer's job specification?	In general yes, but the most employers are asking for at least 1 year experience with framework X. I will continue to work on this and update my resume accordingly. I will try all the different avenues and hoping to make a break soon.
Does it promote me as a well–rounded candidate with both hard (technical) and soft (non-technical) skills? Does my resume reflect my personality?	Yes it does. • Taking on extra responsibilities at SomeFinance Ltd to meet the project deadlines. • Passion and taking initiatives to learn in my chosen career by contributing to open source projects and working on self-taught projects.
Do I have any fluffy statements that can be improved?	No. All of my statements are substantiated with where and how I acquired them.
Do I make my statements credible enough by mentioning a company name, URL, etc?	All my claims are backed up with where, when, how, URLs, and "source code available on request" statement.

What to do if you don't have all the essential and desirable requirements on the job specification?

All depend on how many of the other resumes received address all the requirements and also how strict the prospective employer is with a particular requirement. Certain requirements are more important to an employer than others.

• If it is a most sought-after requirement then make an effort to acquire it by applying it in your current job, self-taught projects, volunteer work, open source project, etc. It is better to have some level of exposure than to have nothing at all.

- If you are lacking in one or two areas, you will have to try to emphasize on the other areas a bit more with effective phrases.

- If you do not have an experience with a particular framework, middle-ware, or technology, but have used a similar framework, middle-ware, or technology then mention it. For example Tapestry instead of JSF, Tomcat or JBoss application server instead of Websphere.

- Finally, you can emphasize that you are a quick learner with work related examples. Counter any negative impact by pointing out a previous situation where you were thrown in at the deep end and you demonstrated a rapid learning curve. For example,

    - Awarded outstanding achievement for coming in just 2 months before the deadline in a development effort that was going on for 18 months to contribute significantly to fast track development where some home grown Java based frameworks and technologies had to be quickly learned.

Chronological vs. Functional resume formats

The chronological resumes are more common and widely accepted by employers. So, use functional resumes only if you are confident that skills-oriented format would exemplify your transferable skills to better advantage, but be sure to include a clear and concise chronological work history. In some countries, the functional resumes are not recommended, considered non-standard, and can be construed as the candidate is trying to hide something with a non-standard format.

Functional format is organized around skills and knowledge rather than positions held, and emphasize your abilities and achievements. This style can be useful where you:

- are making a career change.
- have had a career break or currently not in work.
- have worked in a number of different fields or careers.

Cover Letters

Best cover letters spark the prospective employer's interest and create an impression of competence. Keep it brief and to the point. Also, it needs to be customized to the job specification.

If the job is for a JEE architect, don't tell why your knowledge of CSS is important. You need to emphasize that you are a big picture person who is interested in how things fit in with the whole organization.

How to write an effective cover letter? Here is an example of an ordinary cover letter.

Dear Sir/Madam,

I am looking forward to a job, which matches my qualifications and where analytical skills & logical reasoning are involved. I am a hard worker towards achieving my goals. ………………..

Why the above cover letter is very ordinary?

- Firstly, where possible try to address to a specific individual. Use Sir/Madam only if you don't know who the recipient is. Secondly, you need to take the effort to customize your cover letter based on the job specification, rather than having a "one size fits all" cover letter.
- "I am looking forward to a job, which matches my qualifications…" It is better to say why your skills, experience, and capabilities are suited to the job than to just expect the employer to do this task for you. Employer would not spend more than 20 – 40 seconds on your cover letter & resume.
- "Analytical skills & logical reasoning are involved and I am a hard worker towards achieving my goals". Any one can write this and it is not clearly thought out. Prospective employers are normally interested in how you can achieve their goals not yours.
- "I am looking forward to a job, which matches my qualifications and where analytical skills". Also, shows that the candidate has not done any research on what the company does or eagerness to work for this particular company.

The above cover letter should have briefly mentioned the candidate's capabilities and how the candidate can contribute to the company and convey candidate's eagerness, if real, to work for the company. That's all that is required in a cover letter. Here is the revised example:

John Cover

Mobile: 0123 456 789, **e-mail**: john_intermediate@hotmail.com
Portfolio: www.john.cover.portfolio.com
Australian Citizen

Dear Mr. Abc, (where possible address to a specific individual)

(State position applied for)

As an IT professional with 10+ yrs of Java/JEE experience, I have successfully completed 16 projects for organizations like Big Brand1, Insurance 2, Retail 3, and Telecom 4. I do feel confident of the skills, knowledge, and capability I can bring to your opening for a senior Java/JEE developer.

(Sell yourself with professional summary and achievements)

Career Highlights:

- Experienced in leading(5+ yrs), designing(4+ yrs), developing(10+ yrs), and integrating(4+ yrs) mission critical Java/JEE based systems with other CRM (e.g. Siebel), CMS (e.g. Vignette), and message oriented middle-ware systems like Websphere MQ and webMethod.
- Proven ability in building Java/JEE systems with sought-after technologies/frameworks such as Spring, Hibernate, and JSF using agile development practices with the business focus.
- Extensive experience and take pride in identifying and fixing potential issues relating to performance, transaction management, security holes, memory/resource leaks, and concurrency issues.
- Proven track record in implementing best practices, good architectural principles, and design concepts at XYZ limited and PQR investment bank.
- In most cases, my efforts were recognized and rewarded.

Additional skills, experience, and capabilities are listed in the enclosed resume. Also, feel free to check my blog at http://java-success.blogspot.com. I would appreciate the opportunity to meet with you, in person, to discuss possible ways in which we could work together to provide innovative technical solutions. I can be reached at the number listed above.

Thank you for your attention.

Sincerely,

_____

John Cover
Senior Java/JEE developer

What do you do after submitting your application?

So, you had submitted your job application on time, the application closing date passed a week ago, and you still haven't heard a response? Reiterate your interest in the job with a follow-up phone call to your prospective employer or recruitment agency. Ask if your cover letter and resume were received and gently re-state your suitability for the job, which can increase your chances of being interviewed.

You can't get a job if you don't have enough experience, but how do you get enough experience, if no one is willing to give you one?

If you are a beginner or changing career, you will be caught in this vicious cycle. Most employers are interested in experience than education. Don't make the mistake of acquiring more academic qualifications by getting certified or enrolling for a post-graduate qualification. If the market is hot, a well-rounded candidate with a decent resume and little or no experience could easily walk into an interview, but during a difficult or an ordinary job market one needs to have a highly effective resume with at least 2 year experience. So, how do you beat this vicious cycle? Programming is like riding a car or a bicycle. The only way to break this viscous cycle is to gain some experience at least in the sought-after technologies and frameworks. This experience needs to be complimented with good job hunting, resume/portfolio writing, interviewing, and networking skills. Here are a few avenues to gain the much needed

180

hands-on experience.

- **Try voluntary work** through both non-profit and for profit organizations. Voluntary work shows commitment and initiative, even if it is not mentally stimulating. It can increase your industry knowledge, give you the much needed hands-on experience, enhance your soft skills, and give you something to write in your resume or portfolio without any **prolonged gap of employment**. Since the task of applying for a paid full-time position can take up considerable time, you could start working voluntarily 2-3 days a week, even weekends if required. Even if it does not involve your choice of programming languages like C# or Java, provided you can gain any other sought-after technical skills like SQL, XML,web development with HTML, CSS, and JavaScript, and more importantly valuable soft skills and domain knowledge that are easily transferable to your future dream job. Now, on a more positive note, while gaining hands-on experience and learning on the job, you will likely to uncover paid opportunities by being an excellent contributor with enthusiasm and personal growth or by networking with similar professionals you would not have met otherwise. Voluntary work is generally a win/win situation for both the employer and the employee. Even though larger brand name organizations may look more impressive on your resume/portfolio and can give you a greater chance of potential internal paid opportunities, smaller companies are more likely to offer you a voluntary work, and also in general, you will not only get to learn more things faster, but also your efforts will get noticed and recognized quicker. You can even try contacting your local charities or non-profit organizations for any potential opening to build a website for them. Don't be too concerned about the size or brand name of the organization, but pay more attention to type of skills, experience, and capabilities you will be gaining. Brand name or popularity may take you to the interview stage, but cannot guarantee success in interviews without the right knowledge, skills, capabilities, and experience. If you properly use the guidelines in this book, you can draw on your other strengths and achievements to look more impressive on your resume/portfolio than to just rely on the brand name or popularity of the organization.

- **Contribute to open source projects** to gain much needed hands-on experience in sought-after technologies and frameworks. The choices are plenty ranging from widely used products such as NetBeans, Eclipse, GlassFish, etc to smaller hobby projects, which have been open sourced by their developers. Pick the one depending on your level of experience, interest, and motivation. If your motivation is to learn sought-after frameworks like Spring & Hibernate, then pick a project that uses both. How do you benefit from open source project contributions?

- Gives you a pretty good big picture of different technologies, tools and frameworks used in a typical application.

- You get to read a lot of code and learn from it. You can not only learn the best practices, but also can understand how various artifacts fit together.

- Write your own small programs just to learn the languages and libraries used in the open source projects.

- Learn how to use the tools used for builds, dependency management, code repository, performance testing, security vulnerability testing, and regression testing.

- Experiment by making changes to your local copy of the code.

- **Self-taught projects and tutorials** to build up confidence and acquire some level of experience with the sought-after technologies and frameworks. Some open source projects can be a bit overwhelming for some beginners. So, choose carefully. Alternatively, you could take up some self-taught projects by using sought-after technologies and frameworks. While this can be an easier option, it is not easy to be disciplined and looks less impressive on your resume/portfolio compared to open source contribution. Having said that, this option is better than not doing anything at all. It at least, shows commitment and initiative with some level of familiarity with popular technologies and frameworks. Improve credibility by providing URL to your portfolio or mentioning availability of your source code in a digital media like CD. What is even better is that, if your self-taught project is based on a creative idea and if you think it can be useful to others, you can open source it or even try selling it.

Each approach has its own pros and cons. If you are a beginner and looking for work, voluntary work will not only give you the experience employers are looking for, but also can open doors for paid job opportunities. If you are already in an employment, and either not mentally challenged or not acquiring the required skills and experience, try contributing to open source projects. If you are not in much luck with first two options, and sitting idly or you have a bright idea, then try working on a self-taught project.

Some of the beginners and unemployed are more tempted to get back to school doing a post-graduate study or inclined to gain additional training or certifications with a view of improving their employment prospects. This may not be a bad idea especially for someone who has no basic degree, but for degree holders, this has a lesser chance of improving their short term employment prospects because this won't give you the experience and personal growth what the prospective employers are looking for, and will look less impressive on your resume compared to more hands-on experience driven accomplishments. Academic qualifications should go hand-in-hand with practical experience. Professional experience can help one better identify his or her strengths, weaknesses, and interests, and align appropriately his or her future educational needs. Knowledge is essential, but what is more important is to know how to put it to work because doing is how you learn and how you ultimately prove yourself.

Learning the design concepts and design patterns may look easy enough, until you try to apply it. Once you start applying it in real projects, your knowledge entirely takes a new dimension. Learning gives you the information to act on something, while doing not only makes you proficient at what you had learned, but also helps you learn more things effortlessly. So, don't get overwhelmed by the number of technologies and frameworks relating to a particular enterprise technology. It may look daunting at the beginning, but if you put both learning patiently alongside of applying what you had learned pro-actively and courageously to practice, you will slowly see yourself getting on top of things. You will also start to notice significant improvements in your ability to learn and grasp fundamentals, newer technologies and emerging frameworks. You will soon start to identify potential issues relating to the key areas like performance, concurrency control, transaction management, security holes, etc like the real experienced professionals do to make their marks. These key areas were the motivation for my interview companion book. No book can help you master this, without really experiencing it yourself. Books give you the information and raise the awareness, but it is up to you to act on that piece of information to make it work for you by experiencing when to apply, when not to apply, how to apply, where to apply, what the pros and cons are, and what the potential risks are as things are not black and white in the real world.

How do you showcase your experience acquired via avenues mentioned above?

You do this by creating an online portfolio. In this digital media age, there are so many open-source tools to create a simple website that contains your resume and links to your work, blog, and online profiles. Include the URL to your portfolio site on your resume. This will distinguish you from thousands of other similar job applicants. Your work could include code you wrote, web layouts you had designed, PowerPoint presentations with conceptual diagrams, UML diagrams, and entity-relationship diagrams, issues you had fixed, problems you had solved, applications you developed, etc. When you go to an interview, you could take your code in a CD and an old fashioned paper portfolio containing screen shots of your application you developed, UML diagrams, entity relationship diagrams for the database design, and conceptual diagrams. Not all interviewers will want to view your paper portfolio, but it is a good thing to relate your answers to open-ended interview questions like tell me about yourself to information and samples contained in your portfolio. This will back up your knowledge with actual proof, lending credibility to your work.

Today, you have many choices to create your website from building your own to using open source tools or web design tools provided by your hosting companies. For example

- http://www.portfoliopen.com/
- Blogs: http://wordpress.com or http://blogger.com
- Combine your personal web pages, blogs, and social network profiles with http://ning.com.

The blogs will show off your technical skills, writing skills, and communication skills. Most importantly it shows that you are passionate about your field and sets you apart from all the other programmers. A few minutes on Google will reveal a lot more about creating online portfolios and blogs.

Do you think you are expending 100% of your job search effort by responding to only online and newspaper advertisements?

Job hunting can be emotionally exhausting, especially if the search lasts for a long time. You can increase your chances of finding a job by casting a wider net, writing an effective resume, practicing your interview techniques, and brushing up on the fundamentals. If you rely only on advertised positions through newspapers and online job-sites, you are not only expending 100% of your effort on 25% to 60% of the possibilities, but also will be competing with many other professionals who use the same avenue. It is better to diversify your job search by trying through different channels. A real job search has following main markets:

- **Published Job Market:** Review job leads via offline advertisements in printed news papers, journals, etc and online advertisements through job banks, job networks, recruiter websites, and industry specific forums. This is a very important, but highly competitive and most common channel.

- **Hidden Job Market:** This channel allows you to apply for a job that has not been advertised, and can improve your chances of getting a job by tapping into 40% to 75% of the market. If it has not been advertised, then less people will know about, which means that you are competing against fewer people. The hidden job market is a numbers game and more people are working on your behalf (e.g. friends, former colleagues, former managers, former acquaintances, and recruitment agents), more applications you send out, more phone calls you make, and more targeted your efforts are, the better chance you will have finding a job. You can tap into this market in a variety of ways as described below.

  - **Networking:** Start by asking your existing network, past employers, recruitment agents, past colleagues, friends, etc. It is vital that you build up your network as you progress in your career. Next, expand your network through paid or unpaid work in your field by registering with online network sites like http://www.linkedin.com/, joining relevant professional associations, attending conferences, attending user group events, taking part in industry specific forums, attending career (or job) fairs, etc. Unless there is an urgency to fill the position, employers prefer to try their networks first and rely on referrals to find the right person. Referrals are basically the most popular method in the hidden job market and recruitment agencies' worst nightmare. Referrals can not only save money in advertising cost and commissions, but also can save valuable time in advertising and finding the right person. The resumes brought in via referrals do get a better attention. While networking, remember to apply dedication not desperation.

Write effective resumes to open doors

- **Unsolicited applications:** Make a list of employers you would like to work for and send your cover letter and resume to express your interest in working for them. If you wish to use this method, it's important to target each application carefully and remember to follow up with a phone call or call before sending the application to ensure that some contact has been made prior to your details appearing before someone in print or via email.

- **Cold calling or direct contact:** Cold calling (over the phone or in person) means approaching employers directly and preferably by establishing relationships with people who work for the organization through previous networking activities, to make this technique less daunting. I generally prefer building up a good rapport with a selected number of recruitment agents who had represented me in the past, and getting them to cold call on my behalf. Alternatively, you can contact a number of recruitment agents in your local area and sell your accomplishments along with an impressive resume to perform door knocking on your behalf. This can result in a win/win situation for both. Carefully prepare what you are going to say and be ready to answer some preliminary questions about what you have to offer the organization. Have your resume up to date and tailored to the job you're targeting.

Looking for a job is a long term investment and it is important to develop all the required experience and skills not only in your chosen career, but also in job hunting like writing an effective resume, self-promotion, telephone technique, high-level researching ability, and networking. Remain positive and get busy with applying all different techniques and tips. Perseverance and action are critical to any job hunting efforts and learn to accept rejection. At times it may be necessary to settle for a job that is unpaid, entry-level, less challenging, temporary, less convenient, etc to get your foot in the door. Once you get a foot in the door, you can work harder and smarter with confidence, enthusiasm, and positive attitude to fast-track your career to be where you wanted to be.

Trying via "Jobs Wanted" forums

There are a number of industry specific forums where you can let the industry know that you are looking for work. For example, jobs.dzone.com, www.coderanch.com/forums/f-36/Jobs-Wanted, etc.

I often see in the "Jobs Wanted" forums, where potential job seekers don't really take the effort to promote themselves more effectively. Firstly, they post their threads with very ordinary titles like "Java Job Wanted" or "Certified programmer looking for Java Work". Secondly, if you click on the title half-halfheartedly, there is no evidence of a link to your resume and portfolio highlighting your experience and achievements. Many fail to realize that they are in a very competitive world out there and they are needed to do something different to standout from others who have done exactly the same thing. Here is an example of an "ordinary forum thread" versus an "improved forum thread"

Ordinary Thread:

Title: want Java Job (SCJP)

Content:

I am a Sun certified software engineer with 3+ years of experience, presently located in New York.

I have worked with Java 1.4, 1.5, Eclipse, JavaScript, JUnit, HTML/CSS, Ajax, XML, SQL, Websphere, and Oracle 9i. I am looking for a suitable job in Java/JEE.

I will be obliged if anyone can contact me via private messages or candidate_name@hotmail.com.

Improved Thread:

Title: 4+ yrs track record in Java/JEE – 7 projects completed

Content:

Career Highlights

- 4+ years of hands-on experience in building B2B, B2C, and multi-threaded stand-alone Java/JEE applications and batch processes.

- Successfully completed 7 Java/JEE projects at XYZ Limited and PWG consulting, taking them all the way from requirements gathering to release.

- Highly resourceful in migrating poorly performing Web services by applying strong attention to detail at XYZ Limited.

- Took the initiative and refactored a single threaded polling driven module to an industrial strength multi-threaded module that not only scaled well to growing demand, but also fixed an intermittent stability issue.

- Effectively promoted best practices, design concepts, and agile development practices to build solutions that not only met current requirements, but also adapted well to changing business needs at PWG Consulting.

Presently located in New York, and my portfolio and resume are available at http://www.candidate.com. I have also blogged my experience at myblog.com and can be contacted via private messages or email: candidate_name@hotmail.com.

Once you have an impressive title, pay attention to writing a summary that will motivate the prospective employer to learn more about you via the URL you provide to your portfolio site and blog. [**Don't provide a link to unprofessional or not fully developed blog or website.**]

Even though the job hunting is a numbers game, it needs to be targeted. For example, I do get many linkedin invites from fellow professionals whom I never worked with. Only a very few invites are targeted by saying why they want to link with me like read my books, blogs, worked with a colleague of mine, etc. I always accept the targeted invites. The majority of them are not targeted with just a default message, and whether I accept it or not depends on my mood at that time.

Section-5:

Open more doors by knowing what the prospective

employers are looking for

Understanding what the prospective employers are looking for will help you identify the areas you need changing or improving to open more doors and go places. Even though it is written mainly from a job interview perspective, many of the qualities are very much applicable in your regular job as well. Put yourself in your prospective employers' shoes. If you were a prospective employer, who are the people you want to have in your team.

- People who are technically competent with good grasp of the core concepts in the 16 technical **key areas**.

- People who are passionate about their work and have the right attitude.

- People who demonstrate ability to learn quickly, research, analyze, and problem-solve.

- People who can communicate, work as a team, be flexible, think from both business and technical perspective, and most importantly get things done with the potential to mentor and lead.

- People who can look at things from both technical and business perspective.

Open more doors by knowing what the prospective employers are looking for

Knowing what the prospective employers are looking for.

Before you read any further, imagine yourself as a prospective employer or interviewer for the rest of this discussions, even if you are not an interviewer. Analyze what type of candidates you would like to have in your team. Would you prefer well-rounded contributors or just techies? Some of the ensuing discussions are inspired by a thought-provoking article by Joel Spolsky at http://www.joelonsoftware.com/.

Job interviews are not technical contests to see who gets the most questions right. It is all about ascertaining

- If you have the right technical skills with the good grasp of the fundamentals.
- If you could get the job done with the "pride of performance" as opposed to "fear of consequences".
- If you would be really interested in the role on offer and the organization. For example, some commercial organizations do have locked down environments, and a passionate open-source developer would feel too restricted to his/her liking as frameworks or tools of his/her choice cannot be readily installed and used.
- If you would fit in well with the team.

If you hire someone who is passionate about their work, you will probably get a better worker, someone who comes to work wanting to do a good job, rather than someone who just sees each day as waiting for the weekend. But you might also occasionally get challenged by someone who is not a team player, inflexible, not approachable, perfectionist, and/or can't look at things from others' perspective. For example, someone with the wrong attitude like I would rather write some code than wasting my time attending a business requirements gathering meeting. A well-rounded approach to interviewing with different types of questions can help you distinguish just techies from well-rounded contributors with the right attitude to get the job done. It will also differentiate people who memorize their answers from those who really talk from their experiences and real grasp of the core concepts. Let's look at these types of questions in more detail as it can help you prepare for your job interviews in software engineering.

Open-ended questions

Open-ended questions can reveal a lot about a prospective hire. Open-ended questions are good ice breakers as people are usually comfortable talking about their own work.

For example,

- Tell us about yourself?

  [**Hint**: Focus on your strengths and marry up your strengths with the job specification. For example, 5 year hands on experience in building web based applications to integrating disparate systems using web services, messaging, and XML based technologies; completed 3 projects through full SDLC process using sought-after technologies X, Y, and Z, and frameworks P and Q in 2 of those projects; one of the projects is a mission critical transactional system that handles 300 concurrent users; experience at X, enhanced my skills in SOA based architectures and stand-alone scheduled batch jobs using bulk loads and ETL operations.]

- Tell us about the most satisfying project you worked on in the last year? What were your contributions?

  [**Hint**: Rewriting the whole batch process framework that not only used to take 17 hours to run but also was very hard to maintain as changing one part of the code can break another part of the application. The re-written batch framework with introduction of modular design, multi-threading, distributed caching, and tuned SQL statements, and revised database tables completes in under 3 hours. My contributions involved designing the solution and leading the development.]

- What are the challenges you faced both technically and non-technically in your past assignments?

  [**Hint**: Fixing performance, thread safety, transactional issues and security holes, spearheading process improvements, taking the initiatives to close the gaps in business requirements, convincing the management with the open-source adoption, streamlining the release and deployment processes, and getting the business users to agree on alternative solutions.]

- Why do you like software development?

  [**Hint**: Passion for building things, and satisfaction you get in seeing all the technical key areas like design, design patterns, thread safety, performance, security, etc fit together like a puzzle. Solving problems relating to above mentioned key areas gives me a sense of accomplishment. Like the fact that one needs to look at the big picture as well as pay attention to details. It is also quite interesting to look at things from both business/end user perspective (e.g. user interface design, ease of use, how the business operates) and technical perspective. Derive pleasure in working with people to get things done in a team environment by collaborating, mentoring, and facilitating to get things over the line.]

When you ask open-ended questions, you can sit back and start assessing some of the technical and non-technical qualities you would want in your potential hire with occasional "can you please elaborate on a particular point?" if they are relevant to the position you are hiring for or an important quality you are looking for. Here are a few things you can look for during open-ended questions.

- **Passion**: Good caliber candidates are passionate about the projects they worked on and their past accomplishments. They get very exited talking about the challenges and problems they faced and how they went about solving them. Great engineers know when a small piece of code is shaping up perfectly and when the **key areas** and the pieces of a large system start to fit together like a puzzle. They derive pleasure and take pride in building quality software that meets business needs. Bad candidates just don't care and will not get enthusiastic at all. While interviewing, ascertain not only if the candidate loves to code, but also will the candidate love to code what you want him or her to code? Will the candidate believe in the project or application? Will it excite him or her?

- **Ability to get things done**: Better candidates are not just techies. So, you need to distinguish between candidates who are only passionate about their technical achievements and who take pride in both technical and non-technical contributions in the best interest of the project. Some technically competent candidates can drag the whole team down. They fail to look at the bigger picture. They hate meetings, writing documents, holding conversations with the infrastructure guys and liaising with the business. They prefer being glued to their key boards and want things to be done their way. They are religious about using the frameworks, libraries, and languages of their choice as opposed to willing and able to learn new ways of building systems or adhering to the corporate standards and policies. So, you may want to weed-out those types of candidates who are technically very good, but lack much needed soft-skills and personal attributes to get things done in a team environment. In a real world, things won't always go to plan. For example, requirements might not be clear, getting things done tactically to meet immediate business objectives is more important than getting it done strategically, initiatives need to be taken to get things moving, challenging problems need to be solved in collaboration, deadlines need to be met, etc. So, you will have to ask more questions targeting those areas. For example,

- What do you do when the requirements are not clear?

  [**Hint**: take initiatives to get it clarified and properly documented. Conduct workshops, meetings, and brain storming sessions to gather requirements. Clearly document your assumptions, potential risks, impacts, and mitigation strategies.]

- How would you proceed if you had been assigned a task that involves an unknown technology or business domain?

  [**Hint**: Learn by doing a quick tutorial and grasping its fundamentals. Seek others' help. Take it as a challenge. For example, had to collaborate with the access control team that looks after Siteminder to get SSO (Single-Sign-On) working for our application.]

- In your experience, what are some of the harder issues to resolve, and how would you go about resolving them?

  [**Hint**: Thread-safety and transactional issues. A better candidate will also touch on non-technical challenges like effectively managing changing requirements, proactively gathering requirements, and taking the initiatives to closing the gaps in requirements and technical design. They may also touch on implementing agile practices, recognizing the importance of collaborative effort, following up with the business for clarification or convincing the business with simpler and more effective solutions to meet their requirements. For example, identified an intermittent database deadlock issue by emulating user experience under load, and fixed it by adding deadlock retry service interceptors to address intermittent database lockouts and service outages.]

- Describe the types of teams you have worked in, and tell me what worked well and what did not?

[**Hint**: Team with generalists and specialists who complement each other to achieve a common goal. Team that engages relevant agile practices for better communication and corporation. Well balanced team with right technical skills and good soft skills. Team that hires good caliber people via rigorous screening process.

A team that blame each other, a team that does not communicate well with each other, a team that says "I did it" instead of "we did it", etc]

- What was the hardest "sell" of an idea or method you have had to make to get it accepted?

[**Hint**: Adoption of open-source technologies and agile development practices. Quick win strategies to enhance user experience and website rankings. Convinced the business and the management to rewrite an application as opposed to providing a band-aid solution.

Good programmers are open to new ideas and constructive criticisms. Most importantly communicate their ideas effectively in simple terms with examples, mockups, demonstration, diagrams, and analogy]

- Ability to **communicate** with both technical and non-technical staff: Better candidates have the ability to express their ideas and solutions in simple terms. They can hold effective conversations with the stakeholders, end users, and business analysts regarding the business needs, infrastructure personnel about the platforms and networks, and the designers about the baseline architecture. You can assess a candidate's ability to communicate in simple terms by asking questions like:

  - Can you draw me a high level architecture of the system you were involved in your last or current position?

  [**Hint**: Good candidates are careful to explain things well in simple terms that even a non-technical person can understand. They will start by drawing a simple box diagram of the architecture and elaborate it further based on their target audience – business goals achieved, design alternatives, design decisions, lessons learned, protocols & data formats used, concepts & patterns applied, development methods used, choice of frameworks, etc.]

- Explain how the solution added value to your business and what was the business problem that it solved?

  [**Hint**: Better customer experience by fully automating a number of manual and partially automated systems. Less error-proneness and much shorter lead times leading to more loyal customers, and much happier support staff.]

- Look for **analytical**, **problem solving,** and **researching** skills: Developing a software always has its challenges, and things don't work smoothly in most cases. A better candidate should have skills to divide complex problems into smaller manageable tasks and apply good analytical, researching, problem solving and step-by-step approach to solve bigger problems and challenges in a collaborative effort. A good understanding of the technical key areas will improve a prospective candidate's engineering skills. You can ascertain this from questions like,

  - Tell me about an instance where you had to solve a complex design issue and how did you go about solving it?

    [**My experience**: A customer order with a complex life cycle of state changes like pending, authorized, completed, canceled, amended, partially filled, rejected, purged, etc had to be managed properly by capturing the state changes. A state chart diagram was created to capture and clarify things. Broke the problem into more manageable tasks. Did my own research to get a better understanding and others' perspectives on the problem. Used process flow, sequence, and state diagrams to get better clarity and presented it effectively to others to ensure that we are on the same page. Prepared a matrix highlighting all possible "what if" scenarios. Wrote down the possible solutions. Analyzed the pros and cons of each solution. Listed how my solution addressed each scenario.]

  - Have you ever been assigned a task of optimizing an application, and how did you go about it?

    [**My experience**: Complex online reports generation clogged up the application with high CPU usage. Converted the report generation process to be asynchronous by submitting the report requests captured via online GUI to a queue, and having a separate process pickup from the queue to generate the report asynchronously and make the report available either via emails or file downloads. The report generation failures are reported via emails.]

[**Hint**: Understand user behaviors and gather load requirements. Monitor the application and gather metrics. Identify and isolate any similar patterns or behaviors. Simulate the load in a non-production environment using tools like JMeter to gather benchmarks. Profile the application under simulated load. Identify the bottlenecks. Fix the bottlenecks through relevant design changes, configuration changes, and code changes. Run your simulated load tests again, and compare the results against the benchmarks. Document the results for future tuning and reference.]

• What are the critical factors you look for in evaluating the work of others?

[**Hint**: Ability to look at the bigger picture and drill down to details. Ability to get things done methodically by keeping things simple and asking the right questions – what if an exception is thrown?, What if this method gets accessed by multiple-threads?, etc. Passion to write quality code by constantly improving on the "first-cut" or draft code with proper test cases. Motivation to use code quality and unit test coverage tools like Sonar.]

Note: Remember the fact when you talk about others, the interviewers are thinking about your suitability.

• Describe a situation in which you had to solve a problem without having all the information you needed - what did you do and what happened?

[**Hint**: In larger organizations, knowledge and expertise are scattered. Collaborate within and outside your team to gather relevant information. Organize meetings and send emails requesting for relevant documentation. Conduct work shops and brainstorming sessions to pick others' brains. Come up with all possible causes. A cause effect diagram can come in handy for more complex problems. Identify and isolate possible causes,

196

and try to reproduce it by emulating the real life scenarios with appropriate load.]

Many job interview candidates don't like open-ended questions. This is because many don't prepare for these types of questions. I thrive on open-ended questions as it gives me a great opportunity to sell myself based on the job requirements.

Technical questions

Technical questions are asked to ascertain a candidate's understanding of the fundamentals. A candidate who has a good understanding of the core concepts can learn a new piece of technology, framework, or a tool a lot quicker. A new piece of technology or framework can become obsolete in 1-2 years. So, it is usually better to hire candidates who understand the core concepts and the key areas, and can quickly learn other things, rather than someone who happens to know how a particular framework works or how to deploy an application to a particular server right this minute.

- In an exception, why do we use *ex.printStackTrace( )*, and why is it called a stack trace?

  [**Hint**: A better candidate will not only state that a stack is based on Last In First Out (LIFO) data structure, but also will touch on other details like each thread will have its own stack, and method calls are popped into a stack as they are entered and popped out of a stack as they exit. When an exception is thrown, the information in the stack is printed on the basis of LIFO for debugging purpose.]

This may not always be the case as some requirements may require specific skills and experience with a particular framework/technology to meet tight deadlines or impart knowledge to rest of the team members, who are relatively inexperienced.

Please bear in mind that the approach and the thought process are as important as, if not more important than the details. Don't ask any questions that require memorizing the answers. Prefer asking practical questions that verifies a candidate's thinking, reasoning, and problem solving ability. Questions like what is a unified class loader in JBoss? or what is the difference between *"ClassNotFoundException"* and *"NoClassDefinition-Exception"*? serves no real purpose. Who cares what the difference is? You can just Google and find the answer within two minutes. It is also a futile attempt to ask tricky questions or questions requiring memorizing relating to APIs or libraries. Good caliber candidates not only have good researching skills, but also understand the importance of having the required API documentation handy while coding to reuse proven and well-tested methods as opposed to reinventing the wheel and compromising on robustness, maintainability, and readability of the code by writing their own. Identify candidates with these important traits.

- Is there a default comparator for String, Integer, Float, etc?

  [**Hint**: Check the Java Doc API for *String*, *Integer*, and *Float* classes. Examine the interfaces they implement. Check the field summary for type *Comparator*. Also, worth looking at the *Comparable* interface for their natural ordering.]

A technically competent developer must have a good grasp of the technical **key areas** like language fundamentals, OO concepts, design patterns, concurrency management, transaction management, performance considerations, memory management, exception handling, writing maintainable and testable code, etc. It is also true that a smart candidate can learn quickly and apply these key areas to develop commercial systems. But we all have limited resources like time, and budget, and it takes experience, time, and most importantly proactive learning to get a good handle on these key areas. We all have deadlines to meet and systems to be delivered with best possible quality. So, it is important to hire candidates who already know the fundamentals in these key areas they need to know and know it well. For example,

- Show a piece of code for a class that is not thread-safe, and get the candidate to explain if he or she could fix the issue. Ask the candidate to talk through the approaches and see if he/she touches on synchronization, immutability, and atomic operations. At times, it is more important to know about the alternatives, pros, cons, and how to go about arriving at a solution than to have the right answer instantly due to time limitation and interview nervousness. Prompt the candidate with open questions like how would he/she go about identifying and fixing concurrency issues.

Most candidates think that they can design systems, but only a few can explain in detail with good examples, alternative approaches, pros and cons of each approach and trade-offs. Better candidates understand the importance of gathering requirements prior to start designing a system, and consequently probe the interviewer(s) with more intelligent questions like:

- How many users are likely to use the system simultaneously?
- What transactional volume should the system handle?
- Should the system be highly available (e.g 99.99%)?
- Are there any disparate systems in a heterogeneous environment to be integrated to behave and appear as a single homogeneous system?

Better candidates will also go on to think aloud about the design constraints and key considerations of the system, and continue to ask themselves and others many other questions like:

- Are we going to use the existing infrastructure or build a new one? How many servers are required to handle 2000 concurrent users? Do we need non-stop servers (e.g. HP non-stop servers) for high availability? Where are the disaster recovery servers going to be hosted?
- How is the system going to be monitored and audited? (e.g. NAGIOS, database triggers, splunking the log files, etc)
- How are we going to gather performance metrics? (e.g Introscope, HP SiteScope, etc)
- How is the system going to interact with other disparate systems? What protocols (e.g. HTTPs, SFTP, SMTP, etc) and data formats (e.g. JSON, XML, CSV, etc) to be used? What frameworks and technology stacks to use?
- Should we build a new service/system or can we tap into, extend, or buy an existing services/system?
- What messages need to use a guaranteed delivery mechanism? What operations need to be atomic? Should it be synchronous or asynchronous? Should it be event-driven, scheduled, or constantly polled?
- How to handle exceptional conditions? What service timeout values to use? Can services be retried? If yes, how many retries are acceptable?
- What cross-cutting concerns like logging, auditing, transaction demarcation, gathering performance metrics, security, dead lock or service retry need to be implemented via aspect-oriented programming, dynamic proxies, or interceptors? Do we required dead-lock or service retry interceptors? Do we need to handle concurrent updates to prevent dirty reads?
- Do we require CORS for JavaScript based cross domain ajax requests?

These questions need to be answered in collaboration with the relevant experts in a multidisciplinary team environment. Alternatives need to be considered with pros and

Open more doors by knowing what the prospective employers are looking for

cons in terms of maintainability, scalability, extendability, time to market, and budget. Experienced professionals also understand the importance of building a prototype as a proof of concept and the need to improve it in successive design iterations. So, prioritize candidates based on his/her experience and detailed analysis/approach.

Identify candidates who understand and had applied the best practices like using immutable objects where possible as they are thread-safe and easier to debug. Look for candidates who favor using proven design concepts, principles, patterns and frameworks where it really makes sense to do so.

Scenario based questions

Scenario based questions can judge a prospective candidate's real experience and analytical skills. Some candidates have real 3 year experience, whilst others repeat their first year's experience 3 times. The experienced candidates are most likely to develop efficient, robust, and appropriate solutions to the given problems by drawing up ideas from their past experience. For example,

*   If you have a stand-alone Java based application that is not meeting the service level agreements (i.e. SLAs), how would you go about resolving it?

    [**Hint**: The cause could vastly vary. It could be due to a bad SQL performing a full table scan, a bad physical database design without proper indexing or partitioning, or a frequent back tracking of a regular expression. It could be due to lack of memory, under utilization of CPU, or not enough sockets or file handles due to resource leaks. So, simulate the load by setting up load tests, profile your application, and identify the root cause.]

*   The Java application you had just built is facing performance issues. How would you go about identifying the bottlenecks without using any commercial profiling tools?

    [**Hint**: Unix (e.g. iostat, netstat, vmstat, etc) or Win32 system tools to monitor system resources like CPU, memory, sockets, and number of threads. JMX console to monitor garbage collection and usage of threads, memory, and cpu. Write your own performance monitoring classes using dynamic proxies, aspect oriented programming (AOP), and interceptors. Using open-source profiling tools like Net Beans IDE and Visual VM]

- If you have been assigned the task of designing a stand-alone Java based host server that needs to talk to about 250+ petrol sites, how would you go about designing it?

[**Hint**: Gather functional and non-functional requirements. Identify the communication protocols and message formats between the client and server. Identify internal and external back end systems that need to be integrated. Draw a proposed solution diagram. Identify all the key components of the solution. Identify the design alternatives, and analyze pros and cons of each alternative. Describe how each high level requirement is going to be addressed by the overall solution and its components. Make a decision on technology stack and frameworks to be used. Identify the data requirements, and come up with logical and physical ER (Entity-Relationship) diagrams. Build a vertical slice for a typical use case as a proof of concept for the baseline architecture. Revise and improve on your design in the successive iterations.]

Note: Strike a good balance between being paralyzed by too much analysis to the point to get nothing done or over complicating things and no analysis at all to build a system that does not serve its purpose properly. A good upfront analysis with constant revision and improvement in an iterative manner can not only get things moving, but also is more conducive to better designs as things become clearer from previous iterations or cycles.

- What would you take into consideration in designing an application that has heavy or stringent logging requirements?

[**Hint**: Asynchronous logging is an option. Main application writes to a queue. A second process on a separate machine or the same machine retrieves the messages and write them to a database.

Database triggers can be used to audit inserts, updates, and deletes to a history table in the same database. This is more suited for transactional data to maintain a history of changes.

Creating your own logging class and appender information using the Log4j framework to manage the granularity. In some applications, contextual logging is very beneficial, and Log4j provides a useful feature called Mapped Diagnostic

Contexts or MDC.]

- What would you take into consideration in handling heavy report generation requirements?

  [**Hint**: **Divide and conquer strategy:** Report generation can be resource intensive. So, carefully divide the requirements into online reports and scheduled reports. Bulk report generation can be scheduled to be performed during off-peak (e.g. after midnight) and made available later via email or online downloads. Where possible, restrict the online report data period to say past 12 to 24 months. Reports requiring data older than 12 to 24 months (i.e. historical reports) can be scheduled. A better database partitioning with last 24 months' data in the current active partitioning and archiving data older than 24 months to de-normalized tables for reporting will contribute to better performance.

  When there is a compelling need to provide instant online reporting, the report generation can be off-loaded to a separate server. The online reports can be requested from the main website, but queued and scheduled to be processed asynchronously during off peak.]

- If you have a myapp.properties configuration file for your Java application, how would you go about updating your cache as soon as a property in the configuration file is updated?

  [Hint: **Automatic-update:** Write a file monitor thread that monitors the configuration file for any changes and updates the cache. This could be a JMX managed thread.

  Managed-update: Provide a web page when invoked will reload the cache from the configuration file. Alternatively, have a JMX MBean that will hot reload the .properties file when the *refresh( )* link is clicked via the JMX console by an admin staff.

  Apache's commons configuration framework should provide automatic and managed reloading of configuration files. If a configuration file is likely to be updated more frequently, a database or an ldap server might be a better choice to store the name/value pairs than a properties file.]

Coding questions

Check if the candidate understands the importance of writing maintainable and testable code by asking questions like how would you go about making your code testable?, how will you ensure code quality?, when are mock objects required, and how would you go about making your code easier to mock?

Coding questions can be used to identify a candidate's:

- ability to think logically.
- ability to write maintainable and testable code.
- motivation to write unit tests.
- experience to take key areas like performance, memory management, best practices, thread-safety, atomicity, etc into consideration.
- willingness to take constructive criticism and modify the code without the "I know it all" attitude. Also, look for eagerness to learn and aptitude to grasp things quickly.

Verify the correctness, smartness, and quickness in writing simple code. Good candidates will write the correct code first and then find ways to refactor the code for readability, testability, and maintainability. You cannot expect all the candidates to jump and cover all the five points shown above instantly, but you can go over all the points with a little prompting.

Better candidates will take key areas like performance, memory management, best practices, thread-safety, etc into consideration. While an experienced candidate understands that "premature optimization is the root of all evil", he or she also realizes the importance of performance considerations during coding to prevent "performance death by a thousand cuts". For example,

- A naive approach to spray *Vectors, Hashtables, and StringBuffers* instead of arrays, *ArrayLists*, *HashMaps,* and *StringBuilders* where synchronization is not required. Synchronization overkill can cause performance issues. The Java 5 concurrent collection classes like ConcurrentMap, Copy-On-Write lists and sets can provide better performance. Using the right data structure and initializing it with the right capacity can make your code more efficient.

Open more doors by knowing what the prospective employers are looking for

- Unnecessary instantiation of too many objects will cause garbage collection to run more frequently and consequently impact the response times. Favor using immutable objects where applicable, and reuse them. Think of the flyweight design pattern to improve object reuse through pooling.

- Badly written SQL queries and regular expressions can adversely impact performance by performing a full table scan and frequently back tracking respectively.

A good candidate will also touch on good coding practices like readability, maintainability, re-usability, extendability, and testability. Know the basic algorithms and data structures well. Make use of pseudo code and relevant diagrams to help with writing code.

Example 1:

Q. Write a program that will return whichever value is nearest to the value of 100 from two given int numbers.
A. You can firstly write the pseudo code as follows:

- Compute the difference to 100.
- Find out the absolute difference as negative numbers are valid.
- Compare the differences to find out the nearest number to 100.
- Write test cases for +ve, -ve, equal to, > than and < than values.

```
package chapter2.com;

public class CloseTo100 {

    public static int calculate(int input1, int input2) {
        //compute the difference. Negative values are allowed as well
        int iput1Diff = Math.abs(100 - input1);
        int iput2Diff = Math.abs(100 - input2);

        //compare the difference
        if (iput1Diff < iput2Diff) return input1;
        else if (iput2Diff < iput1Diff) return input2;
```

```
        else return input1;                    //if tie, just return one
    }

    public static void main(String[ ] args) {
        //+ve numbers
        System.out.println("+ve numbers=" + calculate(50,90));

        //-ve numbers
        System.out.println("-ve numbers=" + calculate(-50,-90));

        //equal numbers
        System.out.println("equal numbers=" + calculate(50,50));

        //greater than 100
        System.out.println(">100 numbers=" + calculate(85,105));
        System.out.println("<100 numbers=" + calculate(95,110));
    }
}
```

Output:

```
+ve numbers=90
-ve numbers=-50
equal numbers=50
>100 numbers=105
<100 numbers=95
```

Note: The main method is used for illustration purpose only, and in real practice write unit tests with proper assertions.

Example 2:

Q. Write a program that will return factorial of n?
A. Considerations:

- n! can be written as n * (n-1) * (n-2) ……... * 1. e.g. if n=5, n!= 5 * 4 * 3 * 2 * *1*
- factorials for negative numbers are undefined.
- 0! is equal to 1.

205

Open more doors by knowing what the prospective employers are looking for

- Should be able to handle factorials for large numbers like 20. So, use the right data type to avoid data overflow.
- Write test scenarios for 0, a larger value like 20, and a negative value.

This can be solved either iteratively or recursively (if supported by the language). Recursive functions are more suited in situations where the iterative approach will either be more complex or harder to understand (e.g. nested loops that are more than 2 levels deep). Recursive functions are more suited for composite objects having a tree or hierarchical structure. Here is the iterative solution in Java.

```java
package chapter2.com;

import java.math.BigInteger;

public class Factorial3 {

    public static BigInteger evaluate(long input) {
        if(input < 0) {
            throw new RuntimeException("Undefined for -ve: " + input);   // fail fast
        }
        if(input == 0) {
            return BigInteger.ZERO;
        }

        BigInteger result = BigInteger.ONE;

        while(input != 0) {
            result = result.multiply(BigInteger.valueOf(input));
            input = input - 1;
        }

        return result;
    }

    public static void main(String[ ] args) {
        //zero
        System.out.println("0! = " + evaluate(0));
        //non-zero +ve number
```

```
    System.out.println("5! = " + evaluate(5));
    //Large +ve number
    System.out.println("20! = " + evaluate(20));
  }
}
```

Output:

```
0! = 1
5! = 120
20! = 2432902008176640000
```

The *evaluate(long input)* method can be re-written using **recursion** as shown below. **Recursion** and **Tree** data structures are very popular in coding job interviews as many engineers fail to have good grasp on these topics.

```
public static BigInteger evaluate(long input) {

    //throw exception on -ve numbers
    if(input < 0) {
        throw new RuntimeException("Undefined for -ve: " + input);   // fail fast
    }

    //to handle 0!
    if(input == 0) {
        return BigInteger.ZERO;
    }

    //exit condition for the recursion
    if(input == 1) {
        return BigInteger.ONE;
    }

    //recursion
    return BigInteger.valueOf(input).multiply(evaluate(input-1)); //invoke evaluate again
}
```

Note: It is a best practice to throw exception early. In other words, it must fail fast. The factorial for -ve numbers fail fast. BigInteger is used as opposed to long to handle large results as 21! returns 51,090,942,171,709,440,000, which is greater than max long value of 9,223,372,036,854,775,807.

Example 3:

Q. Can you write a program to evaluate if a given string input has proper closing bracket for every opening bracket?
A. Firstly, think of the pseudo code. The pseudo-code goes as follows.

1. Store every opening parenthesis (i.e. a LHS parenthesis) in a stack. This will enable LIFO.
2. When you encounter a closing parenthesis (i.e. RHS parenthesis), pop the last entry, which should be the corresponding opening parenthesis.
3. If not found, then the parentheses are not matched.

Think of a very simple input string to test

```
public static void main (String[ ] args) {}
```

A simple diagram can become handy to improve clarity

```
Stack: public static void main(String[] args) {}
```

[				
(	(		{	

| Push (and [| When] is the next one, pop out matching [| When) is the next one, pop out matching (| Push { | When } is the next one, pop out matching { |

Determine the test cases required to test your code

The unit tests must cover both positive and negative test cases. The positive scenario will be the correct input text as shown above. The negative scenarios will be

- Missing "]"
- Missing "{"
- Missing "("

Write the code in your language of choice.

The following sample code is written in Java.

Define different types of parentheses as constants.

```java
package lifo;

public enum PARENTHESIS {

    LP('('), RP(')'), LB('{'), RB('}'), LSB('['), RSB(']');

    char symbol;

    PARENTHESIS(Character symbol) {
        this.symbol = symbol;
    }

    char getSymbol() {
        return this.symbol;
    }
}
```

Now, the stack data structure is in action using its LIFO mechanism to marry a closing parenthesis (i.e RHS) with an opening parenthesis (i.e. LHS). If you find any LHS parenthesis, push it into a stack, and when you find a RHS parenthesis, pop the stack to see if you have a corresponding LHS parenthesis.

```java
package lifo;

import java.util.ArrayDeque;
import java.util.Deque;
```

```java
public class Evaluate {
        // stores the parentheses (LIFO data structure)
        final Deque<Character> paranthesesStack = new ArrayDeque<Character>();

        public boolean isBalanced(String s) {

            for (int i = 0; i < s.length(); i++) {

                if (s.charAt(i) == PARENTHESIS.LP.getSymbol()
                                    || s.charAt(i) == PARENTHESIS.LB.getSymbol()
                                    || s.charAt(i) == PARENTHESIS.LSB.getSymbol())
                {

                        // push the opening parenthesis
                        paranthesesStack.push(s.charAt(i));
                }

                // for each RHS parenthesis check if
                // there is a matching LHS Parenthesis
                // if the stack is empty or does not have
                // a matching LHS parenthesis then not balanced, and return false.

                else if (s.charAt(i) == PARENTHESIS.RP.getSymbol( )) {
                    if (paranthesesStack.isEmpty( ) ||
                        paranthesesStack.pop( ) != PARENTHESIS.LP.getSymbol())
                        {
                                    return false;
                        }
                }

                else if (s.charAt(i) == PARENTHESIS.RB.getSymbol( )) {
                        if (paranthesesStack.isEmpty( ) ||
                            paranthesesStack.pop( ) != PARENTHESIS.LB.getSymbol())
                        {
                                    return false;
                        }
                }
```

210

```java
        else if (s.charAt(i) == PARENTHESIS.RSB.getSymbol( )) {
            if (paranthesesStack.isEmpty( )  ||
                paranthesesStack.pop() != PARENTHESIS.LSB.getSymbol())
                {
                            return false;
                }
            }
        }
    }

    return true;

    }//end of method
}
```

Now, write the unit tests.

```java
package lifo;

import org.junit.Assert;
import org.junit.Before;
import org.junit.Test;

public class EvaluateTest {

        Evaluate eval = null;

        @Before
        public void setUp() {
                eval = new Evaluate();
        }

        @Test
        public void testPositiveIsBalanced() {
                boolean result = eval
                                .isBalanced("public static void main(String[ ] args) {}");
                Assert.assertTrue(result);
```

```
        }

        @Test
        public void testNegativeIsBalanced() {
                // missing ']'
                boolean result = eval
                                .isBalanced("public static void main(String[ args) {}");
                Assert.assertFalse(result);

                // missing '{'
                result = eval.isBalanced("public static void main(String[ ] args) }");
                Assert.assertFalse(result);

                // missing '('
                result = eval.isBalanced("public static void main String[ ] args) {}");
                Assert.assertFalse(result);
        }
}
```

Example 4:

Q. Write a method which takes the parameters (int[ ] inputNumbers, int sum) and checks input numbers to find the pair of integer values which totals to the sum. If found returns true, else returns false?

A. [Hint]

Considerations:

- Should it work for negative integers?
- How big is the *inputNumbers* array? How often does this method gets called?
- What scenarios need to be tested? +ve numbers, negative numbers, positive sum, negative sum, etc.?

This can be achieved using a number of different ways and each approach has its own pros and cons.

Approach 1: using nested loops:

- Pick one number from the array of *inputNumbers* and compare against other numbers in the array of *inputNumbers* to see if 2 numbers add up to the given *sum*.
- If the picked number adds up to the given *sum* with at least one other number from the array, return true. Otherwise repeat this process by picking the next number from the array of *inputNumbers* to see if it adds up to the given *sum*.
- If none of the 2 numbers in the array add up to the given *sum*, return false.

Pros: Works for negative numbers as well. Easy to read and understand.

Cons: Not suited for larger arrays and frequent invocations of this method as its maximum loop count is $O(n^2)$. Say for an array with 500 numbers, max loop count is 500*500 = 250000 times. Hence not at all efficient for larger arrays.

Approach 2: using another collection:

- Pick one number from the array of *inputNumbers*.
- Evaluate the *requiredNumber* (*sum* – picked number) to add up to the given *sum*. Store this *requiredNumber* in a set (e.g. a *HashSet*) for later use.
- Pick the next number, and see if it is one of the *requiredNumbers* by checking it in the previously stored set (i.e. *setNumbers*). If found return true.
- Continue this process for all the numbers in the *inputNumbers* array.
- If all the numbers are processed, and no match was found, return false.

Pros: Easy to read and understand. More efficient than nested loops for larger arrays. Its maximum loop count is n. Say for an array with 500 numbers, max loop count is 500 times.

Cons: Require additional memory consumption to store *requiredNumbers* in a separate collection.

Approach 3: using two pointers:

- Sort the array of *inputNumbers* in ascending order.
- Define two pointers – one starts from the beginning and the other starts from the

end.
- Loop through the array of *inputNumbers* until either numbers pointed by start and end pointers add up to the given *sum* or both the pointers point to the same element in the array.
- If the elements pointed by the start and end pointers add up to the given *sum*, return true. If the given *sum* is greater, move the start pointer forward to the next element. If the given *sum* is lesser, move the end pointer backwards to the previous element.
- If sum is found, return true, and otherwise return false.
- A simple diagram would make things clearer.

2	3	7	12	15

↑   ↑

Pros: Easy to read and understand. More efficient than nested loops for larger arrays. Its maximum loop count is n-1. Say for an array with 500 numbers, max loop count is 499. Can be used for negative numbers.

Cons: Array of numbers must be sorted prior to use. Using a quick sort algorithm will incur an additional O(N * log N) performance.

Which approach to choose? Using another collection or two pointers. Incorporate performance and memory usage benchmarks.

You must know your OO concepts

- Brush-up on the OO concepts abbreviated as "a pie", which stands for abstraction, polymorphism, inheritance, and encapsulation.
- Learn the OO principles abbreviated as **SOLID**, which stands for

SRP	Single Responsibility Principle	A class should only have a single purpose (i.e. cohesive), and all its methods should work together to achieve this goal.
OCP	Open Close Principle	You should be able to extend a class' behavior, without modifying it.

LSP	Liskov Substitution Principle	Derived classes must be substitutable for their base classes. Derived classes must have the same intent, but different implementation. Another way to look at this principle is to think of design by contract. A sub class should honor the contracts made by its parent classes.
ISP	Interface Segregation Principle	Make fine grained interfaces that are client specific. While SRP addresses high cohesion in the class level, ISP promotes high cohesion in the interface level.
DIP	Dependency Inversion Principle	Depend on abstractions, not on implementations. • Higher level modules should not depend directly on lower level modules. Both should depend on abstractions (interfaces or abstract classes). • Abstractions should not depend on implementations. The implementations should depend on abstractions.

You will be either asked to comment on a class that is badly designed or asked to design a simple system.

Example 1:

Q. Can you explain if the following classes are badly designed?

The following snippets design the classes & interfaces for the following scenario. Bob, and Jane work for a restaurant. Bob works as manager and a waiter. Jane works as a waitress. A waiter's behavior is to take customer orders and a manager's behavior is to manage employees.

```
package badrestaurant;

public interface Person {}
```

```
package badrestaurant;

public interface Manager extends Person {
```

```
   public void managePeople( );
}
```

```
package badrestaurant;

public interface Waiter extends Person {
   public void takeOrders( );
}
```

```
package badrestaurant;

public class Bob implements Manager, Waiter {

   @Override
   public void managePeople( ) {
      //implementation goes here
   }

   @Override
   public void takeOrders( ) {
      //implementation goes here
   }
}
```

```
package badrestaurant;

public class Jane implements Waiter {

   @Override
   public void takeOrders( ) {
      //implementation goes here
   }
}
```

The *Restaurant* class that uses the above classes as shown below.

```
package badrestaurant;
```

```
public class Restaurant {

  public static void main(String[ ] args) {

    Bob bob = new Bob( );
    bob.managePeople( );
    bob.takeOrders( );

    Jane jane = new Jane( );
    jane.takeOrders( );
  }
}
```

A. The above classes are badly designed for the reasons described below.

- The name should be an attribute, and not a class like *Bob* or *Jane*. A good OO design should hide non-essential details through **abstraction**. If the restaurant employs more persons, you don't want the system to be **inflexible** and create new classes like *Peter*, *Jason*, etc for every new employee.

- The above solution's incorrect usage of the interfaces for the job roles like *Waiter*, *Manager*, etc will make your classes very **rigid** and **tightly** coupled by requiring static structural changes. What if *Bob* becomes a full-time manager? You will have to remove the interface *Waiter* from the class *Bob*. What if Jane becomes a manager? You will have to change the interface *Waiter* with *Manager*. So, when designing systems, ask the "what if" questions.

The above drawbacks in the design can be fixed as shown below by asking the right questions. Basically waiter, manager, etc are roles an employee plays. You can abstract it out as shown below.

```
package goodrestuarant;

public interface Role {

  public String getName( );
  public void perform( );    //perform a task for your role
}
```

217

```java
package goodrestuarant;

public class Waiter implements Role {

    private String roleName;

    public Waiter(String roleName) {
        this.roleName = roleName;
    }

    @Override
    public String getName( ) {
      return this.roleName;
    }

    @Override
    public void perform( ) {
      //implementation goes here to perform the waiter task
    }
}
```

```java
package goodrestuarant;

public class Manager implements Role {

    private String roleName;

    public Manager(String roleName) {
        this.roleName = roleName;
    }

    @Override
    public String getName( ) {
      return this.roleName;
    }

    @Override
```

```
    public void perform( ) {
        //implementation goes here to perform the manager task
    }
}
```

The *Employee* class defines the employee name as an attribute as opposed to a class. This makes the design flexible as new employees can be added at run time by instantiating new *Employee* objects with appropriate names. This is the power of abstraction. You don't have to create new classes for each new employee. The roles are declared as a list using aggregation (i.e. containment), so that new roles can be added or existing roles can be removed at run time as the roles of employees change. This makes the design more flexible.

```
package goodrestuarant;

import java.util.ArrayList;
import java.util.List;

public class Employee {

    private String name;
    private List<Role> roles = new ArrayList<Role>(10);

    public Employee(String name){
        this.name = name;
    }

    public String getName( ) {
        return name;
    }

    public void setName(String name) {
        this.name = name;
    }

    public List<Role> getRoles( ) {
        return roles;
    }
```

```
public void setRoles(List<Role> roles) {
    this.roles = roles;
}

public void addRole(Role role){
    if(role == null){
        throw new IllegalArgumentException("Role cannot be null");    //fail fast
    }
    roles.add(role);
}

public void removeRole(Role role){
    if(role == null){
        throw new IllegalArgumentException("Role cannot be null");     //fail fast
    }
    roles.remove(role);
}
}
```

The following *Restaurant* class shows how flexible, extensible, and maintainable the above design is.

```
package goodrestuarant;

import java.util.List;

public class Restaurant {

    public static void main(String[ ] args) {

        Employee emp1 = new Employee ("Bob");
        Role waiter = new Waiter("waiter");
        Role manager = new Manager("manager");

        emp1.addRole(waiter);
        emp1.addRole(manager);
```

```
    Employee emp2 = new Employee("Jane");
    emp2.addRole(waiter);

    List<Role> roles = emp1.getRoles( );
    for (Role role : roles) {
       role.perform( );
    }

    //you can add more employees or change roles based on
    //conditions here at runtime. More flexible. No structural changes are required
  }
}
```

Q. Is there anything still wrong with the *goodrestaurant* package classes shown above?
A. Yes. A seasoned professional will ask the following further questions. These questions are related to applying the best practices to write quality code.

1. Why does the Employee class need to be mutable?
2. Why aren't the roles defensively copied?
3. Why would the Employee need to know how to add and remove roles?
4. Waiter and Manager are placed in a collection but don't override the methods hashcode and equals. That will cause the contains method on a List to not behave as expected.
5. If the role is null then you should throw a NullPointerException instead of an IllegalArgumentException.
6. The code that checks for null roles being added is duplicated, thus defeats the DRY principle.

Example 2:

Q. What is wrong with the following code snippet?

```
package principle_srp1;

import java.sql.Connection;
import java.sql.SQLException;
import org.apache.commons.lang.StringUtils;
```

```java
public class Animal {

    private Integer id;
    private String name;
    private Connection con = null;

    //getters and setters for above attributes go here..

    public boolean validate( ) {
        return id != null && id > 0 && StringUtils.isNotBlank(name);
    }

    public void saveAnimal( ) throws SQLException {
        //save Animal to database using SQL
        //goes here ...
    }

    public Animal readAnimal( ) throws SQLException {
        //read Animal from database using SQL
        //...
        Animal animal = null;
        //...
        return animal;
    }
}
```

A. The above class represents 3 different responsibilities.

- Uniquely identifies an animal with id and name.
- Interacts with the database to save and read an animal.
- Validates the animal details.

Hence, the above class violates the **Single Responsibility Principle** (SRP), which states that a class should have only one reason to change. This principle is based on **cohesion**. Cohesion is a measure of how strongly a class focuses on its responsibilities. It is of the following two types:

- **High cohesion:** This means that a class is designed to carry on a specific and precise task. Using high cohesion, methods are easier to understand, as they perform a single task.

- **Low cohesion:** This means that a class is designed to carry on various tasks. Using low cohesion, methods are difficult to understand and maintain.

Hence the above code suffers from low cohesion. The above code can be improved as shown below. The *Animal* class is re-factored to have only a single responsibility of uniquely identifying an animal.

```java
package principle_srp1a;

public class Animal {

    private Integer id;
    private String name;

    public Integer getId( ) {
        return id;
    }
    public void setId(Integer id) {
        this.id = id;
    }
    public String getName( ) {
        return name;
    }
    public void setName(String name) {
        this.name = name;
    }
}
```

The responsibility of interacting with the database is shifted to a data access object (i.e. DAO) class. The data access object class takes an animal object or any of its attributes as input.

```java
package principle_srp1a;

public interface AnimalDao {
```

```
   public void saveAnimal(Animal animal);
   public Animal readAnimal(Integer id);
}


package principle_srp1a;

import java.sql.Connection;

public class AnimalDaoImpl implements AnimalDao {

   private Connection con = null;

   // getters and setters for above attributes
   // go here..

   @Override
   public void saveAnimal(Animal animal) {
      // save Animal to database using SQL
      // goes here ...
   }

   @Override
   public Animal readAnimal(Integer id) {
      // read Animal from database using SQL
      // goes here ...
      Animal animal = null;
      // ...
      return animal;
   }
}
```

Finally, the responsibility of validating an animal is re-factored to a separate class that takes an animal object as input.

```
package principle_srp1a;

public interface Validator {
   public boolean validate(Animal animal);
```

```
}
```

```
package principle_srp1a;

import org.apache.commons.lang.StringUtils;

public class AnimalValidator implements Validator {

  @Override
  public boolean validate(Animal animal) {
    return animal.getId( ) != null && animal.getId( ) > 0
        && StringUtils.isNotBlank(animal.getName( ));
  }
}
```

You now have 3 classes that have clear separation of concerns. The Animal class has been decoupled from database concern and validation concern. The above code is also well encapsulated and highly cohesive.

The challenge with SRP is getting the granularity of a responsibility right. One of the most common complaints about SRP is object explosion. This is a valid complaint, but when things are broken down by concern as shown above, it is far easier to consider the concern in isolation and come up with a better design for that single concern. The art of design is all about striking a good balance by asking the right questions and not blindly following a principle.

Example 3:

Q. What is wrong with the following code snippet?

```
package principle_ocp1;

public interface Animal {
   //methods are left out for brevity. Contains attributes & getters/setters
}
```

```
package principle_ocp1;
```

Open more doors by knowing what the prospective employers are looking for

```java
public class Cat implements Animal {
    //methods are left out for brevity. Contains attributes & getters/setters
}
```

```java
package principle_ocp1;

public class Spider implements Animal {
    //methods are left out for brevity. Contains attributes & getters/setters
}
```

```java
package principle_ocp1;

public class Ostritch implements Animal {
    //methods are left out for brevity. Contains attributes & getters/setters
}
```

```java
package principle_ocp1;

import java.util.List;

public class AnimalLegsCounter {

    public int count(List<Animal> animals) {
        int count = 0;
        for (Animal animal : animals) {
            if (animal instanceof Cat) {
                count += 4;
            } else if (animal instanceof Spider) {
                count += 8;
            } else if (animal instanceof Ostritch) {
                count += 2;
            }
        }
        return count;
    }
}
```

```java
package principle_ocp1;
```

```
import java.util.ArrayList;
import java.util.List;

public class Example {

    public static void main(String[ ] args) {
        List<Animal> list = new ArrayList<Animal>( );
        Animal animal = new Cat( );
        list.add(animal);
        animal = new Spider( );
        list.add(animal);
        animal = new Ostritch( );
        list.add(animal);

        int count = new AnimalLegsCounter( ).count(list);
        System.out.println("Total count for " + list.size( )  + " animals = " + count);

    }
}
```

A. The above code violates the open closed principle (OCP). As time goes on, you may want to add more animals like dog, crab, dragon fly, etc with differing number of legs. This will require you to modify the *AnimalLegCounter* class' *count(...)* method with more else-if statements like:

```
if (animal instanceof Cat || animal instanceof Dog) {
    count += 4;
} else if (animal instanceof Spider) {
    count += 8;
} else if (animal instanceof Ostritch) {
    count += 2;
} else if (animal instanceof Crab) {
    count += 10;
} else if (animal instanceof DragonFly) {
    count += 6;
}
```

This shows that the class *AnimalLegCounter* is not **closed for modification** as you will have to modify it in order to extend it. In other words, this means it is not **open for extension**. The above example is a trivial one, but in real world applications, the code base might be 10 to 1000 times larger and modifying a class is not a trivial task.

Any time you see big if/else or switch statements, you should think about polymorphism. The code below shows how the real counting logic can be moved to the *count( )* method in individual animal classes, and the *AnimalLegCounter* classes' *count( )* method only makes use of the *count( )* method in the *Animal* classes to make it adhere to the OCP principle using polymorphism as shown below.

```java
package principle_ocp2;

public interface Animal {
    //other methods are left out for brevity
    public abstract int count( );
}
```

```java
package principle_ocp2;

public class Cat implements Animal {
    //other methods are left out for brevity

    @Override
    public int count( ) {
        return 4;
    }
}
```

```java
package principle_ocp2;

public class Ostritch implements Animal {
    //other methods are left out for brevity

    @Override
    public int count( ) {
        return 2;
    }
}
```

```
}
```

```
package principle_ocp2;

public class Spider implements Animal {

    //other methods are left out for brevity

    @Override
    public int count( ) {
        return 8;
    }
}
```

```
package principle_ocp2;

import java.util.List;

public class AnimalLegsCounter {

    public int count(List<Animal> animals) {
        int count = 0;
        for (Animal animal : animals) {
            count += animal.count( );
        }
        return count;
    }
}
```

Now, if you want to add more animals like dog, crab, etc, all you have to do is add the relevant classes like *Dog*, *Crab*, etc implementing the same *Animal* interface, and provide the *count(...)* method implementation. The *AnimalLegsCounter* class does not have to be modified at all. In other words, the *AnimalLegsCounter* class is closed for modification by opening it up for extension through adding new classes.

Example 4:

Q. How would you go about designing a car parking station?

Open more doors by knowing what the prospective employers are looking for

A. [Hint]

Map out the requirements:

- The car park needs to cater for different types of car parks like regular, handicapped, and compact.
- It should keep track of empty and filled spaces.
- It should also cater for self and valet parking

Map out the classes that would be required. Use a UML class diagram. Here are some points to get started.

- A *CarPark* class to represent a parking station.
- A *ParkingSpace* can be an abstract class or an interface to represent a parking space, and *RegularParkingSpace*, *HandicappedParkingSpace*, and *CompactParkingSpace*, are subtypes of a *ParkingSpace*. This means a *RegularParkingSpace* **is a** *ParkingSpace*.
- A *CarPark* **has a** (i.e. composition) finite number of *ParkingSpaces*. A *CarPark* also keeps track of all the parking spaces and a separate list of all the vacant parking spaces.
- A *Vehicle* class **uses a** (i.e. delegation) *ParkingSpace*. The *Vehicle* class will hold attributes using enum classes like *VehicleType* and *ParkingType*. The vehicle types could be *Compact*, *Regular*, and *Handicapped*. The parking types could be *Self* or *Valet*. Depending on the requirements, the self or valet types could be designed as subtypes of the *Vehicle* class.

Note: There are so many good books and free technical blogs out there that will prepare you for coding job interviews. All it takes is a few minutes on amazon.com.

Impossible or stressful questions

Impossible or stressful questions are asked to test a candidate's creativity, analytical ability, sense of humor, and ability to handle stress by challenging him or her with impossible questions like:

- How many liters of paint is required to paint Sydney harbor bridge?

    [**Hint**: Make a model of the bridge at the scale of 1:1,000,000, and evaluate the requirements for the model and then multiply it by the scale]

- How many petrol sites are there in New York?

  [**Hint**: Determine the number of major intersections in New York, and then multiply the number of intersections with say 2 petrol sites per intersection. Alternatively, ring the relevant authorities to get the information.]

These questions can evaluate how well a candidate can think on his/her feet, and to rattle the candidate to see how well he or she reacts to stress at the workplace. These questions don't really have right or wrong answers. These questions are also very handy to evaluate someone's attitude.

A good candidate will also have the right attitude to stay positive, motivated, and show eagerness and flexibility to learn from his/her mistakes despite his/her average performance to the scenario based, coding, and impossible questions as these are not always easy to tackle in a short time span, especially in an interview. Some interviewers even go to the length of informing the candidates that these are not pass or fail type of questions, but will be used to evaluate a candidate within the overall interview process. These questions will also help an interviewer determine the seniority. For example, junior, intermediate, senior, team lead, etc. In my view, it is better to evaluate a candidate's seniority based on his/her overall interview performance as opposed to just the number of years of experience alone. This is because some candidates are not only more pro-active than others in acquiring the required skills, but also work harder and smarter with lots of passion and enthusiasm to fast-track their careers. So, look for quality not just quantity.

Open more doors by knowing what the prospective employers are looking for

Section-6:

Passing the job interviews with the flying colors

A little preparation prior to job interviews will help you open more doors by being in an enviable position of to be able to choose from multiple job offers. Asking the right questions at the job interviews will help you decide if it is the right job for you without having to let others decide what is best for you.

Passing the job interviews with the flying colors

No one is going to offer a job to someone who sits there and contributes very little to the conversation and who answers each question with a yes, a no, or a brief mumble. The word "interview" itself makes a person tensed and nervous. It is a normal human behavior to become confused or get tensed, but such things can be overcome with the following tips:

- **Treat each interview as a free technical and behavioral training course**. Have an attitude that even if you are not going to get the job, you are going to learn something good out of it. If you go with this attitude, you will put yourself in a win/win situation and you might really get the offer. If you take this attitude, you can learn a lot from your interviews. It also **helps you manage your nervousness.**

- **Prepare to succeed**. Do your home work and this will make a huge difference. It is important to know yourself, know what you have in the way of skills, experience, past accomplishments, and values. The employers are after the solid basics, and in most cases you can give them what they are seeking and clinch the deal if you prepare well and present it effectively.

- **Think aloud**, even if you don't know the exact or detailed answer. Interviewers may want to hear your thought process. It is better to at least know how to go about ... solving a problem or performing a task than to not having any idea at all.

- **Never think that you have to answer all the questions correctly**. Everyone dislikes a person who behaves like they know everything. In information technology, no one person can know everything. If you can get the questions on solid basics right and convince that you are a team player with the core competencies, right attitude, and necessary soft skills like communication and interpersonal to get the job done, then you have a good chance of succeeding.

- **Don't try to make up your answers** if you have no clue. More experienced interviewers can quickly recognize which potential employees are full of hot air, and which are the real McCoy. It is better to be truthful and say "sorry I don't know the answer". If you are not clear about a question, ask for clarifications and make sure that you fully understand the question or problem. If you are very keen to know the answer, ask the interviewer politely, but don't over do it by asking answers for each and every question. You can always find the answers after the interview through your own research and by asking your fellow professionals through technical forums.

- **Do not get put off by a tricky or a difficult question**. Try to maintain your composure, confidence, enthusiasm, and interest in the position throughout the interview. The interviewer might be testing your soft skills, personality, and attitude with tricky questions. What really earns you a job is **not just** the technical skills, but the combination of your

  knowledge + experience + technical skills + soft skills + attitude + genuine interest in the position + professionalism and ethics + general interview etiquette

- **Arrange for a morning interview** where possible so that you don't have to dwell on it all day.

I can't stress enough how important it is to prepare prior to taking interviews. Luck has nothing to do with interview success. Preparation, right attitude, and confidence has everything to do with it. You need to follow a number of steps prior to planning to take interviews. These steps are:

- Know yourself.
- Know your occupation and industry.
- Know the organization.
- Prepare questions to ask.

Let's look at these steps one by one.

Know yourself

The first step in preparing for an interview is to do a thorough self-assessment. It is very important to develop a complete inventory of your technical skills, soft skills, experience, and personal attributes that you can use to market yourself to your prospective employers at any time during the interview process. Also, take a mental picture of the technical and soft skills you would like to acquire from your next job along with your goals and objectives. This will help you ask intelligent questions at the interview to evaluate if this is the right job for you without having to let the recruitment agencies and prospective employers decide what is best for you. Some of the questions you should answer are:

- **What can I offer this particular employer?**

[**Hint**: Similar experience gained from XYZ Ltd, 3+ yrs of experience in technologies M, N, and frameworks A, B, and C. Domain knowledge in finance through project P at company Q Ltd. Client facing experience, analytical, and problem solving skills acquired as a consultant at R Ltd. Demonstrable leadership and team work skills as the school cricket captain. Familiarity and limited exposure with the popular open-source framework "B" by taking initiatives to assist with their documentation and applying it in my self-taught project K]

- **What are my strengths and weaknesses?**

[**Hint:** _Strengths_ → Expertise in areas like design, performance tuning, and applying best practices. Ability to look at the big picture and analyze things from both business and technology perspective. Experienced with design and development of 3-tier JEE based web applications to stand-alone batch jobs, and system integration using data feeds to Service Oriented Architecture (SOA). _Weaknesses_ → (for your own assessment and don't tell these to your interviewers) – get quite bored with repetitiveness, hate spending too much time on documentation, dislike too much support work, etc]

- **What are my short term and long term goals?**

[**Hint**: For a beginner to mid level → In next 2-4 years to become a senior hands on developer with a good grasp in the key areas of software development, and have a well-rounded exposure to the full software development life cycle (SDLC). Also, prefer improving my job hunting, interviewing, and networking skills along with my technical ability to work as freelance developer (for your own assessment only and your interviewer does not have to know this). Simultaneously acquire the much needed soft skills to become a technical or team lead in 4 – 6 years. Continue to gather much needed wider range of hands-on experience and skills to become an architect in 8-10 years.]

- **What can I learn from this particular job role that is conducive to reaching my career goals and aspirations?**

[**Hint**: Opportunity to enhance my familiarity and limited experience with sought-after technology A, framework B and application server C. Opportunity to acquire domain knowledge in equity markets and derivatives. Exposure to customer facing experience and agile development practices. Opportunity to work in a 24x7 mission critical and high visibility project that rolls out the software to 1000+ retail outlets and 800,000+ on-line users.]

- **What kind of environment or team culture do I like?**

[**Hint**: Agile, fast paced, relaxed, smaller teams, larger teams, investment bank, software house, open-desk policy, more comprehensive interviews indicating opportunity to work with and learn from high caliber fellow professionals, flexibility to occasionally work from home, collaborative and supportive team culture, etc]

- **What do I really like doing? What will be my next ideal job?**

[**Hint**: Both hands-on design and coding, nothing but coding, trainer/lecturer, gain more domain knowledge in finance, role that gives exposure to both technical and human side, more business focus, etc.]

- **What type of projects do I want to work in?**

[**Hint**: Service Oriented Architecture (SOA) that integrates with at least two disparate mission critical systems, 24 x 7 3-tier Java/JEE based web application that has 10,000+ concurrent users, Rich web application with JavaScript and CSS, data migration project with heavy use of SQL, XML, and Database management, any Java project that is driven by popular and sought-after open-source frameworks, etc]

- **Apart from my work related skills and experience, what can I bring to this job?**

[**Hint**: Soft skills demonstrated via extra-curricular activities like sports, charity work, organizing cultural and charity events, researching and writing articles and books, maintaining a blog to help fellow professionals, speaking at conferences, maintaining open-source websites and contributing bug fixes, special training and certification, etc]

Your CV or resume has served you well so far because it has got you an interview. So, review your resume very carefully and make sure that you can explain everything on it. Try to predict the questions your resume may prompt and have confident answers to those questions. While going through your resume, for each task or accomplishment ask yourself "What did I learn?", "What skills did I develop?", What problems did it solve? and "What key areas did it cover?" Keep in mind that you have to look holistically at technical skills, soft skills, and personal attributes. Technical skills should include the key areas, the frameworks, and the technologies used. The soft skills should include the transferable skills like analytical/problem solving, interpersonal, oral/written communication, team work, taking initiatives, being a self-starter, leadership, planning/organization, mentoring, and time management. The personal attributes should include handling pressure/stress, tackling tough colleagues, commitment, staying positive, taking criticisms well, motivation, enthusiasm, sense of humor, adaptability, honesty, integrity, loyalty, etc. You can prepare your answers to open-ended questions using the SAR (**Situation-Action-Result**) technique . For example,

Situation: Inefficient implementation of batch runs at XYZ limited exponentially increased from 5 hours to 17 hours with the increase of data.

Action:

- Identified and attributed the key performance bottle-necks to an inefficient SQL query, absence of database partitioning, and a badly constructed regular expression with heavy back tracking.

- Generated SQL execution plan and optimized the inefficient query with the help of DB Artisan query optimizer and partitioned the database based on the created _datetime column.

- Proposed multi-threading to improve the overall performance. This would enable computation intensive threads to run concurrently while some other threads are blocked on long database I/O operations on a multi-core processor machine.

- Took the initiative to communicate my findings to the business and fixed the issues and implemented my recommendations within 9 weeks in collaboration with the database team and in consultation with the business users.

Result:

- The overall batch process was completed within 2 hours.
- Average CPU utilization increased from 72% to 96%.
- Business users and stake holders were happy as it surpassed the required SLA (Service Level Agreement).

Know your occupation and industry

This is necessary because in order to present convincing answers, you need to have the skills and experience required for your occupation and industry.

- **Get a good handle on the 16 technical key areas** described earlier and brush up as much as you can especially on the language and specification fundamentals relating to your mainstream programming language.

- **Know what is required to thrive in your occupation**. Know what the interviewers are looking for. The previous chapter should have given you an insight as to what the prospective employers will be looking for in general.

- **Know the industry trends** in terms of the sought-after technologies, frameworks, development processes, agile practices, etc to keep your knowledge and skills current .

   [**Hint:**

   Industry specific websites → http://www.sys-con.com, www.infoq.com, http://www.theserverside.com, http://www.dzone.com, etc.

   Researching on Google trends to ascertain a particular technology's or framework's popularity by typing your key word to search at → http://www.google.com/trends

   Discuss with your fellow professionals via forums like → http://forums.dzone.com, http://www.javaranch.com, etc.]

- **Know the names** of the industry experts, your role models, sites you visit, and books you read, to show that you are passionate about your chosen career and industry.

[**Hint**: *Industry experts* → Martin Fowler, Robert C. Martin (Uncle Bob), etc *Role Models* → Rod Johnson, Gavin King, Kathy Sierra, etc. *Books read* → "Effective Java" by Joshua Bloch, "Code Complete" by Steve McConnell, "Java Concurrency in Practice" by Brian Goetz, et al, "Head First ...." series of books by Kathy Sierra and Bert Bates, etc]

- **Have a say on your main language of choice**. Know the language features you really love, features you dislike, and features you like to be added or improved. Be prepared to back up your answers with your reasons. Know the differences and improvements between the versions. For example, the key improvements or differences between Java 1.4 and Java 5. **Good caliber candidates are opinionated.**

[**Hint**: *Features you love* → Generics, Annotations, Java Collection API, etc. *Features you dislike* → static imports because you can't immediately tell where the method lies, etc. *features you like to be added* → support for closures, A "Money" class for safe monetary calculations, C# style properties, modularized JRE, USB support, external aliases to solve same qualified names for different classes, etc. *Features you like to be improved* → Support for design by contract beyond a simple assertion facility to improve the robustness of Java applications, removal of deprecated APIs, improved multi-media libraries, and simplified way of escaping characters and line breaks in string literals without having to deal with all kinds of escaping, etc]

Know the job description and the organization

The more you know about the job description and the organization, the better prepared you will be to discuss how you can meet the prospective employer's needs. Some of the questions you need to ask are,

- How big is the organization?
- What are their core products and services, and who does it serve?
- What level of experience are they looking for in technologies, frameworks, and platforms?
- What key soft skills are they looking for?
- What will be my key responsibilities and tasks?

- Why will I be interested in working for this organization? Has there been any recent changes or new developments?
- Are they more business focused or technology driven?
- Why will I be interested in this particular position?

There are a number of ways in which you can access this information. You check the company website, ask your recruitment agent, ask your network of colleagues and friends who are currently working or used to work there, researching on www.google.com, and asking the fellow professionals on industry specific forums. You will also have to pay undivided attention during the interview to get more information about the project and the position as most interviewers will be providing you these details at the beginning. Tailor your answers and questions based on this initial briefing.

Prepare questions to ask

Having completed your research on the organization and knowing the job description well enough will help you prepare for intelligently thought-out questions not only to demonstrate your genuine interest in the position, but also to assess your interest in the position and company. Many people new to the market see interviews only from their own point-of-view, e.g. they only prepare to answer questions, not to ask them. However, despite the pressure of the moment, it is important to remember that it is a 2-way process. They are interviewing you but do not forget that **you are also interviewing them**. Yes, you might want a job, but do you really want this job? Is there a better opportunity somewhere else? Do you really want to get this job and then spend time looking for something else? However, don't ask too many questions as it can imply you feel the interview was not successfully run. Pick your questions with care and avoid sounding negative. Here are some questions to think about,

- Where is the greatest demand for your products or services?
- Who are your major customers?
- What criteria will be used to evaluate my performance?
- What type of people succeed in your organization?
- If successful, what technologies, frameworks, and platforms will I be working on?
- How much responsibilities will I be given in my position?
- Are you following any agile development practices or have any company specific development processes?
- What are the significant challenges affecting your project/business today?

- Are you planning to take any future direction in terms of the development processes, technology/framework selection, architecture and design, in-house versus offshore development, etc?
- Can you describe the project that I will be working on if I am successful?
- How big is the team?
- When can I expect to hear from you regarding this position?

It is very important to ask the last question because employers want to hire individuals who can not only meet their requirements, but also who are interested in the position, and asking this question definitely helps to demonstrate interest on your part. Make sure that you leave the interview feeling confident that the interviewer knows as much as possible about your experience, achievements, skills, and capabilities. If you feel that the interviewer didn't get around asking you any important questions, pose them yourself diplomatically and answer them. For example, if the position you are being interviewed for requires lots of integration work using web services and messaging, and if the interviewer didn't get around assessing your skills and experience in XML based technologies and you feel that you are comfortable with it, you could bring it up yourself by saying – I guess this position requires skills and experience in XML based technologies like XML, XSDs, XPath, XQuery, and JAXB. If you sense any misconceptions, clear them up before leaving.

Watch out for nonverbal clues and be aware of general interview etiquette.

Watch out for non-verbal clues like facial expressions and body movements. Firm handshake at the beginning and end of the interview. Walk, sit and answer questions with confidence. Lean towards interviewer(s) to show interest. Speak with a well modulated voice. Use eye contact when speaking to the interviewer. Listen carefully, keep calm and avoid abruptness. Avoid inflexibility and negativity. Be positive and optimistic throughout the interview.

Concentrate on your strengths and accomplishments, but don't go over the top. Little things like taking some of your past work (e.g. sample code, screen shots, website links, etc) where possible to show that you take pride in your work, smiling, and being extremely well prepared can make all the difference in the world.

Be aware that prospective employers will also size you up based on if you are professionally dressed, if you are showing up on time, if you are greeting them appropriately by their names, if you are thanking them for their time and opportunity at the end, and if you are loyal and not critical of your past employers.

What to do after an interview?

Take some time to write down everything you remember about the interview. Analyze your performance. What questions were you asked? What did you do well? What did you do poorly? What do you wish you had done or said that you did not? This will help you prepare for your next interview. Also, ascertain if you would be keen in the position if you are made an offer.

If possible, send a thank you note to each of the persons who interviewed you. Thank them for the time they spent and tell them that you appreciated the opportunity to share your interests and career goals. Also, make it a point to have your interviewers' contact details handy, even if you are not keen on pursuing it further because these contacts may come in handy in the future, especially in a tougher job market. If you are keen on pursuing it further, follow up after an interview with a phone call in 2 to 3 days. Tell them that you are checking on the status of your application and indicate your interest in the job.

Finally, if you are not successful, be confident that something better will come through. Also, remember that reason for not getting through is not always reflection of your performance at the interview. Employers might be looking for a specific profile or cultural fit. They might even deem that you might not find the job exciting as you may be over qualified for the position. Some employers or interviewers may want just a team player to get some specific tasks done, and deliberately set out not to hire an all-rounder as they may not stay long (loyalty for small companies are important), or occasionally they may even feel threatened of their jobs by your caliber. Also, don't feel overwhelmed or under prepared by these technical questions and answers because a good team should have people with varying strengths and weaknesses to complement each other to ensure as many perspectives are covered. Interviews are not just technical contests. Interviews are more about people, their experience and achievements, willingness to adapt, motivation to learn, being open-minded to new techniques, and add value to the organization.

If the offers aren't flowing, it is vitally important that you work out what it is you are doing wrong. There are no mysterious recipes for success that are beyond the basics discussed here. Are you prepared to put the effort into preparing and presenting your case so that what you can offer becomes readily apparent? And are you prepared to present your case with the honesty, enthusiasm and commitment? You hold the key to your success.

If the interviews and offers are flowing, don't just jump at the very first offer come your way. Take your time to evaluate, and pick the offer that best aligns with your immediate and longer term goals and aspirations. Don't think only in monetary terms. Consider other aspects like

- opportunity to grow within the organization.
- opportunity to acquire new skills and learn sought-after technologies and frameworks.
- type of project, organization, role, and key responsibilities.

Not an easy decision to make, and also a decision that should not be made lightly, so refer to the topic entitled "How to choose from multiple job offers" in section 1 to assist you make a more informed decision.

Don't be afraid of failure

Your CV/Resume didn't get short listed; you didn't get the job you hoped for; you didn't get the raise you deserved. Don't be afraid of failure because

- Failure can help you grow stronger and motivate you more to achieve your dreams. Successful people know that things won't always go as planned. They also understand that self-doubt, indecision, being over cautious, and procrastination, etc are symptoms of fear that can stall their progress. It is through doing, trying, and experiencing things you never did before that you grow and develop.

- Failure can make you think differently or take a different path to get to where you want to be. Ask the right questions -- what did I do wrong? how can I do it differently?, what changes should I make?, what can I do to improve?, what are my strengths and what are my weaknesses?, where can I get help?, and what resources can I use?.

- Failure can teach you valuable lessons of "what not to do" or how to identify potential pitfalls. Sometimes you tend to learn and experience more from your and others' failures than successes. For example, I learned about the importance of writing effective resumes and presenting myself more effectively at the job interviews after being unemployed for about 16 months since completing my master's degree. I thought I was easily employable due to my post-graduate qualifications. I failed miserably to secure a job because I failed to understand what the prospective employers were looking for. I also more vividly remember my interview failures than successes. I also learned a lot about software development and the importance of good understanding of the key areas like security, performance considerations, scalability, memory considerations, transaction management, etc from others' and my failures in getting them right. These failures have taught me to proactively identify and detect serious issues that can arise from not understanding these key areas.

If you have not failed means you have not pushed yourself to the next level. Motivate yourself to continuously improve your competencies. I am a strong believer of the following quote from David Maister.

"The people who win are not necessarily the smartest people, but they are the people who are able to sustain drive, commitment, passion and engagement"

If you did not change in any way in the last year, it's not very probable that you will open more doors and go places. It is important to constantly expand your knowledge and skills. The skills expansion could happen not only through on the job experience, but also through pro-actively applying what you learn through good books, blogs, white papers, forums, observing others who are going places, and getting involved in self-taught tutorials/projects. Most of the good software developers are self-taught. Nowadays, there is no such thing as real job security. The real job security comes from keeping your knowledge and skills current and sharp, presenting yourself in a better light in your CVs/Resumes and job interviews, building a good online persona, and networking. Change yourself not only by acquiring the relevant technical skills, but also by demonstrating the right soft skills, business skills, marketing skills, and attitude. Research shows that the top five skills to have are -- analytical , technical, communication, interpersonal, and leadership skills. While you are at work or being interviewed, you will be judged on these skills along with the other personal attributes. You should change yourself not just as a techie, but as a well balanced professional.

Before success comes in any man's life, he's sure to meet with much temporary defeat and, perhaps some failures. When defeat overtakes a man, the easiest and the most logical thing to do is to quit. That's exactly what the majority of men do. -- Napoleon Hill

Section-7

Why do you need to write a blog?

How do you get out of your comfort zone?

How do you reinvent yourself?

Blogging has a number of benefits.

- It increases your writing and technical skills.
- It acts as a repository of your experience.
- It helps you make powerful connections.
- It helps you promote your books, services and products.
- It makes you popular in your field.
- It advances your career through proactive learning.
- It opens more doors for you without feeling stagnated.
- It creates an additional passive income stream.

Why must you write a technical blog?

Firstly, on a very positive note, some do make a reasonable passive income by blogging. You will find many success stories if you google for "blogging success stories" or "blogging success stories YouTube". But the reality is that these success stories are a minority. For the majority of you, the benefits realized by blogging will include

- **Capturing your experience:** I use my blogs and books to jog my memory prior to my job interviews. I also use my blog as a reference guide in my regular job to get things done. The 650 job interview questions in my books and blogs are something I collected over 12 years from my own and others' experience. When you create a blog post, you could keep it private for your own use until you are ready to share it publicly. Information gathering takes time, so better start early.

- **Writing blog posts isn't easy**. Most posts require lots of thinking, researching, trying out the code, scratching your head when they don't work right, etc. So, it not only widens your technical skills, but also improves your researching and writing skills. By blogging, you will learn what related topics that you need to learn and identify where your understanding is shallow. It also motivates you to self learn and keeps the momentum up when you are feeling stagnated. English was not my first language, and my written communication skills improved a lot by blogging.

- In addition to being the valuable part of your learning process, it helps you **network** and **show off your skills** with a great potential to open doors to earn a **passive income** by promoting yours and others' products, services, and books. People discover information online today, so if you want to be discovered and become a visible expert then blogging and social media will provide you with the **visibility**. Employers are increasingly inquisitive about your **online presence** and good blogs can open more doors in terms of better job opportunities and other collaborative endeavors. Blogging shows that **you are passionate about your chosen field**, which is an attribute most employers value.

- **Venting your frustrations diplomatically and professionally** through blogs as to what not to or how not to do things as opposed to writing inappropriate comments like "this code is rubbish" in code base or sending inappropriate emails like "ashamed to work with this code". I have seen very technically talented professionals being sacked or overlooked for potential promotions due to inappropriately venting their frustrations. Your blogs could also invite different perspectives and solutions to your frustration or problem from your fellow professionals and followers. Blogging for me has not only been a path for self expression, but also a journey of self discovery.

- Finally, I had no excuse to feeling stagnated. Blogging and social media kept me going with improved creativity and focussed passion even when I felt that I had no future in my regular job. When I could do my regular job with my eyes closed, I exercised my brain through creative writing and proactive learning to provide much needed exercise for the neurons. I did not have to wait 1-2 years to get formal recognitions like "employee of the month" or "CIO's contributor of the year" award. Did not have to study and prepare for 3-6 months to get certified. Every creative and quality blog post and article can earn you the recognitions via Facebook likes, subscriptions, comments, Google +1, potential collaboration work and job interview. **Not locally, but globally**.

You have the power in your hands to make a difference. If you embrace this global and interactive social mind by participating actively, you will be surprised and amazed as to how many doors it will open for you.

Think → Research → Learn → Write → Connect → Get feedback → Handle criticisms/temporary failures → Persevere → Acknowledge praises → Grow → Open more doors

Why is it important to apply the philosophy of "give before you take"?

I used to get quite frustrated in the early stages of my career due to not getting any interview calls or job offers. When I started blogging, I used to get quite demotivated due to not getting enough traffic to my blog or not receiving any positive comments or encouraging emails. This derailed my momentum to keep on going. When I started to consciously apply this philosophy, I started to gather momentum again. This philosophy can be applied in a number of scenarios:

- **At your job** give your employers what they need in terms of getting things done, adding value to the business, providing solutions to business and technical problems, becoming a go to person, taking on more responsibilities, and staying visible as a great contributor before you take what you need in terms of recognition, promotion and salary increase.

- **In your resume or CV** give your prospective recruiters a quick snapshot of what they need in terms of quantified accomplishments, experience and capabilities in sought-after technologies, frameworks, and tools, well roundness to get the job done with good technical skills, soft skills and right attitude before you be in a position to take what you need – multiple job interviews. Have customized and targeted resumes to individual employers to give them what they need.

- **When attending job interviews** give your interviewers what they are looking for in terms of

  - Good understanding of the basics (things you must know).
  - Good handle on the 16 key areas and the relevant soft skills to get the job done.
  - Passion for the chosen field and real interest in the job and the organization.
  - Ability to fit in well with the team.

  During your interview preparation ask yourself a few questions like

  - What can I give to the prospective employers that many others can't?
  - What skills, experience, and capabilities can I marry up with their requirements?

- **When blogging**, give your blog readers what they need in terms of

  - steps required to getting a task done or solving a problem.
  - potential pitfalls to avoid.
  - information to improving the technical knowledge or awareness.
  - inspiration to progress in their careers.

before you take what you need in terms of recognition, networking, and monetary benefits. If providing content that is readily available elsewhere, combine it with some creative ideas, so that it will be easy for your readers to grasp. Before you start blogging ask yourself the following questions

- What can I offer others that no one else can?
- Am I willing to invest time and commitment?

- **If you are building an application** for individuals (e.g. mobile apps, games, etc) or business users give what really your target audience need by asking the following questions

  - What problems does it solve?
  - What benefits does it provide?
  - Are there any similar applications and what am I competing against?

  before you take what you need in terms of your market share, revenue, and recognition.

Very often people give what they need without the right skill or know how to put themselves in others' shoes. So, apply this philosophy in your future endeavors as you see fit, and avoid frustrations and open more doors for your success.

Giving makes more sense only when you are reinventing yourself

Reinventing yourself is all about constantly embracing change. It also means being selfish and looking after yourself. Most people dislike or even fear change, but want things to "get better" in terms of promotions, salary, job satisfaction, not feeling stagnated, being recognized, and job security. So, there is no point in keep giving your services in outdated technologies due to fear of change. Reinventing yourself does not just mean changing jobs, but also includes putting your hand up for internal movements, taking on more responsibilities, changing your career focus from being a web developer to a mobile developer, etc to stay relevant in your field. More and more employers are finding their next hire via the online presence of a candidate. So, this requires you to reinvent yourself by giving more towards an online presence to show off your skills, capabilities, and accomplishments. More and more people are getting their daily technical doses and expanding their network with an online presence. People are finding different ways to supplement their primary income with secondary active and passive income. Even though some of those incomes are as little as $100.0/month, it is better to make some pocket money for your coffee/tea while learning and improving your technical, written, marketing, and networking skills. In fact, this is better than preparing for certifications and paying to sit for the exam. The certifications and the skills that are valuable right now may not always be valuable, or valued in the same way in the future. Also, it takes a fair amount of time and investments to prepare for the tests. I am not against certifications. If getting a certificate is what gets you out of your comfort zone to take action and maintain your momentum then go for it. But there are other better avenues to learn and stay motivated. For example, when I self-taught JavaScript a while back, I applied this technique of learn → apply → let the world know by

1. Firstly, learning the fundamentals via a handful of quality blogs and books.
2. Secondly, applying what I had learnt by writing small programs.
3. Finally, letting the world know by blogging about what I know in my own style -- that is questions and answers approach with lots of diagrams, code snippets, and examples to enhance my understandings.

I have not been using much Javascript since I blogged about it, but when I want to brush-up my skills on JavaScript, I know where to go.

I enjoy being a freelance developer working for a single client for 6 months to 24 months for two reasons – **firstly**, I like variety in terms of a bit of coding, bit of designing, bit of blogging, bit of networking, bit of mentoring, lots of challenges, and most importantly learning how to solve similar problems differently in different environments. The added bonus of all this is the job security due to staying relevant, possessing wide range of skills, and having a few valuable networked contacts that I can count on. **Secondly**, it gives me the professional freedom. I can afford to work for a client say for 24 months and then take 1 to 3 months off to pursue my other interests like working on a book to be self-published via POD, laying the ground work for a startup or an application that I always dreamed or taking a well earned holiday. This is mainly possible because the contract based opportunities pay around 1.5 to 2.0 times the permanent salary.

I am not advocating everyone to become a freelance developer, but what I am saying is that embracing change is mandatory and not optional. The big picture diagram will inspire you to try different avenues to reinvent yourself. The few things that you can get started on right a way are writing a blog about a new technology/framework, and learning and using the social media and search engine optimization (SEO) techniques. So, give your time and effort in areas where you can reinvent yourself. The key is to **get out of your comfort zone**.

"If you want something you've never had, you must be willing to do something you've never done" – by Thomas Jefferson

How do you get out of your comfort zone?

The 2 biggest challenges for reinventing yourself are getting started and persevering to keep the momentum going.

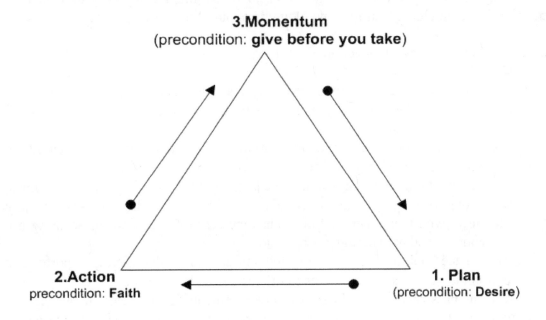

3.Momentum
(precondition: **give before you take**)

2.Action
precondition: **Faith**

1. Plan
(precondition: **Desire**)

Getting out of the comfort zone is hard, but if you don't change, don't expect things to "get better". The real difference in your career will be made by action and momentum to get the cycle going. Blogging and self-publishing books via POD have definitely helped me fast track my career by proactively learning, applying, and blogging on the core concepts and the 16 key technical areas. Blogging helped me further clarify the fundamentals through additional research.

The "Dreyfus Model" defines 5 stages that you need to go through on the journey from novice to an expert,

- Novice

How do you reinvent yourself?

- Advanced Beginner
- Competent
- Proficient
- Expert

If you just rely on your experience alone, it can take a long time to become an expert. The best way to fast track through these stages is by pro-actively applying and blogging what you learn from others' experience by helping them solve their challenges at work and via industry specific forums. Carefully analyzing the quality code written by your peers, superiors and open source contributors to transform that learning to your own experience by researching, learning, and blogging about it in your own style.

The key drivers for me as a blogger are

- Fast tracking my career through proactive learning. As a blogger, I continuously and proactively looking for things to learn and write about. This prevents me from feeling stagnated.
- Positive and constructive comments from my readers and followers increased my self confidence and clarity on a wide range of topics.
- Opportunity to enhance my online presence and stay visible. In recent times, many potential employers had learnt about my blogs and publications prior to my interviews with them. This definitely has increased my chances of securing my next contract and negotiating a better rate.
- More "Face book likes", followers, and subscribers handed me the opportunities to promote my books and services to my readers and followers.
- A small passive income via online advertisements is very easy to get started without much ongoing effort. Isn't it a good feeling to get some passive income deposited into your bank while you are fast tracking your career and making yourself more employable.
- Opens more doors in terms of opportunities to co-author or review books, finding a direct employment without having to go through an agency, and joint investment possibilities.

"Everyone thinks of changing the world, but no one thinks of changing himself."
Leo Tolstoy

How do you find time to blog and write POD books?

I often get asked how I find time to write books and blog posts while working full-time as a freelance Java developer. It is not easy and requires a few changes to your routines.

Change #1: Swapping reading online news and entertainment snippets with researching and experimenting for my next blog post.

Change #2: Swapping the usage of Facebook, Google+ and twitter to socialize and follow others with usage of these media for professional networking and getting others to follow me.

Change #3: Swapping listening to music and radio while commuting to and from work with learning SEO, Google adsense tips on CPC and CTR, Print-On-Demand (POD) – Lulu Vs Createspace, blogging on Blogger versus Wordpress, and other digital media topics via good blog posts and YouTube videos.

Change #4: After putting kids to bed, cutting down on watching TV and replacing it with blogging and POD writing.

Change #5: Making proper use of my idle time in between my contract assignments and disciplining myself to spend around 3-4 hours in the weekends. So, it is not all about finding time, but making time for things you are passionate about.

Reward yourself

All work and no play makes Arul a dull man. So, it is imperative to reward yourself with a well earned break/holiday, a nice meal, a trip to the movies, or a nice Starbucks signature hot chocolate once you reach certain goals like

- publishing your first 10 blog posts.
- completing the first chapter of your POD book if you are in competent to expert level.
- getting a good handle on a particular technical key area or the much needed soft skill
- setting up your accounts in wordpress.com or blogger.com, Google+, Facebook, and Twitter and setting up your profiles in LinkedIn.com, and industry specific

forums for professional networking.
- getting a good handle on resume writing, job hunting, and interviewing skills, especially if you are in novice to advanced beginner level.
- taking the initiative to get the much needed hands-on experience via voluntary work, open-source contribution, and self-taught projects if you are in novice to advanced beginner level

This step of quantifying your accomplishments as a result of your **action** and subsequently rewarding yourself to get the **momentum** going.

Note: It is quite easy to get started with blogging. There are myriads of quality blogs on "how to start blogging". Here are some of my tips from my experience.

My top 10 blogging tips from my experience

1. **You need to be patient and keep at it**: It took me around 9 months to go from 100 to 3000 daily page views. It was a gradual and slow process, and I promoted my blog posts by publishing articles via industry specific sites like dzone.com and helping out fellow professionals via forums like javaranch.com with my signature at the bottom having a link to my blog posts. It also gave me the inspiration for my blog titles by solving others' problems. It is also important to promote your blog via social networks like Facebook, Google+, Twitter and professional networks like LinkedIn.

2. If you are serious about blogging, f**avor your own domain name** (e.g. http://java-success.com) from the beginning as switching domains half way can hurt your SEO ranking. This is one of the mistakes that I made, and my blog is still on the blogspot domain java-success.blogspot.com. Another recommendation is that wordpress.com seems to have good plugins and features, so weight it against blogger.com. Research on the net for other blogging tips before starting.

3. **Pay attention to Google key words** that are not highly competitive and ensure that your blog headings, contents and meta tags had those key words. The google keyword tool or signing up for adwords is the best place to start. I picked "Java interview", "Java Interview Questions", and "Java Interview Answers" as my key words. These key words had "low" competition rating on the google keyword tool. It took me a good 4 to 6 months to get a good ranking on google search. Make use of the free SEO (Search Engine Optimization) tools and tips you can

find on the internet to improve your google search ranking, but the key is to **keep writing quality posts** that invites more dedicated readers and followers. Reader participation via leaving comments and back-linking to your quality blog posts will improve your ranking.

4. Start early and don't wait to be perfect before publishing. You will learn from your mistakes. You will never get it right without making a few mistakes. Any journey requires starting despite being judged harshly and criticized. If you don't start then nothing will happen. Persevere and continuously reinvent yourself and then opportunities will be revealed in time.

5. Sign-up for Google analytics to monitor your progress. Pay attention to "New Vs. Returning Visitors" and the "Bounce Rate". It is a very useful analytics tool to continuously improve your blog by providing what your readers are looking for. Here are some examples from my blog.

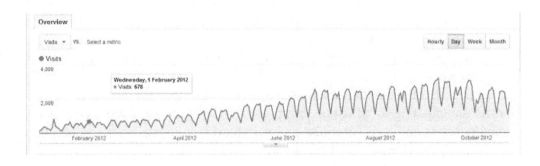

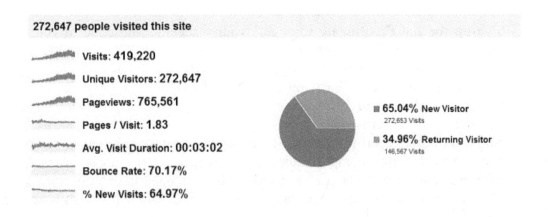

272,647 people visited this site

Visits: **419,220**

Unique Visitors: **272,647**

Pageviews: **765,561**

Pages / Visit: **1.83**

Avg. Visit Duration: **00:03:02**

Bounce Rate: **70.17%**

% New Visits: **64.97%**

- **65.04%** New Visitor
  272,653 Visits

- **34.96%** Returning Visitor
  146,567 Visits

The slow and steady increase in this number indicates that you are getting some loyal readers who like reading your blog posts.

- Jan 2012: **2,825**
- Feb 2012: **4,007**
- March 2012: **7,131**
- April 2012: **10, 321**
- May 2012: **14,304**
- June 2012: **19,122**
- July 2012: **22, 327**
- Aug 2012: **24, 390**
- Sep 2012: **25, 994**

Try to keep the bounce rate under 75%. You can't please everyone who comes to your site. Make sure that the landing page is interesting and informative enough to keep the bounce rate below 75%. If the bounce rate is high, then the possible causes may include irrelevant information, poor design or that your campaign is targeting unqualified visitors, too many advertisements putting people off, the content is not unique enough and freely available in many other sites, etc. You need to come up with an idea that will differentiate both your site and your content from others in the same niche. Not easy as there are thousands of online articles competing for attention, but possible. For example, there are so many matured sites on "Java Tutorials" and very hard to compete on. The small number of tutorials provided on my blog are mainly to provide some familiarity with the sought-after technologies and frameworks. The real differentiating factor for my blog was to provide quality Java job interview questions with concise and easy to grasp answers with lots of code, examples, and diagrams.

6. **Sign-up for the Feedburner** to enable your readers to subscribe to your blog feeds. Also, signup for the adsense to earn a passive income only after building a reasonable size reader base. Don't place any advertisements until you get around 5000+ repeated visitors. Once you get enough repeated visitors you can sign up for "**google adsense**" and "**infolinks**" advertisements to be placed. Don't over do it as too many advertisements can annoy your readers. Generally, vertical and horizontal banners perform better. Set up custom adsense channels to see which advertisements are doing better. Don't expect too much from these advertisements, but can be a good passive pocket money in the order of $5.0 to $20.0 per 4000 page views. So, this income is like a long term savings account

that grows slowly. Some will do much better than others.

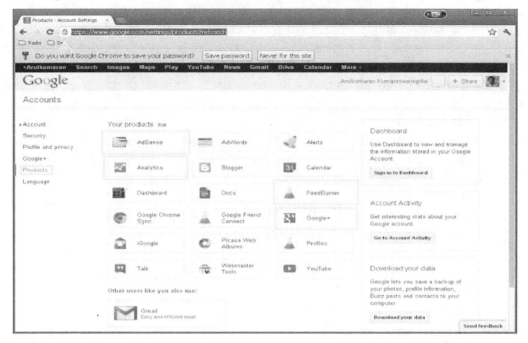

7. **Don't forget that the main reason for starting a blog is to open more doors**. As an independent contractor, my blog helps me capture my experience and stay relevant.

Q. Why capture my own experience?
A.

- Firstly, it serves as handy notes for my future references. It is not easy to remember a vast number of technologies, frameworks, and tools that I had worked on.
- Secondly, I can refresh or jog my memory prior to job interviews to provide a more convincing answers to open-ended questions like -- tell me about yourself? what are your strengths? give me an example where you applied your problem solving skills? what are your recent accomplishments?, etc. Blogging also immensely improved my clarity on the topics due to additional research.
- Finally, my blog contents became my inspiration to self-publish my own books. Publishing my own book has never been easier with the advent of POD (Print On Demand) publishers like *createspace.com*, *lulu.com*, etc. I

had worked with many talented professionals who wished they had written a book too, and attributed not sharing their experiences via books to not having enough time. This problem may have been alleviated if they had recorded their experiences somewhere over a period of time.

It also gives me an opportunity to network. Some of my past and current employers have read my blog posts, and it has certainly helped me win new contracts. Also, it has improved my researching and written skills. In future, if you have a reasonable size followers, you could promote other products and services. You can increase your understanding of the fundamentals from relevant questions and intelligent doubts raised by your readers.

8. **People don't have whole day to read your blogs.** So, it needs to be short and sweet. The headings need to be catchy and informative. For example, I have come across some catchy titles like "How I taught my dog polymorphism", "I quit my job today, and so should you", etc. It needs to be laid out well enough to navigate between topics. Add diagrams and code snippets where applicable. Consult the "google key words tool" to optimize your blog titles for SEO.

9. **You need to consistently post blog entries, and can't afford to be complacent.** The times that I had been a bit slack in posting new blog posts, my google search rank had dropped. Currently, I have about 165 blog entries. Post about 2 to 4 per week. Don't post multiple entries the same day. One entry per day. The way the SEO works for the blog posts, it not only looks at the back-links and the key word concentration, but also the reader involvement in terms of the number of comments posted, site popularity with repeated visits, etc.

10. Finally, there are myriad of blogging tips out there on the internet. Some are very good, but many others are hyped up. Feel free to experiment with the tips, but don't lose focus on the core reason, which is "**writing quality blog posts that help you and others**". Also, for most of you the primary source of income is going to be via your full time job as a software engineer. If you are proud of your blog, have the link to your blog on your resume, LinkedIn profile, and other social media profiles. Freelancers and job seekers can benefit from having a portfolio of their best work online for ease in sharing with potential clients and employers.

Section-7

Recap and quick tips

This section has some quick tips to recap what was discussed in the previous sections. It also has some useful links to acquire further information if you wish to freelance, participate in open-source projects, self publish your book and would like to start blogging.

Do something to standout!!!!

Many software professionals try to concentrate on getting a certification done to standout, but as you had seen in this book, you can do many other things that are more effective to standout without really having to pile up your certifications. Your learning should not stop with certification, but ongoing as technologies, frameworks, and tools change very rapidly. You are only limited by your creative thinking and lack of the industry knowledge. Your top priority must be **experience!**, **experience!!**, **experience!!!** or coding, coding, coding.

Benefits of participating in open-source projects

- You can learn from and enhance your coding skills by looking at others' code.
- You can learn how things are wired up together by looking at the real code base. For example, configuration files, build files, web resources like templates, CSS, JavaScript,   etc and how the artifacts are organized.
- You can get feedback from others on your code.
- You can enhance your ability to understand problems and develop effective solutions for it.
- You can proudly mention your contribution on your resume and online portfolio.
- You can get a good understanding on the software development life cycle by getting into the rhythm of code, build, test, commit, and release.

If you are still not convinced, go to http://seeker.dice.com/jobsearch and search for "open source".

Where do I look for open source projects?

- http://www.freshmeat.net/
- http://www.ohloh.net/
- http://code.google.com/
- http://www.sourceforge.net/
- http://dev.java.net/
- http://jakarta.apache.org/
- http://www.ibm.com/developerworks/views/java/projects.jsp
- http://www.google.co.in/search?q=Apache+Java+projects
- https://www.dev.java.net/servlets/ProjectList
- https://openjdk.dev.java.net/

- http://developers.sun.com/javadb/
- http://www.netbeans.org/
- https://glassfish.dev.java.net/public/devindex.html
-

How to contribute to open source projects without coding?

- Writing documentation, fixing bugs, proposing a new feature, making enhancements, writing unit tests, testing the application, etc.
- http://www.granneman.com/techinfo/linux/contributewithoutcoding/

What to do if you don't have experience with newer technologies?

1. Pick a few newer technologies and learn them from online tutorials, good blogs, and books.
2. See if you can apply them in your current project at work or contribute to an open source project or a self-taught project in a way that uses those technologies.
3. Write a few blog posts about those technologies to increase your understanding.
4. Make sure to list those technologies on your resume and online portfolio, once you have used them in any projects -- paid, unpaid, open-source, and self-taught projects.

Unfortunately most recruiters and hiring managers do keyword searches based on technology lists, and if you want to work with them, you need to play their game.

Don't be overly concerned about your academic achievements

We all get paid based on how we contribute to the bottom-line of the business. The employer pays you a certain salary and expects you to return more than what is invested on you. So, your learning does not stop with your certification(s) or academic achievements. You need to continuously invest in your professional development both technically and non-technically. You need to stay abreast with latest advancements in your field. Set aside some funds for your personal development. Learn to evaluate yourself critically and see where you can improve. Blogging is a useful tool for self realization. Constantly challenge and reinvent yourself to become a well-rounded contributor. Try volunteering on open source projects, community initiatives, taking part in company presentations, and taking on extra tasks whenever you can.

Display great professional ethics. Be punctual, reliable, diplomatic, enthusiastic, and positive. It is a human behavior to err. Learn to accept constructive criticisms and learn from your past mistakes. You do not have to be a team-lead to display leadership skills. Irrespective of your title, display good communication, leadership, and interpersonal skills. Develop an analytical and problem solving mind. Learn to ask the right questions.

Improve your visibility without becoming a politician or a braggart. Attend company events, team meetings, conferences, etc with utmost enthusiasm and contributions. Make sure that your boss knows what results you are producing. Don't just be a quiet achiever. You might be missing out on great opportunities.

Why is it important to network?

If you ask me to list one thing that can make a huge difference to one's career, I would say networking. If you have a proven record with a manager, and this manager wants you when he moves onto a new high profile position or project, do you think that he'll be that concerned with your experience or number of certifications? If he thinks that you get thinks done, he would want to have you on his team. Knowing the right people within and outside the organization can do wonders to your career. Build a good rapport and keep in touch with your present and past managers, work colleagues, and recruitment agents.

Not all job openings are advertised. Networking is a top source for finding a new position. In fact some of the best jobs aren't listed anywhere except in the mental catalogs of development and project managers. Networking is a numbers game. So

- attend professional or trade association meetings.
- take part in industry specific forums and publish quality articles.
- keep in touch with your former work mates and managers.
- Register with online business oriented sites like http://www.linkedin.com/.
- upload your resume to job networking sites like http://www.javajobnetwork.com/, http://www.jvsearch.com/, etc.

Prospective employers tend to pay closer attention or spend more time in reviewing the resumes brought in via networking compared to resumes sent directly as a response to an advertisement.

Where can I find freelance work?

- http://www.guru.com
- http://www.elance.com
- http://odesk.com/
- http://www.getafreelancer.com/projects/by-job/Java.html
- http://www.liveperson.com/experts/computers-programming/programming

What is the difference between a freelancer and a contractor?

Even though these terms are used interchangeably, there is a subtle difference.

A contractor: generally works for **one client** on an exclusive basis for a **longer term say 3 to 12 months**. Contractual agreements may prohibit you to work for other clients. You will get paid on an hourly or daily rate, and **rates are generally 1.5 to 2 times the equivalent permanent role**. You normally work at the client's location. You can find contract jobs through recruitment agencies, job advertisements or your network. You tend to have more security and steady income as a contractor as your contracts can get extended.

A freelancer: generally works for multiple clients on a project by project basis for shorter period. You normally work at your location and visit the client office as needed. You will have to find your work on your own. You could even have overseas clients. There are popular websites like the ones listed below to bid for work. Handy to gain some extra income while gaining much needed hands-on experience.

Which one to prefer? You can't just jump on elenace.com or guru.com and expect to pull jobs that will give you a good income. These are low-dollar markets as you will be competing with people around the world. Especially with people who are prepared to do the job for very low wages to gain much needed hands-on experience or to supplement their more permanent incomes. If your main focus is to gain more practical experience, then freelancing is not a bad avenue. But for a more steady and decent revenue, contracting is the way to go.

Being different

In the "subject" of your email, put something more creative than "Resume Enclosed". Try something like: "Resume showing 7+ years in PHP", "Resume highlighting technical & soft skills", ".Net resume highlighting extensive finance experience", etc.

- Choose an eye catching phrase that best describes your situation, for example

  - Proven track record of/in …
  - Expertise and demonstrated skills in …
  - Instrumental in ….
  - During employment with …, successfully …
  - Spearheaded ……..
  - Successful in/at ….
  - Extensive and diverse practical experience in ….
  - Proficient/Competent at …

- When networking, you should not ask for a job opening but ask for advice. Ask for things like industry advice and advice on career direction. Flatter the people in your network with tactfulness and courtesy. Show interest in your contacts. Send thank-you notes after each networking contact.

- Prepare your interview kit consisting of your certificates, college transcripts, company information (e.g. annual reports, sales materials, etc.), self-taught project(s) in a CD, extra resumes, your letter of references, list of questions you had prepared based on your research and analysis of the company, 5-6 screen shots of some of the websites you had built and anything else you are proud of.

- Your market value depends on your past accomplishments and demonstrable ability to contribute to the bottom line of the business. So, show you can solve organizational problems, improve productivity, meet business expectations, build good rapport and work as a team, improve quality, reduce costs, meet deadlines, motivate and mentor others, etc. Highlight specific achievements. Achievements determine hire ability.

- Delay all salary negotiations until there is an offer on the table. Know your value and research the average salary paid for similar positions with other organizations in your geographic area. Don't be afraid to negotiate, but negotiate in a fair and reasonable manner to have a win-win outcome. Play hardball only if you have multiple job offers and you are willing to walk away from or lose the deal. Never link salary to personal needs or problems. Compensation should always be linked to your value. Be sure to get the offer and final agreement in writing.

- Remember that the salary alone is not everything. If you have multiple job offers, look at other aspects like opportunity to learn new things, likelihood to grow within the company, caliber of the people you will be working with and can learn from, visibility and mission criticality of the project you will be working on, business acumen of the company, will the company name look good on your resume for future prospects, etc to improve your longer term career prospects.

Build a professional online persona for others to discover you

Speaking of being different, building an online persona can help others discover you.

- Create a professional blog. It can help you share your knowledge and experience. It can also serve as a notepad to jog your memory and show off your ideas, accomplishments, problem solving, and findings. It can be used at times to vent your frustrations professionally and warn fellow professionals of any potential pitfalls.

  It is free to get started. Here are some links to get started

  - http://blog-services-review.toptenreviews.com/
  - Google for "How to start a blog"

- Create various online profiles like professional networking via www.linkedin.com, industry specific sites and forums like http://java.dzone.com/, http://php.dzone.com/, http://www.infoq.com/, http://www.theserverside.com/ to publish articles, tips, etc and social networking profiles like Facebook, Google+, tweeter, etc.

Recap and quick tips

- Create an online portfolio and link your profiles and blogs. There are pros and cons in using the hosting services like http://www.portfoliopen.com/ and creating your own from scratch. The portfolio hosting sites were initially created for photographers and web designers to upload and promote their work. This concept is now extended for programmers to upload their resume, code, designs, and provide links to their blogs, and online profiles.

- Provide a link to your portfolio and blog on your resume and email correspondences.

- Sign up for **Google analytics** to see how well your blog is doing. Focus on keeping the bounce rate under 75% with quality content.

- Participate in industry specific forums and provide a link to your blog or website as a signature to drive more traffic.

- Network with your readers via Facebook, Google+ and twitter.

- Your blogs are generally ranked by the search engines based on repeated visitors (**Google analytics** can give you this statistics) and their participation via comments. The Google analytics also shows what key words are driving you the traffic and where the traffic is coming from.

- Use the following tools to see what keywords to use, how competitive a particular keyword is and how your site is ranked for a particular key word.

    - Google keyword tool
    - Google rank checkers: e.g. http://www.searchenginegenie.com/google-rank-checker.html, http://www.seocentro.com/tools/search-engines/keyword-position.html, etc
    - Submit your site for search engines: e.g http://www.submitexpress.com/free-submission.html
    - Submit your site to blog search engines and bookmarking sites like Technorati, Digg, Stumble Upon, and Delicious.

Some companies are already starting to request job applicants for their online presence. So, it is imperative to maintain a professional outlook. Some employers even google your name to see what they can find out about you.

What is POD publishing and how to get started?

It stands for print on demand publishing. I have used createspace.com and lulu.com. Why use POD?

- Anyone can publish.

- Costs you as little as $50.0 to get started. This is mainly for cost of your proof read copy plus shipping. Additional professional services can also be purchased. For example, kindle conversion, designing the book cover, expanded distribution, etc.

- Provides all the necessary tools and distribution services including amazon.com to sell your books.

- All you have to do is upload your interior (book contents) and exterior (book cover) files in the format requested (usually in PDF format), set a selling price, set the channels you want to sell through, fill the necessary details like name, payment method, contact details, etc, order a proof read copy, and start selling.

- The books are printed on demand and on each book sold you get a portion as a royalty and the POD company gets its share to cover the cost of printing and their profit share. They provide a calculator to work this out upfront. As a rough guide you get about 20% - 60% of the selling price depending on the channel (e.g. eBook, printed via eStore, printed via amazon.com, expanded distribution, etc).

Google for "Lulu versus createspace" for more info.

Books can impart knowledge, but cannot give you the much needed experience ...

Most accomplished professionals are self-taught. If you want to really master them, you need to pro-actively apply them to experience it. Once you experience it, you will remember it, and be good at what you do. The technology is so vast. In many cases the decisions have to be made from a number of choices. Firstly, you need to have the knowledge to come up with the valid choices. You will have to work out the pros and cons for each choice. **Nothing is black and white in real world**. There are trade-offs to be made. Only experience can give you the expertise to make the the right decision under a given circumstance. Once you experience it, you may not even agree with what others say. When you start to do so, you start to think and act like an experienced professional. Be passionate about what you do, but don't be inflexible.

Glossary & References

Abbreviation	Description
ACID	Abbreviation for: Atomicity, Consistency, Isolation, and Durability
AJAX	Asynchronous JavaScript and XML
AOP	Aspect-oriented Programming
BPM	Business Process Management. e.g. Pega BPM, Lombardi, Oracle BPM, etc..
CMS	Content Management System. e.g. Vignette.
CRM	Customer Relationship Management. e.g. Siebel, Salesforce, etc.
CSS	Cascading Style Sheet
DoS	Denial of Service
DRY	Don't Repeat Yourself
EJB	Enterprise JavaBeans
EL	Expression Language
ER	Entity Relationship
ERP	Enterprise Resource Planning. An enterprise wide planning system. e.g. SAP.
ESB	Enterprise Service Bus
FIX	Financial Information eXchange. This is a protocol to exchange trade related messages.
GoF	Gang of Four
HTML	HyperText Markup Language
I.T.	Information Technology
JAXP	Java API for XML Processing
JDBC	Java Database Connectivity
JEE	Java Enterprise Edition
JMS	Java Message Service
JMX	Java Management Extension

JNDI	Java Naming and Directory Interface
JSF	JavaServer Faces
JSON	JavaScript Object Notation
JSP	JavaServer Pages
JSTL	JavaServer Pages Standard Tag Library
JVM	Java Virtual Machine
KISS	Keep It Simple and Stupid
LDAP	Lightweight Directory Access Protocol
MOM	Message Oriented Middle-ware
OO	Object Oriented
OOA	Object Oriented Analysis
OOAD	Object Oriented Analysis and Design
OS	Operating System
REST	REpresentational State Transfer
RIA	Rich Internet Application
RMI	Remote Method Invocation
RUP	Rational Unified Process
SDLC	Software Development Life Cycle
SEO	Search Engine Optimization
SLA	Service Level Agreement
SOA	Service Oriented Architecture
SOAP	Simple Object Access Protocol
SOLID	Abbreviation for design principles – **S**ingle Responsibility Principle (SRP), **O**pen Close Principle (OCP), **L**iskov Substitution Principle (LSP), **I**nterface Segregation Principle (ISP), and **D**ependency Inversion Principle (DIP).
SQL	Structured Query Language

SVN	Subversion
TDD	Test Driven Development
UML	Unified Modeling Language.
WADL	Web Application Description Language
WSDL	Web Service Description Language
XML	Extensible Markup Language
XP	Extreme Programming
XSD	XML Schema Definition
XSL	Extensible Style sheet Language
XSL-FO	Extensible Style sheet Language Formatting Objects
XSLT	Extensible Style sheet Language Transformations
XSS	Cross-site scripting
YAGNI	You Ain't Going to Need It.

References

- Perfect Phrases for Resumes – by Michael Betrus, CPRW, 2005 McGraw-Hill.

- The Damn Good Resume at http://damngood.com/jobseekers/tips.html

- HOW TO WRITE A MASTERPIECE OF A RESUME by Rockport Institute at http://www.rockportinstitute.com

- Why Soft Skills? by Jide Awe at http://www.webpronews.com/expertarticles/2005/11/08/why-soft-skills

- 6 'soft' skills you need for success by Rukmini Iyer at http://in.rediff.com/

- Develop the skills and attributes that employers value at http://www.careers.unsw.edu.au

- All employers want the "Balanced Graduate" at http://www.careers.unsw.edu.au

Glossary & References

Please email any suggestions or errors to java-interview@hotmail.com. If you are a Java developer, you will find more info at my blog http://java-success.blogspot.com.

Glossary & References

www.ingramcontent.com/pod-product-compliance
Lightning Source LLC
LaVergne TN
LVHW062309060326
832902LV00013B/2132